THE
ACADEMIC CAREER
HANDBOOK

Loraine Blaxter,
Christina Hughes and
Malcolm Tight

Open University Press
Buckingham · Philadelphia

Open University Press
Celtic Court
22 Ballmoor
Buckingham
MK18 1XW

email: enquiries@openup.co.uk
world wide web: http://www.openup.co.uk

and
325 Chestnut Street
Philadelphia, PA 19106, USA

First Published 1998

A catalogue record of this book is available from the British Library

ISBN   0 335 19828 7 (hb)   0 335 19827 9 (pb)

Library of Congress Cataloging-in-Publication Data
Blaxter, Loraine, 1945–
    The academic career handbook / Loraine Blaxter, Christina Hughes &
Malcolm Tight.
        p.   cm.
    Includes bibliographical references and index.
    ISBN 0-335-19828-7 (hb). — ISBN 0-335-19827-9 (pb)
    1. College teachers—Great Britain—Handbooks, manuals, etc.
2. College teaching—Vocational guidance—Great Britain—Handbooks,
manuals, etc. I. Hughes, Christina, 1952–   . II. Tight, Malcolm.
III. Title.
LB2331.74.G7B53   1998
378,1′2′0941—dc21   97-43057
                                                                    CIP

Typeset by Graphicraft Typesetters Ltd., Hong Kong
Printed in Great Britain by Biddles Ltd., Guildford and King's Lynn

CONTENTS

LIST OF BOXES

1 | INTRODUCTION

What is this book for?

Academic work is generally considered to have changed dramatically in the United Kingdom (and elsewhere) over the last few decades. It has grown substantially, and is now a major industry employing hundreds of thousands of people in an increasing diversity of positions: full-time and part-time, secure and short-term, specialist and generalist, central and peripheral. Box 1.1 provides a breakdown of the characteristics of academic staff employed in universities in 1994/95 for the purposes of teaching and/or research.

In addition to the 114,721 academics recorded in these statistics, there are of course large numbers, working in over 100 universities and colleges, in administrative, computing, laboratory, library and other posts. Outside the higher education system, many in further education colleges or private institutions teach courses franchised or validated by universities, or engage in research. Many of these institutions are leading employers in the towns and cities in which they are located.

The academic career structure is no longer as straightforward (if it ever was) as it may once have appeared, when the clever graduate was first employed as a research assistant while finishing their PhD, then progressed to a lecturership or fellowship, and on and upwards depending on their age, merits and chances. Yet, while there are plenty of directories which list postgraduate courses, or detail the many career opportunities available to graduates as a whole, there is no volume (at least not in the United Kingdom) which discusses the career strategies, opportunities and practicalities for those who are interested in academic work. This book aims to fill this gap.

Box 1.1: Academic staff at United Kingdom higher education institutions, 1994/95

In 1994/95, there were 114,721 academic staff recorded as employed at universities and colleges in the United Kingdom. Of this total, according to the Higher Education Statistics Agency (1996: Table 16):

- 102,701 (90%) were employed full-time;
- 12,020 (10%) were employed part-time;
- 82,203 (72%) had as their primary employment function 'teaching' or 'teaching and research';
- 32,518 (28%) had as their primary employment function 'research only';
- 80,181 (70%) were male;
- 34,473 (30%) were female;
- 7,719 (7%) were professors;
- 19,868 (17%) were senior lecturers or readers;
- 47,597 (41%) were lecturers;
- 29,138 (25%) were researchers;
- 10,399 (9%) were 'other grades'.

Academic staff are defined for these purposes as those whose primary employment function is teaching, teaching and research, or research, and who have either (i) worked in such a capacity throughout the previous academic year on at least a 25% contract, or (ii) joined the staff during the last academic year and worked on at least a 25% contract. The grades listed include analogous grades.

Who is this book for?

This book has been written primarily for those working, or seeking to work, within the British higher education system. It has a particular relevance for those who are just starting, have recently started, or are seeking to start, on academic careers. It should also have much of interest to say to those in more established positions, who want to think about academic work or whose careers may be developing in new directions.

It has been written by a cross-disciplinary team – we initially qualified as an anthropologist, a geographer and a sociologist – and will, therefore, have most relevance for those working in humanities and social science subjects. Much of what is said about processes and roles is common, however, to those based in other disciplines.

British higher education has many elements in common with higher education systems in other countries, particularly English-speaking countries. Indeed, examples and analyses from North America and Australasia are used widely in this text. The guidance given, which draws upon personal knowledge and experience as well as published sources, should be of use to those working in similar systems, though the specific institutional details will, of course, vary.

We also recognize that there are many people working in careers which come into close contact with the academic world. It is not uncommon to find such people moving into and out of academic work, or balancing elements of academic work with other careers. This is especially the case in the professions. Nurses, teachers and social workers, to take just three examples, may make a specialist input to academic teaching or research; while academics in these fields frequently (in some cases, mandatorily) also practise their skills in hospitals, schools or the community at large. This book has much to say to these audiences as well.

Why is career planning important for academics?

Our position, in writing this book, is that academic careers share many characteristics with other employment careers. They are lived within organizational and social networks which have particular rules, hierarchies, cultures and politics. The academic world, like other areas of employment, is highly competitive. It is regulated through legislation. It is taxable and pensionable. It requires, among other things, a similar range of administrative, organizational and personal skills to many other professional careers. Being an academic is a job, with core tasks, as well as a way of life.

To enjoy some success in any career, however such success might be defined, requires a broad understanding of the working environment and a more detailed appreciation of particular aspects of it. This is doubly important at a time when careers are changing rapidly. Even in order simply to survive, academics require an awareness of trends and changing practices. For more senior and established staff, offering sound advice to postgraduate students and new colleagues requires a critical understanding of the changing career context.

Career planning is, therefore, crucial for academics, just as it is for other types of professional. This book aims to provide a solid starting point of information and guidance to support that planning.

The individual and the system

At this point we must enter a cautionary note. Almost without exception, books on career planning and strategies are directed primarily at the individual. This is partly because individuals represent the largest market, but also relates to the difficulty of designing books for anything other than individual use.

This book is really no different, but we are conscious that, in emphasizing the individualist perspective, the importance of collective action may be downplayed. We recognize that:

> Individuals may be able to exert some influence on the culture of an organization, the shape of the hierarchy or the methods of recruitment and promotion, but they cannot, alone, affect the political, welfare or economic contexts in which we all live; only organized collective action can achieve change at this level.
>
> (Shaw and Perrons 1995: 7)

Much of the content of this book is necessarily directed at the individual academic or aspiring academic. We have, however, sought to draw attention, wherever possible, to the importance of collaborating with others within and across institutions, departments and disciplines. This is important for individuals to realize their potential in their employment careers. More pertinently, it can also provide a framework for guarding against exploitation and challenging inequalities.

How to use this book

In composing this text, we have had to try and capture a variety of academic values and a range of experiences and viewpoints. Given this diversity, all of our readers should find aspects of this book provocative. The point of disjuncture between your own viewpoint and experience and the tone or content of the book should have the potential for refocusing your own professional knowledge and understanding.

As you will have seen from its contents list, this book is organized into nine chapters. Aside from this introductory chapter, three chapters (Chapters 2, 3 and 9) consider the nature and development of academic careers, while the other five (Chapters 4 to 8) examine different academic roles or tasks: networking, teaching, researching, writing and managing. Through this form of organization, we aim to inform you about both the general process of being an academic and the major concerns and duties that go with the job.

One problem with books – compared with, for example, electronic publishing – is that their very format suggests a single direction for reading: namely, from start to finish. We doubt that many of our readers will in fact take this approach; indeed, we would discourage you from doing so, unless it seems necessary or appropriate. Rather, we expect you to focus on particular chapters or sections in the light of your immediate interests, though we would hope that you would make use of other parts of the book in time. To facilitate this kind of reading, we have extensively cross-referenced between chapters and sections.

The book also has a number of other features to which we would draw particular attention:

- The main text of the book is supplemented by a series of boxes, which contain information, opinions and examples drawn from a wide range of sources. To some extent, these can be read on their own. By counterpoising them with the text, we hope to get across some of the complexities involved in academic work and careers.
- Within the text and the boxes there are many quotations, from research texts and experiential accounts, which help to illustrate some of the different perspectives on academic work.
- Annotated reading lists and sources of further information are included at the end of every chapter except this one. Much has been written about many aspects of academic life and careers. Clearly, we cannot cover it all in detail in a single book like this. These listings offer a quick and accessible guide to

some of the most pertinent texts and sources for those who wish to pursue particular issues further.

- At the end of the book you will find a list of relevant organizations and journals, with full contact details.

Throughout the text you will also find a series of hints and tips. These are intended to give practical guidance, making clear some of the many 'unwritten rules' of academic life, the kinds of thing you usually only learn by being an academic for some time.

2 | ACADEMIC CAREERS

Introduction

Interest in an academic career can develop at various stages in your working life. You may be coming to the end of a research degree or have just begun academic employment. You may be reflecting on your own experiences of being an academic and wish to reassess or renew your career. You may have assumed responsibility for the development of new academics and wish to broaden your own knowledge. You may have entered university more or less directly from school, and have been there ever since, or you may have experience of working in other forms of employment.

What is academic life really like, and how is it changing? From the outside, or from the perspective of the student, it is easy to get a partial or mistaken perception of what it is actually like to work as an academic. The image of academic life as relatively leisured, quiet and reflective is deeply ingrained in the public imagination, epitomized in the notion of the university as an 'ivory tower'. Like all such images, it contains, or contained, some elements of truth, but could only serve as a very misleading guide to the current reality. This chapter aims to provide a more reliable and up-to-date guide.

The remainder of this chapter is organized into four main sections:

- **The academic life**, which compares the portrayal of academe in literature and the media with the experience of academics;
- **The changing nature of higher education**, which provides a brief portrait of the state of British higher education at the close of the twentieth century;
- **The changing nature of careers**, which considers the characteristics of contemporary careers;

- **Academic roles and careers**, which offers an overview of the different kinds of work undertaken within higher education.

At the end of the chapter a selection of sources of further information is listed.

The academic life

One important source for our popular ideas about academic life is fiction (Carter 1990). A succession of modern novels have used universities and colleges as their backdrop, and many of them have been adapted for television and the cinema, spreading their impressionistic portrayals to wider audiences. Box 2.1 offers a brief selection of vignettes from English academic novels, from Thomas Hardy in the late nineteenth century to Ann Oakley in the late 1980s.

Box 2.1: Literary representations of academia

He always remembered the appearance of the afternoon on which he awoke from his dream. Not quite knowing what to do with himself, he went up to an octagonal chamber in the lantern of a singularly built theatre that was set amidst this quaint and singular city. It had windows all round, from which an outlook over the whole town and its edifices could be gained. Jude's eyes swept all the views in succession, meditatively, mournfully, yet sturdily. These buildings and their associations and privileges were not for him. From the looming roof of the great library, into which he hardly ever had time to enter, his gaze travelled on to the varied spires, halls, gables, streets, chapels, gardens, quadrangles, which composed the *ensemble* of this unrivalled panorama. He saw that his destiny lay not with these, but among the manual toilers in the shabby purlieu which he himself occupied . . .

(Hardy 1974: 135–6)

I called at Brown's rooms, as we had arranged with Chrystal, at eleven o'clock next morning. They were on the next staircase to mine, and not such a handsome set; but Brown, though he went out each night to his house in the West Road, had made them much more desirable to live in. That day he stood hands in pockets in front of the fire, warming his plump buttocks, his coat-tails hitched up over his arms. His bright peering eyes were gazing appreciatively over his deep sofas, his ample armchairs, his two half-hidden electric fires, out to the window and the snowy morning. Round the walls there was growing a set of English water colours, which he was collecting with taste, patience, and a kind of modest expertness. On the table, a bottle of Madeira was waiting for us.

(Snow 1951: 28)

Howard was interviewed in the panelled Gaitskell Room of the Elizabethan hall which had been the original starting-place of the new university, before the towers and the pre-stressed concrete and the glass-framed buildings that were now beginning to spread across the site, the achievement of that notable Finnish architect Jop Kaakinen, had ever been conceived. The interview was affable. The interdisciplinary programme of the university, and its novel teaching methods, excited Howard, after Leeds; he could see he was being taken seriously; the modernistic campus growing on the old estate pleased him, seemed in accord with his sense of transforming history.

(Bradbury 1975: 34)

'Bitter? Of course I'm bitter!' he repeated to himself each morning as he made his way across the ring-road which separated the Polytechnic car park from the Polytechnic. The wind was always especially sharp and bleak here and the lights were always against him. The students coming to and from lectures were dowdily dressed and looked slow-witted. At the bus stop long queues of Wrottesley working people muttered and complained through running noses, and the Jamaican bus drivers had mad glints in their eyes, as if they were thinking of ploughing their vehicles into the lines of waiting passengers.

(Jacobson 1984: 22)

She had been lecturing in the Life Sciences department of the university for two years. The thesis was simply a part of the process; a continuation of a career that hardly needed planning, an academic progress that, barring accidents, just happened. The choice of what she wanted to do in life having been made (and barely made, it had been so obvious) at school, everything else followed unsurprisingly.

(Diski 1988: 20)

She arrived at the department at ten o'clock. A corner building in a Georgian square, with newly painted blue and white woodwork, it housed the overflow from Regent's College, one of the colleges of London University. As the college had grown, its premises had not, and the sociology department had been moved round the corner to a separate residence. The reason why sociology had been singled out for this special treatment was not that the other departments thought especially highly of it, but rather that they tended to discount it and could do so more easily if it wasn't there any more. But the effect on the sociologists of having a separate existence was to give them a quite audacious sense of their own grandeur.

(Oakley 1989: 6)

We can trace in their descriptions the changing nature of both the university as a place of work and the wider society within which it exists. A sense of architecture seems very much to the fore. The earlier accounts focus on the glittering spires of Oxford, or the clubby, male atmosphere of college accommodation, while later stories use modern campus universities or urban polytechnic sites as their settings. We are presented with 1960s or 1970s images of the university as the centre of radicalism, with 'heroic' male dons ferociously coupling with students and staff alike; and with 1980s reactions to these lost worlds. As with the imagery of the ivory tower, these accounts have some grounding in the realities of academic life, though they by no means tell us the whole story.

Box 2.2: Higher education in the headlines

Surrey reveals crisis fears
Research formula will reward elite
Notts prods 'poor' staff to early exit
Dons tell Oxford to go private
Rich robbed to prevent collapse
Bullies in the common room
Student rents soar
Research value 'in doubt'
Glasgow warns 'passengers'
Five-star funding for fab four
The urge to merge
Strike threats issued
Lancaster admits reckless spending
Student loans to be means-tested
Fees: there's no limit
Staff pay the price in jobs

Source: *Times Higher Education Supplement*, 10/1/97; 24/1/97; 7/2/97; 21/2/97; 28/2/97; 14/3/97; 4/4/97; 18/4/97; 25/4/97; 9/5/97; 16/5/97; 13/6/97; 18/7/97; 1/8/97; 22/8/97.

Another source for understanding academe is, of course, the press. Box 2.2 reproduces a series of headlines used in 1997 in the British academics' professional weekly paper, the *Times Higher Education Supplement*. From glancing through these, and from reading the stories attached to them, one might well get an idea of British higher education as a sector in crisis, subject to rapid structural change and just barely coping. There is something in this perspective as well, and the *Times Higher Education Supplement* can at times be a very depressing read for insiders and outsiders alike. Further inside the paper, however, in the lengthier reviews and reflective sections away from the immediate news stories, one can find more optimistic, challenging and engaging accounts.

For many years, the *Times Higher Education Supplement* has been running a weekly column, 'Don's Diary', in which individual academics summarize their week's work. For some years, this appeared to be stuck in travelogue mode, with one lucky academic after another reporting on work in ever more opulent or exotic locations (indeed, academics junketing around the world is another popular image of our profession). In the last few years, however, the column has come down to earth and offered accounts which most of those working in higher education can relate to. Box 2.3 offers a weekful of 'Don's Diary', with each day taken from a different column published in 1997. The contrasting accounts – some individually accredited, some understandably anonymous – offer serial insights into what it feels like to work in a British university or college in 1997. There are high points: engaging in research, delivering successful teaching sessions, networking with others at conferences. And there are also low points: the treadmill of research

Box 2.3: A week in the life of a don

Monday
Work begins at 8.40 am. After picking up the morning papers to scan (and produce a cuttings sheet for top management), there is a work report meeting with my female boss. These encounters have become progressively more fraught over the past few months. I have been given only in-post training and am being subject to a prolonged, subtle bullying campaign. The usual tactics are employed. Times of meetings are often changed with little warning, rules are altered at whim (most notably when, after weeks of producing presumably satisfactory news releases, I was told, very crossly, that they should always be double-spaced), instructions are forgotten. It is what you might call the mobile goalpost syndrome. My boss also loves acronyms, power-speak which leaves the uninitiated out in the cold, and it becomes difficult to ask what these arcane utterances mean – 'The v-c is heading up the NYPD at the BU conference next month – that will, of course, need flagging in our paper'.

Tuesday
This week, like the semester, is dominated by Shakespeare. I begin teaching a module called 'The Shakespeare Phenomenon' which considers the place of Shakespeare in late 20th century culture. There is considerable contemporary interest in the phenomenon and I receive a regular supply of material on email from the United States following a lecturing visit to California last autumn. We consider why an advertisement for tea can use a speech from Richard II, yet change the final words from 'this England' to 'this Britain'; we observe a film that quotes a speech from Shylock to great effect, but in fact contrives this by weaving in a totally different speech from Antonio; we look at the marketing of the BBC *Animated Tales*; and we set up our work for the week to come. The task is simply to collect examples of the use of 'Shakespeare' and to attempt to classify them.

Wednesday
Civil war has erupted. Everybody is blaming everybody else for what has happened. The senior members of the department are accusing the junior members of not having been productive enough, or producing work that was not sufficiently scholarly. They are claiming it is our fault for getting a 3a rather than a 4. The junior members are insisting it is the fault of the senior members for not taking a lead with research. Some members of staff think that the administration does not like our subject and that's why we are being axed. Little cliques are meeting in the corridors. Everybody looks ashen. I am trying to keep well out of it. I have a book to finish and the publishers are pressing. But I just cannot concentrate.

Thursday
Meet Anglia TV people again, to learn that the person I was going to shake hands with has discovered an urgent appointment elsewhere. Lost opportunity to make the visual point that this is a mature democracy in which we can have a good row with good humour. Mark examination papers for external examiner's meeting next week in Dublin. See former doctoral student applying for a job, and do my best to keep his courage up. Write three references for

another doctoral student with two infant children and desperate need of an income. Suspect their chances would be improved if their referee could sign self 'Professor'. Talk to doctoral student who wants to know where commentary of Albertus Magnus on Aristotle is to be found in edition more modern than 16th century. Comfort distressed examination candidate.

Friday
By car to visit the most remote of the schools in the study – a tiny village primary in the snow-covered hills. Three other village schools should be joining us here today, but two of them have sent word that the journey is too risky on the icy roads, so we have just two schools combined. We are able to use every child on the premises for the questionnaire – including a couple of five-year-olds who manage pretty well. The discussion task is about reality and fantasy. The eight to 11-year-olds involved in it are certain that no real-life headmaster would be allowed to behave as *The Demon Headmaster* does, much as they enjoy the programme. 'Nobody would really want to take over the world with technology' . . . The snow does not prevent my return to London.

Saturday
Kids, gardening, swimming and, of course, email. Work never goes away and I usually take time over the weekend to make some quality inputs on my course monitoring. I monitor one course for third-level students which means I look in on the student and tutor and try to be helpful. Sometimes I just add an endorsement to a tutor comment or pass on some information, sometimes I need to let people know quietly that bad behaviour (flaming as we call it) is not acceptable. The amazing thing is that the email coffee shop works well. Students chat and share ideas, tutors make some interesting comments and the sense of community is very powerful. The way of things to come? I hope so.

Sunday
Due to a little-known clause in the Ten Commandments, the rules of the Sabbath do not apply to post-doc research fellows. Not only is the flow of work continuous, but it is so engrossing that it is impossible to leave alone. The more you find out, the more you want to find out; the fights, tensions and struggles pieced together through archival records become compulsive dramas in their own right, commenting upon an entire history of representation and of sociocultural movement; the series and serials viewed nightly for 'relaxation' purposes increasingly slot into a framework of dramatic development and trigger new ideas for research avenues.

'Don's Diary', *Times Higher Education Supplement*, 10/1/97, 7/3/97, 28/3/97, 11/4/97, 6/6/97, 20/6/97, 27/6/97. Quotes from contributions by 'Georgina Riley, information officer'; Geoff Ridden, principal lecturer in cultural studies, King Alfred's College; 'an author working at an English university'; Gillian Evans, lecturer in history in the University of Cambridge; Maire Davies, director of studies, London College of Printing and Distributive Trades; Simon Bell, Instill lecturer in the Systems Department, Open University; Madeleine Kavanagh, postdoctoral research fellow, University of Reading.

Box 2.4: Myths in academia

1 The myth of meritocracy.
2 The myth of objective standards and neutrality in the classroom and in hiring, promotion and tenure.
3 The myth of non-discrimination and fairness.
4 The myth of democracy.
5 The myth of collegiality.
6 The myth of liberalism and openness.
7 The myth that, in academia, the primary goal is the search for knowledge.
8 The myth that, in academia, people's search for knowledge is done coopera-tively, not competitively, and that this cooperation is rewarded.
9 The myth that 'they' really want you to do service, teaching and research in equal amounts and that, when it comes time for tenure and promotion, they will count all three as equally valuable.
10 The myth of individualism.
11 The myth that all teaching and scholarly work, regardless of its content and methods, will be regarded as equally important and valuable, as long as it is of good quality.
12 The myth that partial acceptance in academia means full acceptance.

Source: Caplan (1994: 48–55). For a comparable list of myths, see Millard (1991: xiv–xix).

---

and teaching assessment, the constant pressure of doing more with less, and the difficulties of dealing with awkward or unpleasant colleagues.

The experience of academic work is, of course, different for each academic. Much depends on the seniority of your position, the nature of your contract, the kind of institution you are working in, and your relationships with your immedi-ate colleagues. Academic employment, like any other, is also mediated by issues of 'race', class and gender. The overall experience, therefore, has much in com-mon with that of working in any modern large organization. There is a lot of uncertainty, there are many pressures and challenges, and much of the day is spent in fairly mundane activities. What is different is the core activity, the focus on developing and disseminating knowledge and understanding. While this is not unique to higher education, universities and colleges remain at the centre of this intellectual life.

Given these circumstances, it is hardly surprising that higher education re-mains a land mapped by myths: commonplace understandings which, whatever their reality, many take to have some truth. Box 2.4 summarizes many of these myths. While the source is American, almost all of the myths referred to have their counterparts in Britain. Many academics undoubtedly feel that things were better in the past, that most of the changes being pressed upon them are wrong, that universities and their component departments are best left to themselves, and that nobody outside is capable of understanding their work. These and other myths are yet another source influencing our image of academic work.

The changing nature of higher education

The contemporary condition of British higher education has been extensively studied by a small, but persistent, body of researchers. Their analyses offer a useful complement to the literary representations included in Box 2.1 and the myths listed in Box 2.4. From their publications, one can build up a picture of both the nature of higher education and how it is changing.

One of the key points made by those who have studied academics, in Britain and in other countries, is that their discipline or subject is at least as important to their working lives as is their institution:

the discipline rather than the institution tends to become the dominant force in the working lives of academics. To stress the primacy of the discipline is to change our perception of enterprises and systems: we see the university or college as a collection of local chapters of national and international disciplines, chapters that impart and implant the orientations to knowledge, the norms and the customs of the larger fields.

(Clark 1983: 30–1)

While the recent rise of managerialism in British universities and colleges (see Chapter 8) may have altered this balance somewhat in favour of the institution, the pull of the discipline undoubtedly remains strong. The tension between institution and discipline is, however, only one element of the multiple fragmentation of academic life:

The British academic profession has at least six important features . . . It is split between different sectors and kinds of institutions . . . It is . . . divided . . . hierarchically into layers of different prestige and importance, according to a rigid pecking order. It is fragmented yet another way by specialization and departmentalism, and often the specialists can no longer talk to each other. It is unrepresentative of the population as a whole, and particularly neglects talent among the working class, women of all classes, and immigrants of different race and colour from the majority. Its salary structures discourage mobility between institutions. And finally the principle of tenure, one of the best safeguards a profession might have, also entails costs in discouraging effort and innovation.

(Perkin 1987: 29)

Since that was written, tenure has been replaced by normal security of employment for new appointments, and the former polytechnic and university sectors have been combined. Nevertheless, the notions of hierarchies and grading are, arguably, more firmly embedded within our higher education system than in almost any other activity. What, after all, would be the point of higher education without grading?

One of the striking features of academic life is that nearly everything is graded in more or less subtle ways. People are quite open in designating the leading journals in their discipline, about which there is virtual unanimity; they are willing, when pressed, to list institutions and departments in order of intellectual precedence; there is a constant process of implicit and explicit ranking of individuals (the outstanding scholar, the student with the 'first class mind', and, more often by implication or omission, those who are less well regarded).

(Becher 1989: 56–7)

The importance, both historically and currently, of the two oldest English universities, Oxford and Cambridge, within these hierarchies remains undeniably strong:

career patterns for academics are entwined in an evolving hierarchy of institutions, with Oxford and Cambridge exerting a disproportionate influence at both the point of entry and as the preferred occupational destination.

(Halsey 1995: 200)

The British higher education system also remains, to a large extent, a system dominated by and working in the interests of men:

It is tempting to regard universities as hospitable places for women – places where academic excellence and the merit of an argument are the overriding values, places where there is a detached and impartial consideration of issues, and where argument is least likely to be *ad hominem* or *ad feminam*. Yet there has long been evidence to suggest that this is not so. Twenty years ago, when the idea of sex discrimination legislation was still under discussion, the universities were singled out for criticism for their low proportions of female staff and students. By the mid-1980s, a decade after the legislation was put in place, it was clear that the Higher Education sector had been slow to act.

(Davies and Holloway 1995: 11–12)

As Box 1.1 indicated, only 30 per cent of academic staff in the United Kingdom are women. The proportion is highest at the lower grades of employment, and decreases with each promotional step. Thus, only 8 per cent of professors are women, and in no university does this proportion exceed 30 per cent (Griffiths 1997).

Against this picture of strong, 'traditional', repressive structures we must, however, set another, more dynamic, story. This is a story of recent, rapid change. Box 2.5 illustrates the massive expansion in student enrolments between 1970/71 and 1994/95. It shows that, during that period, total enrolments increased nearly threefold. While much of this growth was among the full-time undergraduate population, other aspects of provision actually grew faster. Thus, postgraduate numbers increased fivefold, while part-time student numbers increased fourfold. The representation of men and women among the student body also changed dramatically, from a position where there were twice as many men as women to one where women now outnumber men.

The recent changes which have affected the British higher education system are not, however, simply a matter of expansion in student numbers. They have also involved related developments in institutional and student financing, and in the oversight of the system's performance:

Box 2.5: Enrolments in higher education, by sex, level and mode of study, United Kingdom, 1970/71 and 1994/95 (thousands)

	Men	Women	Total
1970/71			
Full-time undergraduate	241	173	414
Part-time undergraduate	127	19	146
Full-time postgraduate	33	10	43
Part-time postgraduate	15	3	18
Total	**416**	**205**	**621**
1994/95			
Full-time undergraduate	513	511	1024
Part-time undergraduate	210	273	483
Full-time postgraduate	74	56	130
Part-time postgraduate	92	84	176
Total	**889**	**924**	**1813**

Source: Central Statistical Office (1997: Table 3.16).

Within the space of a few years the internationally recognised British model of higher education based on short, well-financed, full-time undergraduate courses for a comparatively small proportion of the population has changed irrevocably. Since 1980, full-time student numbers have doubled; public expenditure per home student has fallen by one third; overseas student fees have been set at full cost levels; links between teaching and research have been seriously questioned and their funding almost completely separated; loans for students have begun to replace maintenance grants; and a unified system of financial allocation and academic accountability has replaced the binary system . . . The expansion of the past ten years amounts to the advent of mass higher education in quantitative terms. The prime concern of the next ten will be coming to terms with the qualitative consequences.

(Williams and Fry 1994: 8)

A similar analysis of the recent 'radical transformation' of higher education identified the following key changes:

- substantial and rapid *growth in student numbers* . . .
- substantial and rapid *decline in per capita funding* . . .
- *changes in resource allocation*: the previous formula of a simple block grant, based on historic costs, has been replaced by separate resource streams for teaching and research, each competitively awarded . . .

- *structural change*: in 1992 the polytechnics ... and a number of larger colleges of higher education were redesignated as universities ...
- *managerialism*: government pressure has been applied to reshape the administration of the 'old' universities from a collegial style to the managerial models in operation in the former polytechnic sector.
- *inspection and accountability* ...
- *conditions of service for academic staff*: formal academic tenure has been abolished ... salary levels have declined.

(Fulton 1996: 391–2)

We might add to these listings many other detailed changes affecting the operation of higher education in the United Kingdom, and with which academics have had to come to terms. For example:

- the introduction of national vocational qualifications;
- the rise of access programmes;
- the creation of credit accumulation and transfer schemes, and the widespread modularization of teaching programmes;
- the growth of franchising and validation arrangements, linking universities with local further education colleges;
- the replacement in some institutions of terms with semesters;
- the introduction in all institutions of formal schemes for staff appraisal.

In summary, it has been argued that:

external changes have produced a mass higher education system whilst the lack of internal change has resulted in the retention of the values of an elitist system. This imbalance is the cause of many of the tensions and dysfunctions which higher education presently experiences.

(Wagner 1995: 15)

Clearly, with these pressures, further changes in higher education policy and practice are only to be expected in the coming years.

Despite these recent changes, the British higher education system remains structured and fissured. This is illustrated in Box 2.6, which reproduces a contemporary typology of universities and colleges. This kind of typology asserts the continuing importance of both geography and history. Scottish, Welsh and Northern Irish institutions are recognized as in some way different from those in England. The English universities are grouped in order of foundation, from the medieval beginnings of Oxford, Cambridge and Durham, through the nineteenth-century foundations in London and the major cities, the early twentieth-century redbricks, the technological and 'new' universities which opened in the 1960s, to the new 'new' universities (the former polytechnics) designated in the early 1990s. The colleges are classified separately in terms of the nature of their curriculum offer.

If you doubt the continuing relevance of this typology, take a look at Box 2.7, which presents a league table of excellence. This is derived from the 1996 research assessment exercise, and lists all of the 102 British universities and colleges which are represented on the Committee of Vice-Chancellors and Principals in

---

Box 2.6: Sub-sectors of British higher education

1 Oxford and Cambridge universities
2 The University of London
3 The Victorian civic universities (Birmingham, Bristol, Leeds, Liverpool, Manchester, Sheffield)
4 The redbrick universities (Exeter, Hull, Leicester, Nottingham, Reading, Southampton)
5 Durham and Keele universities (both *sui generis*)
6 The technological universities (Aston, Bath, Bradford, Brunel, City, Loughborough, Salford, Surrey)
7 The Scottish universities
8 The Welsh universities
9 The Northern Irish universities
10 The Open University
11 The old 'new' universities (East Anglia, Essex, Kent, Lancaster, Sussex, Warwick, York)
12 The new 'new' universities (Anglia, Bournemouth, Brighton, Central England, Central Lancashire, Coventry, De Montfort, Derby, East London, Greenwich, Hertfordshire, Huddersfield, Humberside, Kingston, Leeds Metropolitan, Liverpool John Moores, London Guildhall, Luton, Manchester Metropolitan, Middlesex, North London, Northumbria, Nottingham Trent, Oxford Brookes, Plymouth, Portsmouth, Sheffield Hallam, South Bank, Staffordshire, Teesside, Thames Valley, West of England, Westminster, Wolverhampton)
13 Multi-faculty colleges (e.g. Bolton, Nene)
14 Liberal arts colleges (e.g. Bath)
15 Further/higher education colleges
16 Specialized colleges (e.g. Royal College of Music)

Source: Scott (1995: 43–53).

---

terms of their overall performance. This table is also headed by Oxford and Cambridge, closely followed by three University of London colleges, and then a mixture of older and newer university foundations. The first new 'new' university does not appear until 60th place, and there is virtually no overlap in placings between the pre-1990 universities and the more recent foundations. Interestingly, a very similar league table could be, and has been, constructed from the results of the teaching quality assessments carried out in individual university departments over the last few years.

The use of the term 'league table' is, of course, both conscious and deliberate. The parallels with the football world were made closer by all the talk regarding an academic transfer market in the months preceding the research assessment exercise. The university in which the authors are based, Warwick, which is graded eighth in the table given in Box 2.7, was once memorably described in the *Birmingham Post* newspaper as the 'Wimbledon of the premier league' of British universities. More generally, the use of terms such as 'world class', 'international

Box 2.7: League table of excellence

1 Oxford	34 Reading	71 Oxford Brookes
2 Cambridge	35 Glasgow	72 West of England
3 London School of	36 Heriot-Watt	73 Manchester
Economics	37 Aston	Metropolitan
4 Imperial College	38 Liverpool	74 Sunderland
London	39 Salford	75 Robert Gordon
5 University College	40 Newcastle	76 Liverpool John
London	41 Stirling	Moores
6 UMIST	42 Leicester	77 Glamorgan
7 Bath	43 Queen Mary &	78 East London
8 Warwick	Westfield College	79 North London
9 Lancaster	44 Dundee	80 Thames Valley
10 York	45 Strathclyde	81 Middlesex
11 Essex	46 Open	82 Northumbria
12 Sussex	47 Exeter	83 De Montfort
13 Edinburgh	48 Swansea	84 Glasgow
14 Bristol	49 Belfast	Caledonian
15 Cardiff	50 Bradford	85 Lincolnshire and
16 St Andrews	51 Wales, Bangor	Humberside
17 Cranfield	52 Kent	86 Leeds Metropolitan
18 Durham	53 Keele	87 Central Lancashire
19 Sheffield	54 Brunel	88 Huddersfield
20 Southampton	55 Aberdeen	89 Kingston
21 Royal Holloway	56 Ulster	90 Coventry
College	57 Hull	91 Staffordshire
22 King's College	58 Wales,	92 London Guildhall
London	Aberystwyth	93 Derby
23 Manchester	59 City	94 Paisley
24 Birmingham	60 Sheffield Hallam	95 Anglia Polytechnic
25 Leeds	61 Wales, Lampeter	96 Bolton Institute
26 Goldsmiths College	62 Westminster	of Higher Education
27 Royal Veterinary	63 Nottingham Trent	97 Bournemouth
College	64 Greenwich	98 Abertay Dundee
28 East Anglia	65 Hertfordshire	99 Central England
29 Surrey	66 South Bank	100 Wolverhampton
30 Nottingham	67 Portsmouth	101 Teesside
31 Loughborough	68 Plymouth	102 Luton
32 Birkbeck College	69 Napier	
33 Wales, College of	70 Brighton	
Medicine		

Source: Times Higher Education Supplement, 20/12/96, p. xvi.

Box 2.8: Institutional diversity

- Of 180 publicly funded institutions, around 100 are universities (the precise figure varies according to how one counts the constituent institutions of the University of London and certain other federal or collegiate institutions). The remainder are either small specialist institutions – many of which concentrate on postgraduate work – or larger multi-purpose colleges of higher education, many of which might be considered to be aspirant universities.
- There are 20 institutions with more than 15,000 full-time equivalent (FTE) students; 35 institutions have 1000 or less.
- Three institutions have 60% or more of their FTE students enrolled on part-time study; 98 have less than 10%.
- There are nine institutions with 80% or more of their students on postgraduate courses; 63 have less than 10%.
- Thirty-two institutions obtain more than 20% of their total income from research grants and contracts; 110 get less than 10%.

Source: Brennan and Ramsden (1996: 3–4).

---

standing' and 'centre of national excellence' make the importance attached to grading and status crystal-clear. While we may still hold to the belief, at least at a superficial level, that all degrees, wherever and however earned, are more or less equivalent, universities and colleges are by no means equal.

In addition to being unequal in terms of their standing, British higher education institutions also vary considerably in their other characteristics. Box 2.8 summarizes some of this diversity, covering a larger number of institutions than appear in Box 2.7. It focuses on size, specialism, the modes and levels of study offered, and the importance of the research function. Anyone looking at Box 2.8 who still has an image of the university as a full-time, residential finishing school for the children of the middle classes is in for something of a shock, though that role is certainly still important. Indeed, many degree courses are now partly or wholly taught in further education colleges, while other courses offer clear progression routes from local colleges to universities.

In case this section has given too strong an impression of British higher education as being an environment subject to continuing change, it may be as well to emphasize the concurrent importance of continuity in many key aspects of academic life and work. Box 2.9 provides two sets of aims for higher education as a whole, formulated thirty years apart. The more recent version has obviously been influenced by the earlier one (taken from the Robbins Report), whether directly or indirectly. While the former is expressed in a more contemporary language, there is little here that is different, apart from the explicit reference to lifelong learning.

The fundamentals of academic work, and its commitment to the intellectual life, arguably, therefore, remain much the same as they did generations ago. What has changed is the size of the enterprise and the intensity of the work involved.

Box 2.9: Aims of higher education

- instruction in skills suitable to play a part in the general division of labour;
- what is taught should be taught in such a way as to promote the general powers of the mind;
- the advancement of learning;
- the transmission of a common culture and common standards of citizenship.

(Committee on Higher Education 1963: 6–7)

- the development of the 'trained mind', i.e. critical thinking and reasoning skills, independence of thought, an ability to think conceptually and to bring an intellectual perspective to bear on issues;
- the acquisition of knowledge needed to be an educated person arising from exposure to different domains of knowledge, to different cultures, and to the important contemporary theories in the arts and sciences;
- personal development for adult life which values the affective, moral and creative aspects of personality as well as the cognitive, and pays attention to educating the future citizen as well as the future employee;
- establishing a base for lifelong learning.

(Atkins 1995: 26)

The changing nature of careers

If one reads the popular management literature, there's no shortage of advice as to what people and their organisations need to do to be successful in this fast changing world. The messages are forceful ones:

'Become flexible.'
'Adapt.'
'Self-organise.'
'Thrive on chaos.'
'Develop a learning orientation.'
'Become more creative.'
'Be market driven!'
'Foster entrepreneurship.'
'Empower your staff.'
'Decentralise.'

One may want to debate the buzzwords and the precise directions given, but there's a consistent theme here. In the new global environment, old styles of organisation and management no longer work. We have to find alternatives.

(Morgan 1993: xxvii–xxviii)

Careers, like higher education and most other aspects of the modern world, are changing. The idea that a man might enter an organization or occupation as a youngster, and spend a whole working life within it, receiving occasional promotions along the way, while a woman would take 'a little job' and concentrate

---

Box 2.10: The meaning of careers

The term 'career' can mean a number of things. It can imply advancement – persons move 'up' in their career rather than 'down', although we refer to 'career moves', which may also be lateral. We also refer to people 'having a career in' some form of profession, such as medicine, banking or management, and there is an implication, if now largely out-of-date, that a career is likely to be stable over time. In fact it is becoming more common for people to think in terms of 'career portfolios', interrelated sets of work experiences that may be combined to provide career evidence for a range of jobs. Because of this, we shall define career as 'the pattern of work-related experiences that span the course of a person's life'.

(Thomson and Mabey 1994: 123)

By career I mean that trajectory through life which each person undergoes, the activities he or she engages in to satisfy physical needs and wants and the even more important social needs and wants. The career, then, is activated in the service of both the physical being and the symbolic self.

(Goldschmidt 1990: 107)

Organisations are not pyramids, they are scattered encampments on a wide terrain of hills and valleys, and careers are not ladders, but stories about journeys and routes through and between these encampments . . . Careers, as stories of these journeys, often get better with the telling . . . They provide cognitive structures on to which our social identities can be anchored.

(Nicholson and West 1988: 94)

---

on family responsibilities, is now outmoded, though it still represents many people's assumptions.

Within higher education, the traditional male career is best exemplified in the idea of moving from postgraduate study to become successively a research officer, lecturer, senior lecturer, reader and, eventually, professor; though few, of course, would make it that far. While some people may take that route, and more of those over 50 who are currently working in higher education did, the opportunities today tend to be less linear, secure and straightforward. For those who are in or approaching mid-career, this means they may need to renew their engagement with their own career identity. For newer entrants it means career planning takes on a whole new resonance.

Box 2.10 offers three quotations on the nature of careers in general, each of which has relevance for the particular case of higher education. The first recognizes the varied and changing meanings applied to the term, but opts for an employment-based or work-based definition. The second suggests a broader interpretation, linking career to the whole of the life course, something which probably has resonance for most academics. They are unlikely to go to the university to work in the office, lecture room or laboratory from 9.00 a.m. to 5.00 p.m., five days a week. The intellectual calling is a vocation, in an older sense of that term. Academic work tends to invade and structure all aspects of your life: you take it home with you, you take it on holiday, and it enters your dreams (and nightmares).

The third quotation given in Box 2.10 identifies the perceptual and individual nature of the career, relating this to the organizational location. Careers seem very different in retrospect than they do in prospect, and vary as they are presented to different people. If you doubt this, think about how you alter your curriculum vitae to suit different job applications (the curriculum vitae is considered in detail in the section on **Applying for a Job** in Chapter 3).

Some of the imagery associated with our varying career perceptions is summarized in Box 2.11. This list contains both expressions used in everyday speech and terms which have been given specific meanings by career theorists. The range of metaphors which have been, and are, applied to our understandings of career is clearly extensive. It can be seen that, while some of these metaphors construe careers as being about progression, construction and building (ladders, fast tracking), others reflect the necessity of compromise (moving sideways, running with the wolves), or the reality of frustration and disappointment (the glass ceiling, on hold).

Some of the general changes in career patterns, indicated in the quote from Morgan with which we opened this section, are summarized in Box 2.12. All organizations are under pressure to become 'leaner', more efficient and more productive, if they are to survive, far less develop, in an increasingly competitive world. These strictures also apply to universities and colleges, which have shown an increasing willingness in recent years, under the pressure of the changes sketched earlier in this chapter, to adopt business management practices. After all, if the idea of the learning organization (one of the key concepts in the contemporary business and management literature) has any meaning, one might expect universities to become leading exponents.

Academic roles and careers

As the organization of this book makes clear, academic careers can be thought of as involving work in one or more of five broad roles:

* networking;
* teaching;
* researching;
* writing;
* managing.

What may be called the classic career model of academic life – a secure lecturing or professorial post – would involve doing some of all of these things, though with a focus on teaching, researching and writing. Entry, following academic qualification (in the more recent period, typically at postgraduate level), would normally have been through an initial focus on either teaching or research. Other activities, notably managing or networking (as a representative), might come to assume a dominant role later on in one's career, particularly for the minority who had built a reputation within their institution or discipline.

Box 2.11: Career metaphors

Career elements
career building
career blocks
career barriers
career breaks
career bottlenecks
career anchors
career portfolios
career patchworks

Career as progression
streams
ladders
routes
paths
the seven-year itch
on a roll
fast tracking
ahead of schedule

Career as frustration
stuck in a rut
the glass ceiling
the slippery pole
plateauing out
on the scrap heap
retiring on the job
dead man's shoes
moving sideways
promoted beyond your abilities
hitting the buffers
slipping away
the forgotten army

Career seen in a wider context
on the back burner
on hold
in the pending tray

Male dominance metaphors
the boys' club
the men's room
the old school tie

Playing organizational politics
playing the game
heat in the kitchen
running with the wolves

Box 2.12: Changing career patterns

Organizational imperatives
flatter structures
flexible workforces
downsizing
outsourcing
just-in-time
efficiency/productivity
high involvement
globalization

Individual perspectives
career portfolios
uncertainty
adaptability
self-belief
ability to collaborate
willingness to keep learning
commitment to achievement
balancing careers
composing a life

Nowadays, entry to the academic life may be through proficiency in, and/or practice of, any of the five main activities identified, though teaching and research remain of primary importance in recruiting staff in most disciplines and institutions. Careers can be made almost wholly in any one of the five activities, though combinations of them remain more common. The importance of networking throughout one's career must, however, be stressed. Constructing careers from combinations of roles is, of course, even more the norm in the varied professions and activities which 'surround' academic work – for example, further education, journalism, libraries and museums – and also contribute to the intellectual life.

Box 2.13 summarizes what is currently known about variations in academic employment characteristics in terms of subject area, job role, sex and age. It confirms, among other things, the continuing importance of teaching and research as the major roles for many academics.

Box 2.14 presents a complementary, but rather more complicated, picture of academic work in terms of the use of time for different activities. While this does not separately distinguish two of the five academic roles we have identified – writing and networking – it does indicate much else. The academic workload is shown as being, on average, significantly heavier than the conventional 35- or 40-hour working week, whether that week is in term time or not. About one-third of this workload is characterized as administration. During term, another third is allocated to teaching and a fifth to research. Outside term, the balance switches, with about one-third of the average academic's time spent on research, and less than one-fifth on teaching.

Box 2.13: Major subject differences in higher education staffing

1 'Teaching only' staff predominate in certain specialist subjects, e.g. agriculture, languages, the creative arts and education.
2 'Research only' staff predominate in the sciences and technology.
3 The possession of a doctorate or any higher degree is more common among those who teach or research in the sciences; overall, 'teaching only' staff are less likely to possess a higher degree.
4 Female staff are comparatively few in departments of engineering and physical sciences; but they predominate in nursing, and are in equilibrium with male staff in departments of education.
5 Staff who do both teaching and research in clinical departments and in departments of science (but less obviously engineering) tend to be more highly paid than those in other disciplines.
6 It appears that staff working in arts and social science departments are somewhat older than staff working in scientific and clinical departments.

Source: Ramsden (1996: 29).

Box 2.14: Use of time by academic staff

Activity	Term week		Vacation week	
	Mean hours	% of total	Mean hours	% of total
Teaching undergraduates	16.1	29.3	7.1	13.9
Teaching graduates	3.0	5.5	1.6	3.1
Graduate research	2.7	4.9	2.7	5.3
Personal research	8.5	15.5	13.8	27.0
Other internal academic work	2.6	4.7	3.0	5.9
External academic work	4.1	7.5	5.8	11.3
Administration	18.0	32.7	17.2	33.6
Totals	**55.0**	**100.0**	**51.2**	**100.0**

Source: Court (1994: 6).

With higher education institutions seeking to maximize the use of their resources throughout the year, we should question the distinction suggested by this table between 'term' and 'vacation'. The table does show that the average workload is much the same at all times. The days when academics could expect long vacations during the summer are long gone!

What has changed most significantly in academic careers over the last few decades, and is not apparent in either Box 2.13 or Box 2.14 (or Box 1.1), is the reduced availability of full-time and permanent positions within universities and colleges. Much of the growth in academic employment necessary to cope with increasing numbers of students and other activities has been in short-term and part-time contract posts. There have always been a lot of these, of course, but their numbers have mushroomed as the system has expanded and become less generously resourced. While it is still possible to move from a part-time or short-term contract to a permanent position, the opportunities for doing so have shrunk, and many academics may spend most if not all of their working lives in relatively insecure positions.

The other significant change in recent years in academic employment patterns also relates to the expansion of the higher education system. As higher education institutions have become larger and more complex, there has been a related rise in the importance of the management and networking functions. More people now choose careers in academic management, while national, international and disciplinary organizations employ many others.

For anyone, the choice of academic career will already, of course, be shaped by their educational history (see also the section in Chapter 3 on **Evaluating your present position**). This will affect not only the departments or subject areas they might work in, but also the level at which they might enter. The choice of an academic career should also be guided by interests and skills. While these may have to be adapted and developed to match the opportunities available, if your interests and skills lie in teaching, you would be best advised not to enter institutional management, and vice versa. There may be opportunities to shift career between academic roles later on, particularly between research and teaching, but this cannot be relied upon in advance.

As Box 2.15 indicates, the standard salary scales for university academic, research and related staff (which includes administrative, computer, library and other categories) are exactly parallel, so that everybody in academe should know their place in the relative pecking order. The senior grades are much more negotiable in terms of remuneration. These salaries are far from munificent, and have fallen behind recently in comparison with other white collar professions. Indeed, salaries are one aspect of the job with which academics are least satisfied, as a 1994 survey showed:

> We found from our survey that, on the whole, university teachers were generally fairly satisfied with their job. They were particularly satisfied with teaching and, to a lesser extent, research. Another area where they also derived great satisfaction was the interaction with their colleagues . . . However, the university teachers derived only moderate satisfaction from the behaviour of their head of department and from physical conditions and the working facilities which existed in their universities. The three aspects of their job from where they derived dissatisfaction are pay, promotion and, to a lesser extent, the performance of their administrative and managerial duties.
>
> (Oshagbemi 1996: 398)

There may, however, be some scope for increasing one's earnings on the side. Institutional and departmental practices on this do vary, however: most expect to

---

Box 2.15: Salary scales for university academic, research and related staff, 1997/98

Point	Salary(£)	Academic grades	Research grades	Related staff
4	15,159			
5	16,045		I B	1
6	16,927			
7	17,606			
8	18,494	Lecturer A	I A	
9	19,371			
10	20,103			2
11	21,016			
12	21,894			
13	22,785			
14	23,691		II	
15	24,600	Lecturer B		
16	25,552			3
17	26,508			
18	27,985			4
20	29,380			
21	30,318		III	
22	31,269	Senior		5
23	32,238	Lecturer		
24	33,202			
25	34,038			
26	34,901			
27	35,893			
		Professorial minimum £33,882	Grade IV minimum £33,882	Grade 6 minimum £33,882

Note: Job titles, and salary minima and maxima, vary from institution to institution, particularly between old and new universities. There is no point 19.
Source: Association of University Teachers.

be informed, some require that you seek their permission, some expect a proportion of any additional earnings.

Further guidance on which sort of academic career might best suit you may be found throughout this book, but particularly in Chapters 3 and 9. Chapter 3 considers the issues involved in starting an academic career, while Chapter 9 focuses on developing an academic career from that starting position.

Sources of further information

In this section we list a range of materials in which you may follow up in more detail some of the issues discussed in this chapter. The emphasis is on recently published books in English. In each case, brief details are given as to contents and approach. Most of the sources given here are either contemporary analyses of the state of higher education or guides to working in it.

For an immediate guide to developments in British higher education, the best source is the weekly *Times Higher Education Supplement*. The daily broadsheet newspapers all carry major higher education stories as well, and usually have a special education section once a week. For research-based and analytical accounts of the changing higher education scene, there are a number of academic journals – for example, the *Higher Education Quarterly*, the *Higher Education Review* and *Studies in Higher Education* – typically published three or four times a year. The Open University's Quality Support Centre publishes a very useful *Higher Education Digest*, summarizing current issues and publications, a few times a year.

Further details of these publications, and of relevant organizations concerned with higher education, are included in the list of organizations and journals at the end of the book.

Arnold, J. (1997) *Managing Careers into the 21st Century*. London, Paul Chapman.
This text discusses career within an international and organizational context. The chapters are concerned to demonstrate the connections between the individual and the organization and include work-role transitions, making career decisions, developmental and organizational approaches to career management. Outsourcing, delayering, performance appraisal, personal development plans, self-efficacy, ageing and dual career are among those issues discussed in detail.

Becher, T. (1989) *Academic Tribes and Territories: Intellectual Enquiry and the Cultures of Disciplines*. Milton Keynes, Open University Press.
Study of academics working in 12 subject areas in prestigious departments in the United Kingdom and the United States. Considers disciplines, boundaries, specialisms, community life, communication, careers and the wider context.

Becher, T. and Kogan, M. (1992) *Process and Structure in Higher Education*, 2nd edn. London, Routledge.
Offers a general model for higher education, considers post-war developments in Britain, analyses the workings of the system and its component institutions and units.

Bianco-Mathis, V. and Chalofsky, N. (eds) (1996) *The Adjunct Faculty Handbook*. Thousand Oaks, Calif., Sage.
American text aimed at part-time and short-term staff.

Brooks, A. (1997) *Academic Women*. Buckingham, Open University Press.
Comparative study of the representation and experience of women as academics in the United Kingdom and New Zealand.

Caplan, P. (1993) *Lifting a Ton of Feathers: A Woman's Guide to Surviving in the Academic World*. Toronto, University of Toronto Press.
Reviews the myths underlying higher education, gender bias in academia and the different forms which the maleness of the environment takes. Contains many suggestions as to what you might do to deal with particular situations.

Clark, B. (1983) *The Higher Education System: Academic Organization in Cross-national Perspective*. Berkeley, University of California Press.
Analysis of the organization of higher education in Western countries. Includes chapters on knowledge, work, authority, values and change.

Clark, B. (ed.) (1987) *The Academic Profession: National, Disciplinary and Institutional Settings*. Berkeley, University of California Press.
Considered study of the structure and organization of the academic profession, focusing on the United Kingdom, the United States of America, France and Germany.

Cuthbert, R. (ed.) (1996) *Working in Higher Education*. Buckingham, Open University Press.
Includes sections on the workers, the work and the work context.

Deneef, A. and Goodwin, C. (1995) *The Academic's Handbook*, 2nd edn. Durham, NC, Duke University Press.
American text, with sections on the academy and the academic, issues in the academy today, academic employment, teaching and advising, funding academic research, publishing research, academic communities and administrations.

Frost, P. and Taylor, M. (eds) (1996) *Rhythms of Academic Life: Personal Accounts of Careers in Academia*. Thousand Oaks, Calif., Sage.
Over 50 chapters, principally by North American organizational scientists, offering personal reflections on career rhythms, becoming a teacher, doing research and getting published, working with doctoral students, getting tenure, integrating work and personal lives, working collaboratively, becoming a reviewer, a journal editor, a department chair, a full professor, working as a consultant, developing innovative teaching materials, taking a sabbatical.

Hall, D. (ed.) (1996) *The Career Is Dead – Long Live the Career: A Relational Approach to Careers*. San Francisco, Jossey-Bass.
This takes the perspective of the career as a series of lifelong employment-based experiences and personal learnings. The book has been written primarily for human resource professionals and career counsellors. The three parts discuss organizational changes, relational approaches to career development and diversity issues.

Halsey, A. (1995) *Decline of Donnish Dominion: The British Academic Professions in the Twentieth Century*, revised edition. Oxford, Clarendon Press.
Places the development of the university in its historical perspective, examining academic career patterns and their changing place in society.

Johnson, L. (1996) *Being an Effective Academic*. Oxford, Oxford Centre for Staff Development.
A useful source of guidance on self-organization, priorities, decision-making, action planning, reading and writing, people, motivation and other day-to-day aspects of the academic job.

Rose, S. (ed.) (1986) *Career Guide for Women Scholars*. New York, Springer-Verlag.
Drawn from the experience of North American women academics. 'Behind the scenes' accounts of job hunting, publishing, networking, career transitions, 'race' and gay issues.

Scott, P. (1995) *The Meanings of Mass Higher Education*. Buckingham, Open University Press.
Examines the evolution of British higher education and its component institutions; its political, social and economic context; and the relation between massification and other developments.

3 | STARTING AN ACADEMIC CAREER

Introduction

This chapter focuses on the strategies which might be adopted to enter academic life, and on the variety of initial experiences. It also offers ideas on the kind of support established academics and institutions may offer to novice scholars and new colleagues.

Starting any career, whether it is a first entry into paid work or a follow-up to a previous career or careers, can be a nerve-wracking experience. You may not know until a number of years afterwards, and perhaps not even then, what the unwritten rules of practice are. The purpose of this chapter, then, is to provide some insights and encourage reflection, in the belief that this may make the rites of passage into academe a more pleasurable and less worrying period.

The chapter is organized into six main sections, the first four focusing on the processes involved in obtaining an academic post, the last two considering what may be involved in the initial period of entering academic work:

- **Evaluating your present position** encourages you to review the kinds of qualifications, skills and experience which academic posts require, and what you might have to offer;
- **Where to look for work** identifies the main sources of information about available academic posts;
- **Applying for a job** describes the components and strategies involved in putting together a good job application and curriculum vitae;
- **The job interview** considers the varied nature of job interviews and how best to approach them;
- **Negotiating transitions** focuses on the shift from student or non-academic status to becoming an academic, and looks at the induction and initial experience of new academics;

- **Balancing careers** considers the strategies involved in reconciling academic with non-academic work and family life, and in maintaining two academic careers within the same household.

At the end of the chapter, a selection of sources of further information is listed.

Evaluating your present position

Career counsellors advise that one of the key elements of career planning is a high level of self-awareness and self-evaluation. Various diagnostic instruments used in career counselling can aid this process. These include tests and inventories, cognitive and behavioural assessment, guidance interviews, self-assessment exercises and interactive computer guidance systems. The purpose of these is not only to raise your awareness of the skills and knowledge you currently possess, and their transferability to a range of domains, but also to stress the importance of identifying the kind of post which would suit your qualifications, interests and values. Evaluating your position is a craft which can be learnt.

If you have a PhD or are just completing one – a typical position for those seeking their first academic post – you should have developed many transferable skills which can be applied to academic or other work:

> being able to see any prolonged task or project through to completion . . . the abilities to plan, to allocate time and money and to trouble-shoot . . . to set their work in a wider field of knowledge . . . to sift through large quantities of information, to take on board other points of view, challenge premises, question procedures and interpret meaning . . . Dealing with criticism and presenting cases ought to be second nature . . . the skills needed for composing reports, manuals and press releases and for summarising bulky documents . . . the skills of coping with isolation . . . self-direction; self-discipline; self-motivation; resilience; tenacity and the abilities to prioritise and juggle a number of tasks at once. Students working on group projects should be able to claim advanced team-working skills . . . networking with others, using project management techniques, and finding their way around specialist libraries or archives.
>
> (Cryer 1997: i)

The necessary skills and knowledge for an academic post clearly rest on postgraduate activities. In reviewing these, be careful not to overlook relevant experience, whether paid or unpaid. It is not uncommon, for example, for postgraduate students to help one another out, and to provide support and encouragement. You may, in helping a friend finish a piece of work, have been acting as a research assistant. When a colleague asked you to look over their thesis you may have done some peer-tutoring. When you were asked by an acquaintance for help and advice in completing a portfolio, were you perhaps acting as a mentor? That time when you committed three days to helping someone get a conference ready: was that conference administration? In addition, therefore, to being pragmatic in applying for academic posts, you should also be careful not to undersell yourself.

Box 3.1: Advertisements for academic posts

Lecturer in English
Manchester Metropolitan University, £13,493–£22,493. As well as having teaching experience, it is essential that you are an active researcher who will have publications available for inclusion in the next research exercise.

Research Associate
University of Cambridge, Department of Geography. SMEs, Networks and Local Economic Development. One year. Applicants should have experience of basic data and statistical analysis, and may be at pre- or postdoctoral level with a degree in geography, economics or a related discipline. The salary will be in the range £14,732–£18,825 (subject to review) depending on age and experience, plus USS benefits.

Teaching Fellowships in History
University of Essex. To replace colleagues on leave. Fixed term teaching fellowships in British history (late 18th to 20th centuries). Candidates must have completed, or be close to completing, a PhD on any period of British history between the late 18th and 20th centuries. Appointment will be until 31 July 1999 with the possibility of a further year's renewal. Salary £15,159–£22,785.

Faculty of Arts British Academy Institutional Fellowships
University of Manchester, for a period of six years. Applicants should preferably hold a PhD or equivalent qualification and will have started to publish, or be able to demonstrate the potential to publish, in their specialist field. A good understanding of and interest in recent syntactic theories as they apply in the historical domain will be important. Initial salary in the range £14,732–£22,143 per annum (under review).

Lectureship in Social Policy
University of Bath. Applications are invited for a Lectureship in Social Policy in this Grade 5 department. Candidates must be committed to high-quality research and teaching. Lecturer A scale £16,045–£21,016 per annum.

Source: summaries of advertisements appearing in *The Guardian*, 17/6/97, and the *Times Higher Education Supplement*, 25/4/97, 9/5/97, 23/5/97, 13/6/97.

A second important element in career planning is that of job knowledge (see also the next section, on **Where to look for work**). Advertisements for academic posts offer a way of assessing the qualifications, experience and skills sought or expected from applicants. Browsing the job pages of the education press, even when not actively seeking employment, is a useful exercise for evaluating present and future skill requirements. Box 3.1 gives some examples from recent advertisements: more specific details would typically be given to potential applicants who made further enquiries. As might be expected, the requirements vary depending upon the level of the post, its subject area, the institution involved and the specialization of the post (e.g. whether it focuses on research or teaching). The examples chosen also reflect the present realities of

British higher education: some are short-term or replacement posts, while others refer to the requirements of the research assessment exercise.

Clearly, in applying for any of these posts, you would be well advised to have qualifications, knowledge and skills which more or less match those being sought. You might not have everything asked for – such an applicant might not exist or might not be attracted to the post – but you should have most of it. Thus, if the advertisement asks for a PhD, those who are near to completing one might still be positively considered. If there are requirements which you don't meet – a particular subject specialism, facility with a specific computer package – you should at least be able to demonstrate an interest in these areas, and be prepared to develop new skills.

One of the most valuable ways in which you can gain advice about your readiness for a particular post is by using your networks. Nearing the age of 40 and with a recent sole-authored book, one of us was advised: 'go for the permanent job *now*, if you wait another couple of years you'll be over 40 and your book will be out of date'. Among the obvious people whose advice you might seek, both in general and about specific posts, are:

• the person, or persons, who supervised or tutored you when you last engaged in academic study;
• colleagues and other people you know who work in universities or colleges in similar positions or subjects;
• the head of department or centre advertising the post you are considering applying for, or any other named contact.

Finally, bear in mind two key points. First, you are unlikely to be offered the first post you apply for. Getting an academic job is a competitive business, so you should treat it as a campaign. Once you have got a job, the campaign is unlikely to stop, but will continue with more or less intensity for much of your academic career. Second, be honest, both with yourself and about yourself. Misrepresenting your interests or plans might help you to get a post, but it is less likely to form the basis for a happy and successful career.

Where to look for work

Having undertaken a preliminary evaluation of your skills, competencies and interests, and having begun to learn how best to present your experience (see also the next section on **Applying for a job**), the next stage is to seek out vacancy information. Box 3.2 contains some interesting advice on job searching. It stresses the importance of being concurrently pragmatic and idealistic, of tailoring your approach to each application, and of being willing to take some risks.

Academic posts are advertised in a variety of places: Box 3.3 summarizes the main sources in the United Kingdom. For most posts in most subject areas, the two best sources of information nationally are the *Times Higher Education Supplement*, published each Friday, and the Education supplement included with *The Guardian* each Tuesday. Both of these publications also include their advertisements on their Internet sites, which are updated before publication. In the

---

Box 3.2: Dos and don'ts of successful job searches

• Do evaluate your assets brutally, because others will.
• Do as much as possible to overcome weaknesses in your record.
• Do work with advisers and senior colleagues to help you obtain interviews.
• Do tailor your approach to each employer.
• Do practise your presentation and take it seriously.
• Do realize that your graduate school's reputation will have a bearing on your job search.
• Do remember the importance of attitude and appearance.
• Do realize that previously unappealing job vacancies look more attractive later in the year.
• Do remember that another job search can occur next year, especially if you end up in a temporary or one-year position.

• Don't underestimate the competition.
• Don't restrict your search to only safe or sure options.
• Don't forget that universities and colleges have their own interests and peculiarities.
• Don't pretend to be someone you are not.
• Don't act as if you are too good for certain places or tasks; don't put others down.
• Don't appear too eager or desperate.
• Don't lose needed energy near the end.
• Don't expect to find the perfect job the first year.

(Kronenfeld and Whicker 1997: 94, 95)

Spring, the *Times Higher Education Supplement* carries a 'Research Opportunities Supplement', which contains details of some research posts alongside fuller details of postgraduate studentships. Bear in mind the cycles of the academic year when jobs are most likely to be advertised: spring vacancies, for example, will often have autumn start dates.

In addition to published advertisements, the other key way of checking on academic job opportunities is through direct and continuing contacts with prospective colleagues. Indeed, as Box 3.4 indicates, the more informal routes of job searching are often the most successful. This is where identifying your skills and interests, matching these to a university or department, and then making suitable approaches can be highly successful. Here, the importance of networks and networking in providing 'insider' knowledge and access cannot be underestimated.

Many university and college departments have short-term and part-time opportunities which come up at various times during the year and need to be filled quickly. Such jobs can lead on to something more permanent or full-time. These posts may not be advertised, or at least not widely, so you need to make your skills, interests and availability known. Ask friends and colleagues, contact the heads of likely departments (not just the one where you did, or are doing, your PhD), or other key staff, and send them a copy of your curriculum vitae. Visit

---

Box 3.3: Where to look for academic advertisements

* The *Times Higher Education Supplement*
Published weekly on Fridays, this has the most comprehensive collection of academic advertisements for the United Kingdom, and also carries some for Commonwealth and European countries. Also available on the Internet:
http://thesis.newsint.co.uk
For North American opportunities, the *Chronicle of Higher Education* is the standard source.

* The national quality press
The Guardian on Tuesdays has the widest collection of academic advertisements, and these, like those in the THES, can be accessed through the Internet:
http://recruitnet.guardian.co.uk
Other quality dailies (*The Independent* on Thursdays, *The Times* on Mondays, the *Daily Telegraph* on Wednesdays) also carry some. Academic posts in particular fields (e.g. computing, social work) may also appear in the weekly features which some newspapers include on other days. Quality Sunday news-papers, such as the *Sunday Times* and the *Observer*, also carry some academic advertisements.

* Quality weekly papers
Some specialist weekly papers contain some relevant academic advertisements. Thus, *The Economist* carries details of some posts in economics and related areas, the *Times Literary Supplement* carries some for humanities and social sciences, the *New Statesman* carries some for sociology, social policy, politics and cognate subjects.

* Institutional notice-boards
University and college departments often circulate details of new posts among themselves, so departmental notice-boards can be a good source of informa-tion, particularly for short-term and part-time positions.

---

such departments when you can, get to know the secretarial staff, participate in seminars, be pleasant, make yourself useful if you can, and keep your eyes and ears peeled!

Applying for a job

While acquiring work through informal networks, particularly on a short-term or temporary basis, may get around some of the standardized procedures associated with job applications, for those seeking longer-term employment the submis-sion of an application will normally be required. Don't hold back from making informal enquiries to the head of department or professor responsible prior to application: these are likely to be welcomed as an indication of serious interest, rather than seen as awkward or time-consuming. However, as Box 3.5 indicates, it pays to plan and prepare before making that telephone call.

Box 3.4: The least and most effective methods of job hunting

The least effective

1 Using computer bank listings or 'registers'.
2 Answering local newspaper advertisements.
3 Going to private employment agencies.
4 Answering advertisements in professional or trade journals within your field.
5 Mailing out curricula vitae by the bushel.

The most effective

1 The so-called 'creative job-hunting approach' – figuring out your best skills, and favourite knowledges, and then researching any employer that interests you, before approaching that organization and arranging, through your contacts, to see the person there who has the power to hire you for the position you are interested in.
2 Applying directly to an employer, factory or office in person, without first having done the homework just described.
3 Asking friends for job leads.
4 Asking relatives for job leads.
5 Using the placement office at the school or college that you once attended.

Source: Bolles (1996: 27, 57, 58).

Submitting an application for an academic job is much the same process as for many other professional posts. Consequently, the normal rules apply. The university or college to which you are applying should provide you with at least basic instructions as to what your application should contain. They may ask you to fill in a standard application form, or to submit a completed application form together with supporting materials, or simply to send in an application in the form you think best. Within those constraints, it is up to you to make the best impression possible. This is known to be difficult: handbooks for job hunters can be helpful in providing positive strategies and words!

If you are sent a standard application form to complete, you should obviously follow any instructions given as closely as possible. Most institutions will prefer you to send back a typed or word-processed form. Unless otherwise invited, you would also be advised to fit your replies neatly into the spaces allowed, which may not be generous. You are usually allowed or encouraged to submit a more detailed curriculum vitae and statement together with the completed form.

If there is no standard application form, or additional material is asked for, you will need to set out your application yourself in an acceptable and attractive format. Box 3.6 lists the contents common to most academic job applications: just what you include may be adjusted as appropriate in the light of the job applied for and such instructions as you have. We will consider each of the elements involved in crafting your application in turn.

You need to get your application noticed in order to have a chance of being interviewed. There are two craft skills which are critical here. One concerns how

---

Box 3.5: Hints and tips for making telephone enquiries

1 Have a positive mental attitude before you call. Take a few deep breaths to help prepare yourself.
2 Be prepared and organized. Have a copy of the advertisement to hand with relevant points highlighted. Have pen, paper and diary handy.
3 Think about exactly what you want to know. Prepare key questions in advance, and also any information you may be required to give to the other party.
4 Make sure there are no distracting background noises. It is best to wait for a quiet settled period before calling.
5 It is always preferable to address the person by name as this helps to establish rapport.
6 Use your normal tone of voice and natural vocabulary. Any special 'telephone voice' will sound affected. Convey your personality through your voice, attitude and speech.
7 Don't be afraid to ask relevant questions, as this may be the only way to acquire the information you need, even if it means hearing negative comments.
8 Take notes, but concentrate on what is being said, particularly the intention and attitudes behind the words.
9 Don't interrupt; wait until the other person has finished speaking. This is an important interpersonal skill, so train yourself if necessary.
10 Conclude the call by confirming any details. Remember to say thank you and to express enthusiasm for the post.

A conversational opener:
'My name is——and I am ringing regarding the [name of position] position you advertised in [source of advertisement and date].'

Some possible questions:
'Could you please tell me the qualities you are seeking in the applicant?'
'Could you please tell me exactly what the job entails?'
'What qualifications and skills are required?'

Source: adapted from Shmerling (1993: 142–7).

---

you write about your work and achievements. The second has to do with managing and presenting your personal and social identity.

Your *covering letter* is often the most important part of the application. It is here that you have an opportunity to make a good initial impression. As suggested in Box 3.6, this letter should both express an interest in the post you are applying for and summarize the contents of your application. It might also indicate why you think you are well suited to and qualified for the post: in other words, draw attention to your strengths and say why you should be given the job. This is the place where you tailor your experience to the requirements of the post and identify the relevant transferable skills you have developed. Both flexibility and coherence are important.

A key quality of the covering letter is its brevity and accessibility. Ideally, you should take no more than one side, certainly no more than two. Personnel

---

Box 3.6: Contents of a job application

- Covering letter: 'a short formal statement of your interest in the position and a very brief list of the enclosed documents'.
- Curriculum vitae: 'a factual outline of your life as a scholar', containing personal information and details of your education, positions held, awards, societies joined, teaching experience, papers delivered and publications record.
- Statement of research interests: 'a concise presentation of what your research has been about and where you see it heading'.
- Statement of teaching interests: 'an honest evaluation of your qualifications to teach courses at the graduate and undergraduate levels'.
- Letters of reference

Source: Wilbur (1995: 118–20).

---

officers and heads of department, the people who are initially most likely to review your application, are busy people. Your task here is to organize your letter in such a way that their attention is easily drawn to the connections between your ability to do the job and the job requirements. You should, therefore, reuse key words from the advertisement or further particulars. In the advertisements summarized in Box 3.1 you will see phrases such as 'active researcher', 'experience of basic data and statistical analysis', 'British history between the late 18th and 20th centuries', and 'demonstrate potential to publish'. In response, you need to use personal examples to indicate to potential employers your ability to fulfil such requirements.

The *curriculum vitae*, by comparison, is likely to be the most substantial part of your application. It will give details of your:

- educational qualifications (focusing on higher education),
- employment experience (again focusing on higher education),
- papers and publications (organized by date and kind of publication), and
- other relevant experience (e.g. professional work, involvement in societies, awards, languages, computing).

Your curriculum vitae embodies a tension which will be present throughout your application – between, on the one hand, brevity and clarity, and, on the other, comprehensiveness. If you have already published a good number of papers, and given presentations at a variety of conferences, you will want to include full details. However you structure it, it is critical that anyone examining your curriculum vitae should be able to find their way around it quickly. So don't make it longer than necessary, include short summary sections, and lay particular emphasis on key aspects of your academic and work histories.

Box 3.7 encourages you to think about the presentational aspects of compiling a curriculum vitae in terms of impression management. In addition to the general comments given, it is worth considering the ways in which the titles of publications and conference papers, and current and past research, convey your intellectual

---

Box 3.7: Writing your curriculum vitae creatively

- make it results-orientated, not just a recitation of what you are/were responsible for
- you can influence the content of your interview by what you put, and don't put, on your application form
- describe career breaks as you would a period of paid employment. Refer to them as, for example, 'managing a home', and describe what you did: 'organized finances, managed changing priorities', etc
- the different bits of experience that you've had are increasingly described nowadays as your 'portfolio'. This may be something you consciously work on extending, or a pattern that you identify with the benefit of hindsight

(Willis and Daisley 1990: 218–19)

Box 3.8: Rewriting your curriculum vitae for particular audiences

Mary's doctoral research was on an American author who lived and wrote in France. Her use of historical literary sources could have placed her for a post in English literature, comparative literary studies, European studies or American studies.

I received my PhD in social psychology, held a three-year pre-doctoral traineeship in cross-cultural child development (which included a dissertation on Mexican families), and did a pre-doctoral and post-doctoral clinical internship with special emphasis on family therapy and ethnicity and mental health. I was at first hired for a one-year position teaching personality psychology, and then later seriously considered for jobs in clinical, community, personality and developmental psychology, in ethnic studies, and in family and sex roles in several sociology departments.

(Bronstein 1986: 11–12)

Jeff had a BA in sociology and politics, a PhD in social anthropology, and had undertaken research on local politics in rural France. His supervisor was based in a school of African and Asian studies. He could, therefore, consider jobs in one of three disciplines (sociology, politics, anthropology), or with a regional or sectoral focus (e.g. Europe, Africa, rural).

---

interests. These are crucial shapers of your public career identity. What do they say about you? How do they fit the intellectual interests of the department to which you are applying? Examples of the ways in which employment identities have the potential to be shaped to alternative posts are given in Box 3.8.

In preparing for job applications, you may also want to decide whether you should be ready to cope with bias or prejudice. Do you think your age or marital status might count against you? Is it possible to omit or disguise these on your written application, and so get through the first hurdle?

There are a number of professional agencies, whose advertisements you may have seen, who specialize in producing curricula vitae for people like you. You might consider using one if you can afford it, and have little experience in putting these key documents together. You should certainly take advice from supervisors, colleagues and friends, where you can, as to how your curriculum vitae looks and how it might be altered. A good deal is riding here on the quality of your presentation, and how good it looks – though this will not, of course, compensate for inadequate content.

Your *statement of interests* will vary depending upon the nature of the post applied for – whether it involves research, teaching, management, other activities, or some combination of all of these – and your previous experience. This statement is important for indicating that you have some idea of where your career is going, what you would like to do in it, and how you are planning ahead. Potential employers are unlikely to be impressed by applicants without a sense of direction, or who do not intend to develop their portfolio of activities. Your statement, of course, provides a further opportunity to demonstrate that you have researched the interests of the department to which you are applying and will fit in with them.

The fifth item of a standard academic job application indicated in Box 3.6, is also of critical importance: your *references*. Typically, you will be invited to name two or three people to whom your potential employer can apply for references. These referees should include reputable academics who are familiar with you because they taught or supervised you, or employed or otherwise worked with you in a university or college. If you are seeking to move into academic work in mid-career, your references will also normally include your current employer or manager, and possibly your mentor (see the section on **Mentoring and partnerships** in Chapter 4). Whoever your referees are, you want them to appear credible in the eyes of those reviewing your application. Including one or more professors, and/or other senior and well-known academics, from reputable British institutions is, therefore, highly advisable.

There is an etiquette in using referees. They are an important part of your network, and need careful cultivation. You should ask their permission initially, and take that opportunity to sound them out on their opinions of you and what kinds of post you might be well suited for. Ideally, you would like your referees to give you glowing references, praising your achievements to date, linking your skills closely to the job applied for, and asserting that no other candidate should possibly be considered. To help them to do this it is a good idea to keep them as up to date as possible about your career and job applications as you put them in. It is even better, of course, if you can, to discuss each application with them before you submit it, or to provide them with a written synopsis which highlights the parts of your experience which you feel are relevant to the employment particulars. Thank them, of course, for the work they put in on your behalf and keep in touch afterwards.

Whatever you do, keep a copy of any application you make, at least until you know you have been unsuccessful. Even then, you should find it useful to refer to when you make further applications. Finally, remember that you will only have a chance of getting the job if your application is good enough to get you on to the shortlist.

The job interview

> While casualness reigns in academia, there are times when it is more appropriate to dress more formally. It would be foolish for anyone wishing to get a job at a university to turn up in a T-shirt and jeans. The interview situation is always a formal one, even in academia, and requires formality in dress. The casually dressed applicant may just be inexperienced in the art of dressing or interviewing but the overall impression created is one of disrespect for the occasion or straightforward arrogance.
>
> (Entwistle 1997: iv)

> Overall, the research findings reveal that despite anti-discrimination legislation in the mid-1970s, a substantial number of employers, many of whom publicly subscribe to equal opportunities, are still 'managing to discriminate' on the grounds of sex through a variety of recruitment practices.
>
> (Collinson *et al.* 1990: 192)

These two quotations portray continuing aspects of recruitment and selection processes: abiding inequalities and conventional or conservative attitudes. We place them here to remind you that despite the educational language of meritocracy and egalitarianism, and despite pockets of goodwill to bring about change, universities remain places of status and hierarchy (see the section on **The changing nature of higher education** in Chapter 2). The job interview is one place where conventional attitudes emerge, and there are still many members of university interview panels who have had no training in equal opportunities. Prepare to handle, with dignity, any inappropriate questioning. It would not be unusual to become a member of interview panels later on in an academic career: now might be a good time to take an interest and obtain guidance in good practice for equal opportunities.

Job interviews and their associated processes vary. You may be the only candidate called for interview, or there might be several candidates: either way, the panel still might not make an appointment. The panel might consist of only two or three people, or could contain a dozen or more. The panel might consist wholly of staff from the department or centre in which the appointment would be based; or might have representatives from other parts of the university or college; or, and this applies particularly to more senior appointments, might contain one or more experts from other institutions. However it is composed, it is likely to be supported by a representative from the institution's personnel office.

You might be asked to submit further documentation before the interview, perhaps an outline of your ideas for development or an example of your work, such as a key publication. You might also be invited to visit the department or institution before or after your interview: clearly, any reluctance to do so is likely to count against you. There might be two or more stages to the interview

---

Box 3.9: Hints and tips for presentations

- If you are given a remit for your presentation, make sure you keep to it and cover the issues raised. If you are unclear about what is expected, check out the details beforehand.
- Try and find out as much as you can about who will be at the presentation, so that you can focus your talk appropriately.
- Practice your presentation with a colleague, friend or partner, and make changes as necessary. Make sure you can deliver it comfortably in the time given.
- Take a little time before your presentation, if you can, to relax and prepare yourself.
- Begin your presentation with a personal anecdote, or a pertinent quotation, to engage your audience's attention. Then summarize what you are going to say.
- As you talk, engage different members of your audience in passing eye contact. Don't talk to just one person or never look at the audience.
- Make use of familiar technology (e.g. overheads and slide projectors, flip charts) if it is available and adds to your presentation. Don't do so, however, if you are unfamiliar with the technology. Make sure any visuals you use are of good quality. Consider making copies to circulate.
- End your presentation with brief conclusions, and then invite questions or comments.
- Respond to questions in a friendly manner. Don't feel that you have to have all of the answers. Thank your audience before you leave.

---

process, with the number of candidates whittled down from stage to stage. The whole process might take just a few weeks or several months.

A half-hour interview with an appointment panel might be all that is expected of you, or you might also be asked to give a presentation to, and answer questions from, a larger group drawn from the department or university concerned. This is often the most anxiety-provoking aspect of the interview process for applicants. The presentation may be intended to illustrate your competence in teaching, or it may serve to indicate areas you would identify for future research. Box 3.9 offers some hints and tips for such presentations. They draw on the principles underlying any other form of presentation, such as a teaching situation or a conference paper.

However the selection process is constructed, at its core is likely to be an interview of less than an hour with a panel responsible for recommending or making the appointment decision. Box 3.10 lists some of the questions such panels typically ask, with an emphasis on initial appointments. At the heart of these and similar questions are three key concerns:

- with your experience, and how it fits you to do the job in question;
- with your understanding of the job, subject area, department and institution;
- with how you see yourself and the job developing in the future.

In preparing yourself for the job interview, you would be best advised to spend some time thinking through the messages you want to get across in answering

---

Box 3.10: Questions for job interviews

Common questions include:
- Will you have finished your dissertation by the start of the next academic year?
- What are your plans for submitting articles for publication from the dissertation?
- What direction do you expect your research to take in the future?
- What areas of teaching do you want to work in and what could you handle if you had to?
- What has been your prior experience with teaching?
- What are other special strengths and interests of yours?

Other issues often talked about include:
- The teaching load and expectations for staff.
- Your familiarity with the institution.
- Your familiarity with the department and the kinds of student they have.
- The kinds of activities you like when not working.
- Your familiarity with the area in which the job is located.

Source: Kronenfeld and Whicker (1997: 46).

---

questions like these. If you can, set up a mock interview, using your friends or colleagues as an interview panel, so that you can practise your answers out loud and get some feedback. Don't over-practise, as you will want to sound fresh. Focus on how you can best present yourself and your ideas. Remember that if you find a theme or a topic 'difficult' – for example, if your breadth of experience is likely to be interpreted as a lack of direction – working out the confused feelings associated with the topic can help to resolve defensive incoherence.

Box 3.11 provides some guidance on behaviour in the interview itself, with the objective of helping you to present yourself as well as you possibly can. The selectors may be looking for someone who will 'fit in'. If, by virtue of your age, race or gender, you fear that you may not obviously do so, then aim to demonstrate your skills and the capacity to develop them further. If you have the requisite qualities, are prepared to be flexible in terms of where you work and have a bit of luck, you are in a better position to be offered an academic post sooner rather than later.

You should be told the decision of the panel soon after the interview. Our experience would suggest that the successful applicant receives a telephone call during the evening after the interview. No call, no job; though this may not be confirmed for weeks. If you have been unsuccessful, try and get some feedback on your performance, in what areas you were judged to be good or lacking, and on how you might improve your future employability. Use this information to improve subsequent applications and presentations. Remember also that sometimes an institution will offer an unsuccessful candidate a post, perhaps at a lower grade, either immediately or at a later stage; so it is worthwhile maintaining good relations wherever possible.

> **Box 3.11: How to behave at the interview**
>
> - Dress smartly but comfortably. If you are wearing one, keep your jacket on.
> - Aim to arrive early.
> - Check out the detailed arrangements after arrival.
> - Go to the toilet shortly before you are due to be interviewed.
> - Engage in deep breathing or other relaxation exercises before you go in.
> - As you are introduced to each member of the interviewing panel, engage them in eye contact and nod or smile. If the opportunity presents itself, shake hands and greet people individually.
> - Pause for a few seconds before answering any but the simplest questions. This suggests careful thought, and does also give you time to think.
> - Don't, however, delay more than a few seconds before answering. You can play for time by repeating the question back or asking for clarification, but, if you are really stumped for an answer it is probably best to say so.
> - In answering, direct your gaze mainly at the questioner and whoever is chairing the panel, but be sure to make eye contact with each member from time to time.
> - Speak clearly and naturally, and at an easy listening pace.
> - Keep your arms and legs under control.
> - Don't be afraid to ask questions in return. This will probably be expected towards the end of the interview, but may be done at any appropriate time.
> - Remember to thank the panel and smile before you leave.

If, on the other hand, you have been successful, and you are offered the post you have applied for, be aware that you have entered one of those brief moments in the employment relationship where you have most of the power. Generally speaking, it is best to accept the post immediately it is offered to you, unless, that is, you have definitely decided that you don't want the job.

There then follows a brief period of negotiation, in which you can have some influence on the terms and conditions of the post. These will include not just the salary to be paid, but also the period of the appointment, what you will be expected to teach, who you will work with, accommodation, how much time you will be allowed for personal research and writing, and so on. The last of these is likely to be particularly important for the subsequent development of your career. Stand up for what you think you are worth, plus perhaps a little bit more, and the arrangements that would best suit you, but don't push your luck too far. If the deal is not good enough, withdraw.

Negotiating transitions

Almost half of the interviewees found difficulties with aspects of large lectures, citing time keeping, speed of delivery, over-dense material, student passivity, mindless note-taking (on the students' part) and inadequate preparation time . . . All interviewees except one regarded seminars as problematic. The key issue for most was to ensure that all group members participated in discussion . . . Half the interviewees identified time management as an issue. One aspect of this was the need to keep a balance between teaching and research . . . Perhaps predictably, there were tensions involved in working with colleagues . . . Some interviewees spoke of joining a tightly-knit team, of gaining a great deal of support and practical advice, and of quickly coming to identify with immediate colleagues. Others found themselves left very much to their own devices, with the apparent assumption that they would be able to deal with the job . . . All were highly aware of the expectation to publish . . . Most complained of the difficulty of finding time.

(Blackmore and Wilson 1995: 228, 229, 231)

Starting a new career – along with moving home (which you may have to do at the same time), overcoming a serious illness, getting married, getting divorced and dealing with the death of someone close to you – is often stated as being one of the most stressful events you have to cope with in life. This may seem less so with academic careers given prior experiences of student life. Yet the academic world can seem very different when it becomes paid employment, with all the connotations that that implies, or when beginning employment is associated with feelings of not 'fitting in'. Many people entering academic work also come from working in other organizations, and may not have been in universities or colleges for more than brief visits for a considerable time. It is wise, therefore, not to underestimate the extent to which starting a new career, and possibly other concurrent transitions, may affect emotional resilience.

Box 3.12 indicates some of the features associated with transitions. The four phases are not, however, mutually exclusive or linear. The need to learn the nature and content of a job quickly, often at the same time as doing it and with little support available, can collapse the four phases into one. Short-term or renewable contracts necessitate continuing negotiations for extension or renewal, and/or finding the next post. In such circumstances, the 'transition cycle' may be experienced more as a circle or spiral. The added stress of completing a PhD, getting published, discovering hidden unwritten rules or dealing with the chronic burden of prejudice, will make the transition experience even more complicated.

It is hardly surprising, then, that the initial experience of academic life can often be disorientating, lonely and rather bleak (see Box 3.13). In part, this is because universities and colleges, like many other employers, often devote little attention to, and consequently are not very good at inducting and supporting, new employees. Moreover, while formal schemes may exist to induct new employees into the institution, a new recruit's greatest reliance will be on their immediate colleagues, many of whom will be too busy to help or be unaware of this critical period in another's career.

Since career transitions are known to be difficult, there has been considerable research on this theme, including research specifically on academic workers. There are also self-diagnostic materials available to help identify your own customary way of handling stress and recommend coping strategies for transitions:

Box 3.12: The transition cycle, associated tasks, problems and strategies

Phase	Tasks/goals	Pitfalls/problems	Strategies/remedies
Preparation	Developing helpful expectations, motives and feelings	Fearfulness, reluctance, unreadiness	Realistic preview, advance contacts, self-appraisal
Encounter	Confidence in coping, enjoyment in sense-making	Shock, rejection, regret	Social supports, slack in the system, safety, freedom to explore and discover
Adjustment	Personal change, role development and relationship building	Misfitting, degrading, grieving	Real work to do, early success, useful failure, fast feedback, mutual control
Stabilization	Sustained trust, commitment and effectiveness with tasks and people	Failure, fatalism, faking	Goal-setting and appraisal for role evolution and discretion management

Source: Nicholson (1990: 87–92).

If you are considering a career change, you might want to reflect on your own coping style. Are you a creator, maintainer or conventionalist or reactor? Creative coping includes personal, psychological and social resources which can be utilised to ease the strain of transitions ... if you aren't already a creator, you might try to develop or acquire resources associated with this style.

(Ackerman 1986: 106)

Box 3.14 summarizes these social and psychological resources. The first creative task is to work out which of these can be cultivated in your own situation!

The transition period may have not only social or psychological implications but also contractual ones. For example, those who are fortunate enough to secure 'permanent' contracts may be initially designated as a 'probationary' member of staff, which can have advantages and disadvantages. On the one hand, this may mean a somewhat reduced workload and less responsibility, though there is no guarantee in these 'more for less' days that this will be the case. On the other hand, there is less employment security and there are the associated requirements of 'passing' successfully through the probationary period, through, for example, satisfactory appraisal reports.

Box 3.13: Initial experiences of academic life

Unfortunately there was a temporary lecturer who was occupying my office (until the end of September) and I was placed in another office for the first month. However I was not given a key to the building, the computer room or the library as they wanted to give me the set of keys held by the temporary lecturer. As he had applied for the job to which I was appointed this was extremely embarrassing as well as inconvenient for me.

(Quoted in Rust 1991: 10)

I might just mention one last aspect of the junior lecturer's world: the bare and bleak office. My department is arranged around a long corridor. This is the public space and it is unloved, dressed in linoleum and swabbed down every morning by the cleaning staff. The rooms off it have, however, been turned by their long-term inmates into varied bowers of comfort. Sometimes a door will be left ajar and one will glance a plush sofa, or some monstrous pot-plant ... My room, however, having been vacated, or rather, *stripped*, by its last occupant, is a space of echoing, blue-grey minimalist purity. White walls, two filing cabinets, a collection of chairs (ten, for seminars, none comfortable).

(Janes 1996: 80–1)

As far as general academic procedures and regulations were concerned I had to 'feel' my way as I went along. The main problem with this situation appeared to be not how to get information (which was readily given if asked for) but what information to ask for in the first place.

(Quoted in Rust 1991: 20)

Box 3.14: Resources associated with a creative style of coping with career transitions

- Financial and emotional support.
- A social network of friends, community members and colleagues.
- A moderate degree of optimism.
- Healthy self-esteem.
- Ingenuity and flexibility in generalizing old learning to new situations, to train for new positions, and to use all the resources to hand.

Source: adapted from Ackerman (1986).

Entry into a new work role brings with it a list of new tasks and learnings. Box 3.15 lists some learning tasks for new academics. These can be considered before taking up a post, and worked on further in the first few months of academic employment. The suggested tasks involve building up an understanding of the formal and informal working arrangements within your department, centre, university or college. Some of your new colleagues may invite you into their

---

Box 3.15: Learning tasks for new academics

1 Get hold of copies of, and read the following:

(a) The history of your university or college. In most cases at least one has been published; for others an internal publication may be available. Check with the library. This will help you to understand where the institution has come from (some of its older staff may still be there).

(b) All of the main prospectuses which your university or college publishes each year. This will give you an appreciation of the breadth of the institution, and of its particular specialisms.

(c) The university or college calendar, which will typically include a staff list, details of committee structures and meetings, and a list of regulations. This may seem dry fare, but some appreciation of it is essential if you want to understand what is going on in your institution.

(d) Recent reports on the work of your department, centre or unit. These may include its annual report, internal evaluation reports, research assessment and teaching-quality documents. These will help you to understand how your department rates within the institution and nationally, and what its priorities are.

2 Arrange to meet several people in your department or centre individually and informally, perhaps over lunch, to talk about their work. Most people should be quite happy to spare you the time, but don't be put off if some rebuff you. Get them to talk about their careers and interests. Lots of interesting gossip about your colleagues, department and institution is bound to come up. Treat this cautiously. You should also begin to make some friends and learn who to be wary of.

3 Discuss what you have learnt with your partner and close friends. See how well you can explain your job to them. Listen to what they say in response, particularly to any questions or misunderstandings they may have. This should give you suggestions for further learning you need to undertake.

---

rooms, but you will also need to be proactive in establishing your initial departmental networks. As a complement, Box 3.16 identifies 20 very practical tasks which might be undertaken in the first days and weeks as a newly appointed academic employee. These tasks relate to a basic knowledge of where things are and who to turn to for what, and tend to be underestimated in their role in making life at work comfortable!

Of course, many, if not all, of the items identified in Boxes 3.15 and 3.16 would be covered by a good departmental or institutional induction programme. Most higher education institutions do now run formal induction programmes for new members of staff. These are usually compulsory, and may involve regular attendance at training sessions for a year or more, with associated reading and written work, and observation of teaching. In some cases these programmes are certificated, and may lead, after further formal study (these later stages are not usually compulsory), to the award of a diploma or master's degree.

Box 3.16: Twenty practical tasks for new academics

1 Find the departmental office, and introduce yourself to the secretarial and other support staff.
2 Find your office.
3 Get a key to your office and any external door(s).
4 Find out who to contact about the furnishings and decoration of your office.
5 Locate the nearest toilets (both female and male) and kitchen (these may be the same place).
6 Find the staff common room (if there is one), and the nearest refectory, shop, snack bar or coffee machine.
7 Get yourself a university or college identity card.
8 Find out when you will be paid, and inform the personnel or staff office of your bank details so that they can pay you.
9 Visit the university or college library, or the nearest branch of it.
10 Locate any other rooms you are likely to be using for teaching, research or meetings.
11 Find out where your colleagues' offices are.
12 Find out where and when the mail is delivered.
13 Get yourself an institutional telephone directory.
14 Get yourself a computer terminal (and printer if possible), and make sure it is networked internally and externally.
15 Find out how to get your travel and other expenses reimbursed.
16 Find out how to apply for conference funding.
17 Find out where you can park for free, and/or how to get a parking permit.
18 Check out your telephone, fax and e-mail numbers.
19 Find out from where you can telephone internationally.
20 Check whether calls home are charged or not.

The impact of quality assessments and concerns about standards in teaching have led to much greater emphasis on training new academics in these ways. Beyond the increased knowledge they bring, such programmes also offer opportunities to develop relationships with other newly appointed academics across the institution. New members of staff may be offered, or even obliged to have, a mentor (see the section on **Mentoring and partnerships** in Chapter 4 for a fuller discussion). In each of these ways the vocabulary of higher education is becoming peppered with the language of personal development.

This section has emphasized the importance of paying attention to those aspects of transition associated with entry into academic employment. We conclude with three strategies identified by Cooper (1990) for minimizing the associated stress:

• Plan your life, don't let your life plan you. Try and increase your sense of control. This will involve organization and time management.
• Manage your lifestyle. Structure your lifestyle in ways that help to minimize stress. This will involve making choices about your life beyond work (see the next section on **Balancing careers**).

• Practise relaxation techniques. Learn how to unwind rather than simply to pause.

Balancing careers

In Chapter 2 (see especially Box 2.10), we put forward a broad definition of career which encompassed not just paid work but also other aspects of one's life course. This seemed particularly appropriate to academic life, which potentially extends far beyond the confines of the office, lecture theatre or laboratory to infiltrate a large proportion of our waking hours. From such a perspective, it is difficult to conceive of academic careers as simple or one-dimensional: pursuing such a career is a balancing act.

The language of balancing competing interests is closely associated with employment in the 1990s. There are several reasons for this. One is that the notion of a job for life has become one of a job for now, changing with it the social contract between employer and employee. This change has been summarized as follows:

• from an expectation of long term to a transitory relationship;
• from perception of entitlement to shared responsibility;
• from employees being part of an organization to being a factor in production;
• from corporations taking a patriarch's [sic] role to employees bearing more of the responsibility.

(Altman and Post 1996: 51)

Given the inherent insecurities implied by this position, employees would be well advised not to invest too much of their identity in a paid work role.

There has also been a greater recognition in recent years of the interconnections between family and employment. In part this is a result of increasing numbers of women entering the labour force; in part it is due to the growth in dual-career households; and in part to the shifting imagery of fatherhood, which has given greater legitimacy for men to be open about their wish for involvement with their children (Finch and Morgan 1991). Lambert has identified three ways of characterising work/family linkages:

The earliest view of the relationship between work and home is that they are segmented and independent, that work and home do not effect each other. This view has been applied most frequently to workers in blue-collar occupations which are often uninvolving and unsatisfying and for whom the segmentation of work and home is seen as a natural process ... The idea that workers actively respond to occurrence in both spheres led to the view that they may try to compensate for lack of satisfaction in work or home by trying to find more satisfaction in the other ... The most popular view of the relationship between work and family is that their effects spill over from one to the other.

(Lambert 1990: 241–2)

Box 3.17: Work, family and career: some findings from research

Often, women only pursue their careers fully if their husband's self-esteem is not threatened.

(Russell 1994: 292)

Couples often wish to give equal weight to the interests of both partners. In reality, locations and relocations among heterosexual couples often are based on the husband's opportunities ... locating or relocating is further complicated for partners in lesbian couples who may be reluctant to mention their dual-career situation to employers.

(Gilbert et al. 1994: 153)

Men's career decisions are being influenced by the fact that in dual income families the prospect of moving to gain promotion is not economically feasible ... Men's career decisions are becoming sensitive to family needs as more emphasis is placed on parenting in our society. Fathers are becoming less willing to move their families at key periods in the development or schooling of their children and they are questioning the unreasonable hours that are often demanded if they are to be taken seriously as career ambitious.

(Limerick 1995: 69)

The ability of both partners to give and receive support is a major factor determining the quality of the dual-career relationship.

(Lewis 1994: 234)

It will avail little to restructure work to ensure more contact between family members if work experiences are sufficiently negative to ... exert a negative and indirect effect on family functioning.

(Barling 1994, p. 69)

Increasing labour market participation and demographic change are building pressures on women to do everything ... the place of caring as work and obligation in women's and men's lives has far from adequate recognition.

(Pascall 1997: 107)

The men simply had no experience of trying to juggle roles ... and reported that they did not want it ... The difficulties of balance between the public and domestic spheres of activity were seen as belonging to women and being largely up to women to solve.

(French 1995: 58)

Universities and families are both what have been called 'greedy institutions'. They demand as much time as it is possible to give, and then some more. In practice, therefore, most academic careers involve striking a balance between academic work and family life. It is also not unusual for both of the partners in a household to be working in academe, sometimes at similar levels, sometimes not. Box 3.17 highlights some of the research findings from studies which have focused on the relationships between family and employment in dual-career households. The mix of personal and professional tensions which can be present is clear, tensions which require constant negotiation and renegotiation.

While much research has focused on the relationships between couples, less attention has been given to the institutional and collegial relationships of dual-career couples. Here concerns about matters such as independence of judgement, confidentiality and nepotism can be added to the personal and professional jealousy which can occur when one career advances more quickly than the other or there are disputes over the household division of labour. Most often these institutional or collegial concerns are not voiced. They may remain relatively hidden in the language of academic employment, which you would be well advised to learn.

A final aspect of balancing careers which we wish to highlight is that related to academic and non-academic work. In some subjects it has long been common (indeed, expected) for professionals to mix academic and non-academic work. This pattern has become more widespread as full-time and secure contracts have become less available. There are four main forms which such balancing may take:

> First, in most professional disciplines or subject areas, such as architecture, education, management and planning, it is normal for individuals to move between academic work and professional practice, and vice versa, and to maintain some involvement in both fields simultaneously. Thus, departments of architecture and management make considerable use of professionals, both to supervise students in the field and to give specialist lectures or seminars. Conversely, academics who teach and research nursing, education or planning are expected or encouraged to engage in regular or continuing professional practice. These relationships are essential for maintaining both credibility and an up-to-date understanding of practice.
>
> Second, it is not uncommon for intellectuals to have political, public or social service commitments. Indeed, some academic disciplines set out to develop values of active citizenship in their graduates. Academic employment may, therefore, be combined with community leadership roles such as school governorship, voluntary organization management, being a local councillor, justice of the peace or lay visitor.
>
> Third, academics in some departments have opportunities to engage in consultancy work. This may be funded by business, government or international organizations. Such work brings useful contacts, access and experience, though the outputs may be controlled by the funder concerned. It can also bring additional income for the academics concerned, though this may be subject to agreement with the department or institution. Some departments or institutions are open and encouraging about such arrangements, others less so: the advice is to check out expectations and reach any necessary agreements before you get involved.

The first three forms of balancing academic and non-academic work identified are widely practised and accepted within the academic world. They also mainly affect established full-time staff. The fourth form is rather more problematic:

It impacts upon those who have only short-term or part-time academic contracts. In such cases, it may be desirable or necessary to take on a number of part-time academic contracts simultaneously, or to balance part-time academic and non-academic employment.

Those in part-time posts are in a particularly difficult position:

Part-time academic employment rarely gives rise to an academic career for at least five reasons. First, rarely does a career ladder exist for part-timers . . . Second . . . part-time positions . . . [do] not carry tenure . . . Third . . . part-timers do not have normal salary progression over the course of their career . . . Fourth, opportunities for promotion are limited or non-existent. . . . Finally . . . part-timers are not full fledged members of their employing departments.

(Tuckman and Pickerill 1988: 109)

While all such arrangements for balancing different kinds of work are a logical outcome of the 'portfolio' careers identified and advocated by contemporary management theorists (see the section on **The changing nature of careers** in Chapter 2), this does not mean they are easy. Most employers, whether they hire you full-time or part-time, long-term or short-term, continue to assume that your relationship with them is your only priority. They will act as if you are free to meet at any time convenient to them, and to shift your working patterns about on demand.

Managing such relationships will be something of a nightmare unless you are able to agree specific and stable patterns of working with each of your employers. It is not, in our experience, likely to be a long-term pattern of working unless there is no alternative.

Sources of further information

In this section we list a range of materials which you may find of interest in following up in more detail some of the issues discussed in this chapter. The emphasis is on recently published books in English. In each case, brief details are given as to contents and approach.

In addition to the limited literature on starting academic careers, there is a vast general literature on what to do after graduation, and on general career strategies and options. Some representatives from this broader literature are also included below.

Bolles, R. (1997) *What Color is Your Parachute? A Practical Manual for Job-Hunters and Career-Changers*. Berkeley, Calif., Ten Speed Press.
Annual American publication full of practical advice about job hunting, finding a new career, securing and conducting interviews. Extensive appendices list career counsellors, books and other sources of relevance.

Collins, H. (1995) *Equality in the Workplace: An Equal Opportunities Handbook for Trainers*. Oxford, Blackwell.
This text has been primarily designed for human resource professionals. Nevertheless, it is useful for those who wish to update their knowledge and skills in this area. It considers

training-needs analyses, methods and approaches to equal opportunities training, and how to enhance the effectiveness of training programmes. There is a glossary of terms and a listing of British equal opportunities legislation from 1944 to 1994, together with an address list of key organizations.

Collinson, D., Knights, D. and Collinson, M. (1990) *Managing to Discriminate*. London, Routledge.

This text explores the operation and management of sex discrimination practices, with a particular focus on recruitment. The text includes theoretical and empirical studies.

Diamant, L. (1993) *Homosexual Issues in the Workplace*. London, Taylor and Francis.

Based on North American sources, this text addresses lesbian and gay concerns in career development, recruitment and promotion, and human resource policies and practices.

Kronenfeld, J. and Whicker, M. (1997) *Getting an Academic Job: Strategies for Success*. Thousand Oaks, Calif., Sage.

American text which discusses job searches, interviews, landing the right job, dual careers, senior and non-academic jobs, dos and don'ts.

Parkinson, M. (1994) *Interviews Made Easy: How to Get the Psychological Advantage*. London, Kogan Page.

Considers job searches, making an application, handling references, psychological tests, interviews, dealing with stress, assessment centres and handwriting analysis.

Shmerling, L. (1993) *Job Applications: The Winning Edge*. Melbourne, Macmillan Education.

This book covers the whole process from relating your employment skills to job planning through to writing your curriculum vitae, making direct approaches to organizations when seeking employment, the interview and starting a new job.

Walsh, W. and Osipow, S. (eds) (1994) *Career Counseling for Women*. Hillsdale, NJ, Lawrence Erlbaum Associates.

The chapters in this text take a range of positions on career counselling. The discussions focus on basic issues and concepts in career counselling, dual-career families, ethnic minority and gifted women, science, engineering and management.

White, B., Cox, C. and Cooper, C. (1992) *Women's Career Development: A Study of High Flyers*. Oxford, Blackwell.

Based on a sample of 48 women who had achieved career success in a range of fields, this text discusses childhood, personality and motivation, work and family, power and politics. The book concludes with a portrait of the successful woman.

Yate, M. (1992) *Great Answers to Tough Interview Questions: How to Get the Job you Want*, 3rd edn. London, Kogan Page.

Why do you want to work here? How much money do you want? What is your greatest weakness? What will your references say? These are some of the many questions dealt with in this book.

4 | NETWORKING

Introduction

This chapter considers the role of networking in academic careers. This is a role which is of critical importance to the development of an academic career as past, current and future networks impact on access and progression. This does not mean, of course, that performance in other academic roles – teaching, researching, writing, managing – is unimportant, or that it is possible to have a successful career purely on the basis of networking abilities; rather, it acknowledges that the work associated with being an academic is embedded in a social context.

Black professionals and women academics have paid close attention to networking. One way, informally, to counter social exclusion is to work actively on inclusion, developing a voice, professional friendships and a career by consciously cultivating people to share and exchange information with. To point out that women academics are frequently more explicit about the potentiality of networking is not to say that men do not also make use of this strategy. Of course they do. The difference is that they tend not to call it networking, or anything in particular, with the consequence that the activity is less open and more insiduous. One has only, however, to recall phrases like 'old boy network' to realize the importance of this role for both sexes.

The chapter is organized into five main sections:

- **Thinking about networks**, which considers the different sorts of network relevant to academic careers;
- **Approaches to networking,** which focuses on the processes involved;
- **Conferences, seminars and societies**, which discusses involvement in these presentational networks in terms of organizing as well as participating;
- **Journals and newsletters**, which looks at involvement in publishing networks from the perspective of the editor rather than the writer;

- **Mentoring and partnerships**, which examines two key kinds of personal networking arrangements.

At the end of the chapter a selection of sources of further information is listed.

Thinking about networks

Networking is mentioned more and more frequently as a significant explanation of career success. Admonitions to would-be managers include the advice that 'networking, nurturing and self-consciousness . . . are all important strategies' (Powney 1997: 53). Box 4.1, derived from a recent book by two American business academics, clearly links networking with success. Their seven 'secrets' are all considered in this chapter or elsewhere in this book (see particularly the sections on **Balancing careers** in Chapter 3 and **Academic managerial roles** in Chapter 8). These lessons are as important to academics as they are to other professionals. Thus, in a study of British academics, Heward *et al.* (1997: 214) comment: 'In the later stage of careers, invitations to apply for posts and recommendations by senior academics for posts became the most important aspect of the processes of mentoring and networking.'

What, then, are networks, and how does networking operate? Lankshear *et al.* (1997) note that it is an umbrella term for diverse practices. Networking can operate interpersonally in face-to-face networks, or take the form of technologically mediated relationships at a distance. Arnold (1997: 83) provides a definition linking networks to career development:

> The effective initiation and maintenance of social relationships for career-related purposes is often termed *networking*. The obvious key idea is that the more people who know and like an individual and respect his or her competence, the more successful that individual's career will be, other things being equal . . . the pre-emptive and proactive use of networking is key . . . One aspect of networking sometimes forgotten is that it involves giving as well as taking. To be involved in social networks means that one can be expected on occasions to offer help, information, support or advice as well as to receive it . . . to some extent networking appeals beyond simple reciprocity to a wider morality involving perhaps a sense of duty or humanitarian concern. It also tends to involve people of approximately equal status, or at least people who might plausibly be of equal status in the foreseeable future.

The network as a metaphor has been used to extend understandings of organizational formation:

> In contrast with the view that organisations are integrated rational enterprises pursuing a common goal, the political metaphor encourages us to see organisations as loose networks of people with divergent interests who gather together for the sake of expediency (e.g. making a living, developing a career, or pursuing a desired goal or objective). Organisations are coalitions

---

Box 4.1: Seven secrets of success

1 Successful people realize the importance of a mentor/advocate/cheerleader/ coach.
2 Successful people know how to increase their visibility.
3 Successful people know how to develop an effective network.
4 Successful people have learnt to communicate effectively.
5 Successful people know how to balance work and home.
6 Successful people know when to take smart risks.
7 Successful people understand the politics of the organization.

Source: Brooks and Brooks (1997: vii–ix).

---

and are made up of coalitions, and coalition building is an important dimension of almost all organisational life.

(Morgan 1997: 166)

This analysis has particular resonance for higher education systems, when their graded and hierarchical nature is taken into account. Moreover, the relation between discipline and institution (see the section in Chapter 2 on **The changing nature of higher education**) is an example of the more general phenomenon of the borderless organization. Such an organization considers that:

Strategic networks are long-term, purposeful arrangements among distinct but related for profit organizations that allow those firms in them to gain or sustain competitive advantage *vis-à-vis* their competitors outside the network, by optimizing activity costs and minimizing coordination costs.

(Jarillo 1993: 149)

As Jarillo indicates, it is the search for competitive advantage which is the primary motivator for developing strategic networks. In the academic context, strategic networks enable the individual to keep well informed about developments nationally and internationally, in their institution and in their discipline. They also provide the individual with group support and offer scope for collaboration in different aspects of their work. The competitive advantage enjoyed by 'old boy networks' and 'invisible colleges' is one of the reasons why attention is now paid by groups excluded from institutional power and privilege to the significance of networking.

This reflects, of course, the prevailing gendered, ethnic and class-based power relations within academic life. In response, women and minority ethnic groups have deliberately adopted networking strategies in trying to overcome the structural disadvantages they face. In part, this has been due to a recognition that the secrecy associated with 'old boy networks' is inimical to equal opportunity practice.

In summarizing research into women's organizations, Colgan and Ledwith draw attention to the role of politics and values when they distinguish between 'women-aware' and 'fuller feminist' perspectives:

A 'women-aware' perspective can be further differentiated from a fuller feminist one in terms of the aims, strategies and actions prioritised to challenge gender inequalities within organisations and sectors . . . Thus the more 'conservative' or 'women-aware' organisations, recognising the barriers faced by women, set out to create self-help networks rather along the lines of the 'old boys' network'. These organisations (and the women within them) sought to pursue liberal equal opportunities policies and promote a positive and 'sensible' image of women, particularly to management, and were keen to have men as members and patrons of their groups. The feminist groups in the study adopted a more separatist strategy consciously choosing to operate as women-only self-help networks, they sought to improve women's position by creating a women's network, but also sought to operate as pressure groups, challenging gendered organisational structures and cultures and campaigning around women's employment issues.

(Colgan and Ledwith 1996: 28)

With few exceptions, most academic networking activities in Britain have been little studied. One recent project has, however, examined disciplinary networks:

One phenomenon is clearly evident in the testimony from members of virtually every discipline; namely, the existence of an inner and outer circle of professional acquaintance. The outer circle is in many cases quite large in compass, numbering somewhere between 100 and 400 people, with a norm of about 200. Its members comprise those colleagues with whose names and work one is more or less familiar . . . The inner circle is usually surprisingly small, ranging from half a dozen to a score, with a dozen as a fairly common average. The bonds here are tighter and more resilient, singling out those colleagues with whom one has a direct affinity and a closely shared interest; those critical friends to whom one would send papers for comment and whose own drafts one would take some trouble to read.

(Becher 1989: 66–7)

The figures quoted are interesting, as they give an impression of the size of disciplinary networks. It is possible to compare the figures with personal experience, noting also differences in status. Obviously, it takes time to build up such networks, so that those academics in the early part of their careers may have fewer contacts than those who are in established positions. Younger male academics may, however, find it easier to develop relations with more senior staff, who are predominantly male. There will also, inevitably, be changes in networks as careers and interests develop, and individuals move apart or come closer together. Particular academics might manage perfectly well with fewer people in their networks, while some others clearly have far more within theirs.

The numbers which Becher quotes as typical for the outer circle of disciplinary networking are analogous to what might be expected at a good-quality specialist conference (see the section later in this chapter on **Conferences, seminars and societies**). This grouping could be thought of as the potential audience for specialist research and writing. The much smaller number in an inner network would probably include a mentor, if you have one, and any partners you work with closely (see the section later in this chapter on **Mentoring and partnerships**).

The importance of communication to the maintenance and development of networks is stressed in the following quotation, along with an emphasis on the growing significance of international, and particularly European, networks to British academic life.

> At least within the European setting, university research is moving towards large-scale, international and multidisciplinary networks which by their organisational structure can be very complex. Poles and satellites emerge and change within these networks over time, and network leadership involves organising research, finance and work with a number of satellites. Frequent communication within the network is thus essential for its smooth functioning. Computer-based storage and retrieval systems allow international participation from home base. Also, in addition to the regular stand-bys of the international postal and telephone systems, electronic mail, fax machines, and tele-conferencing have all accelerated the exchange of ideas and information between nodal points without the requirement for physical movement, although they have not obviated either the need for or the desirability of direct personal exchanges, where feasible. Both short-term physical mobility (conferences, workshops) and longer-term mobility (exchange or secondments as part of collaborative research programmes, sabbaticals, etc.) remain important parts of international research activity.
>
> (Skilbeck and Connell 1996: 73)

As indicated in Chapter 6 (see the section on **Research funding**), European and international networks may involve teaching and development work as well as research. This quotation also exemplifies one of the points made in Chapter 8 (see the section on **Academic managerial roles**), namely that pursuing a managerial career within higher education should not be seen solely in terms of increasing departmental, faculty, institutional or inter-institutional authority. It might instead be concerned with developing a managerial role, primarily based on research and writing, within your discipline or subject area, nationally and internationally.

Approaches to networking

In the particular context of higher education, networking may operate on a wide range of levels. These include:

- networking within a department, particularly where it is a relatively large one, both to build up specialist subject interests and to establish a more secure working base;
- networking within a university or college, either to create cross-disciplinary linkages or to achieve political and managerial support;
- networking within a discipline or subject area, to enhance an academic reputation and/or seek to develop partnerships, both nationally and internationally;

- networking between institutions, to enhance political status and build up influence in national or international bodies;
- networking between higher education and other organizations, to link up with, for example, business and government for research, teaching, managerial or other purposes;
- networking for support purposes, with people who share an interest in giving and receiving personal and professional information, guidance and advice (e.g. women in management; black social workers).

All such networking activities may either make use of existing, perhaps institutionalized, arrangements, or seek to build new structures, or may involve an element of both. They may also, of course, involve individuals, departments and institutions of equal or differing status. Box 4.2 gives a number of examples of academic networks, illustrating some of the possibilities. Some others are listed and described in the list of organizations and journals included at the end of this book.

How you develop and use networks depends partly on your purposes and the stage you have reached in your career. O'Leary and Mitchell (1990: 58) suggest that there are five main benefits associated with networking:

- information exchange;
- collaboration;
- career planning and strategizing;
- professional support and encouragement;
- access to visibility and upward mobility.

Information exchange and collaboration may be characterized as being about 'getting on' with the job: establishing necessary and useful working relationships, learning from others and letting your peers know about your own work. These kinds of networking might take place within any of the other four academic roles we have identified: teaching, researching, writing or managing. For example, as discussed in Chapter 6, getting advance warning of new research priorities, and perhaps participating in the development of their terms of reference, is more likely when you are suitably networked.

Professional support and encouragement relates to what is commonly termed 'mentoring'. Mentoring and networking are often considered together, as the titles of some of the books referred to in this chapter indicate. Mentoring may be of critical importance in getting your first job and during promotion (see the section in Chapter 3 on **Applying for a job**, and the section later in this chapter on **Mentoring and partnerships**).

Career planning, access to visibility and upward mobility have to do chiefly with career advancement or change. For example, moving out of academic employment can be aided by appropriate networks. Networking has, therefore, both more static and more dynamic elements in establishing and maintaining an academic position, and developing this further. It would be foolish for any academic to ignore either of these elements.

We would add two additional benefits to the five identified by O'Leary and Mitchell:

Box 4.2: Examples of networks

An email discussion group for all academic and related staff on fixed-term contracts, including contract research staff, was set up in March. The purpose of the list is to allow staff to share information about issues that concern them. This could be an enquiry about some aspect of working on a fixed-term contract, a comment on how AUT could improve its services, or even advertising a job vacancy. The group is open to all and is unmoderated, that is, what you write is what appears. Many staff have already joined the list and had informative discussions on a wide range of topics. If you would like to join, e-mail: majordomo@leeds.ac.uk with the message: subscribe ftcs.

(*Research Staff News*, Association of University Teachers, Spring 1997, p. 4)

At the end of the 1980s, a group of us who were newly appointed to positions of leadership within the then polytechnics and colleges sector within the UK came together to formalize and extend to others the support network we were starting to develop between ourselves. We were heads of departments and deans, some were professors; all of us were conscious of being fairly unique in our own institutions. We shared the fact that we faced new challenges daily, in new jobs and in a rapidly changing sector. We were aware, although not in any campaigning sense, that our solutions, separately developed in each of our own situations, were often very different in content and style from those being operated around us by our male colleagues. We were aware of doors closed to us and, indeed, closed to at least some of the men we worked with, and we were conscious of the need to articulate and share some of the thoughts and experiences which we, as women managers, were having.

(King 1997: 93)

People ask you to do things; Australian males value 'mateship' highly, so if my mates ask me to do something for them I usually say yes. A lot of things have got written that way.

(Clegg 1996: 53)

The chapters in this edited collection derive from a series of feminist working papers produced under the auspices of the Sociology Department at the University of Manchester, England. 'Studies in Sexual Politics' (SSP) was set up to give 'a voice' to feminist sociological work produced in the tradition of the Manchester Department . . . one of detailed, particularly but not exclusively ethnographic, styles of research.

(Stanley 1990: 3)

- intellectual stimulation;
- personal support for special interest groups.

Paying attention to these aspects of networking enables academics to recognize the value of those more general issues associated with professional development, and with the political and ethical dimensions of collectivities. Developing networks which take account of all these dimensions has, therefore, a further facet, namely

---

Box 4.3: Tips for networkers

- You must develop and use your contacts.
- You must try to get along to meetings, even if the topic is not of direct relevance to you, to meet other people.
- Make sure you *always* have a supply of business cards to distribute at meetings, or to send to people from whom you extract cards, possibly with a curriculum vitae to show your own interests.
- Send cards at Christmas or New Year to remind your new contacts that you exist.
- Ask around to find out who has the information and influence that you need.
- At all times keep your eyes and ears open for anything that is useful, follow it up and use it, or store the information away for future use.

(Segerman-Peck 1991: 54)

- Are your contacts up-to-date ones, or do they go back a long way? A bit of both?
- Are they work people?
- Are there enough 'outside work' people for you?
- Are they spread around all the departments at work?
- Are you networking with people away from work?
- When do you meet people who are totally different from you?
- In which areas do you want to build up your contacts?
- Do you have a contact who can help you do that?
- Are you adding new contacts to your list?
- What do you do to keep in contact with all these people? See them, send them a Christmas card, phone them regularly?
- Are you tending to network with all the same sort of people?
- Which people do you need to or want to make contact with?

(Willis and Daisley 1990: 98)

---

creating and maintaining associations of shared values. Rose (1986: 53) discusses this in terms of likeability:

> *The goal is to find likeable colleagues.* Basing the quest on liking rather than utility is more compatible with most people's value system. Try to find people with enough in common both academically and interpersonally to warrant developing that connection. It's not necessary to ingratiate yourself to anyone to develop useful connections. There are enough people that are both likeable *and* helpful that you do not have to base your search solely on self-interest.

Understanding the processes of effective networking is clearly an important skill for career development. Box 4.3 contains two complementary sets of tips for academic networking, which should help as an aid to reviewing current practices and developing future approaches. It should also be useful in guiding new colleagues, for those who have such responsibilities.

Thinking, first, of who you currently network with, you might like to consider them in terms of:

- older and newer contacts;
- contacts of similar, lower and higher status;
- their age, ethnicity and sex;
- contacts within and outside your discipline or subject area;
- contacts within and outside your institution;
- contacts in this country and overseas;
- contacts within and outside higher education.

Networks have the potential to enable sharing of benefits, with established academics assisting new colleagues. At every stage of a career it is possible to introduce new professional contacts to others in established networks. Networking with a variety of people facilitates hearing a range of perspectives, as well as opening up options in a volatile working environment. Ensuring that networks are continually reviewed and renewed is, therefore, a significant process in personal and professional development.

Box 4.3 also suggests some techniques for maintaining, renewing, developing and changing the balance of networks. These are basically simple but a little time-consuming, indicating the necessity for being conscious and proactive about the processes involved. These techniques might include the following:

- Using business cards (it is surprising how many academics do not have these) and Christmas cards for establishing and maintaining contacts. You might also regularly make telephone calls or send e-mails to update your contacts on your work and seek information on theirs. Another technique is to circulate widely copies of everything you publish. You will be surprised how welcome colleagues will find this 'free' source of intellectual sharing.
- Treating meetings, whether institutional or interest-based, as a necessary part of the job rather than a chore (see the section on **Committee work** in Chapter 8). If you don't attend regularly, you will not be seen as a serious player by other members and will miss chances to hear the latest news, influence decisions or learn of interesting opportunities.
- Keeping a diary or notebook (as well as business cards) to hand at all times so that you can note down ideas, opportunities and contact details as they occur. You need also to develop the habit of regularly reviewing what you have noted down, and then following up those ideas or contacts which seem potentially fruitful.
- Seeking out contacts in areas in which you would like to develop your interests or career. This may involve reading less familiar literatures or attending conferences you have not been to before. You might also circulate your existing networks for suggestions and information: if you don't know whom to contact, it is very likely that someone you know will know, or at least have a good idea.
- Actively networking other people. Recommend colleagues for seminar or conference presentations. Put people in touch with each other when you think

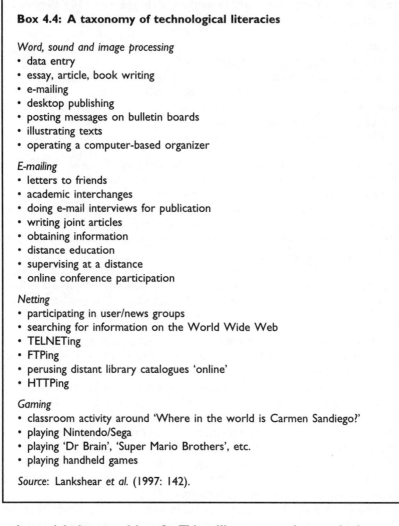

Box 4.4: A taxonomy of technological literacies

Word, sound and image processing
• data entry
• essay, article, book writing
• e-mailing
• desktop publishing
• posting messages on bulletin boards
• illustrating texts
• operating a computer-based organizer

E-mailing
• letters to friends
• academic interchanges
• doing e-mail interviews for publication
• writing joint articles
• obtaining information
• distance education
• supervising at a distance
• online conference participation

Netting
• participating in user/news groups
• searching for information on the World Wide Web
• TELNETing
• FTPing
• perusing distant library catalogues 'online'
• HTTPing

Gaming
• classroom activity around 'Where in the world is Carmen Sandiego?'
• playing Nintendo/Sega
• playing 'Dr Brain', 'Super Mario Brothers', etc.
• playing handheld games

Source: Lankshear *et al.* (1997: 142).

there might be mutual benefit. This will encourage them to do the same for you when the opportunity arises.
• Keeping in mind the five 'Cs' of connections and contacts: conferences, collaboration, correspondence, collegiality and community. Set yourself targets for networking activities of one kind or another.

All of these networking activities may now be done electronically as well as by conventional means. Box 4.4 indicates some of the possibilities.

You will probably, of course, already be using at least some of these approaches. Unless you are an extremely good networker, however, you will likely find that your work and career benefit from a careful review and development of your approaches to networking.

Box 4.5: A sample of societies

Anthropology in Action
Association of Law Teachers
Association for Management Education and Development
British Academy of Management
British Educational Research Association
British Psychological Society
British Sociological Association
Political Studies Association
Royal Anthropological Institute
Royal Geographical Society
Social Policy Association
Socio-Legal Studies Association
Women's Studies Network Association

Conferences, seminars and societies

As an academic, part of a networking strategy is likely to take the form of regular participation in relevant conferences, seminars and societies. Conferences, seminars and societies describe an overlapping continuum of presentational activities. Conferences, seminars and related events tend to be organized by, or associated with, professional societies. Such societies also commonly publish academic and/or popular journals (see the next section on **Journals and newsletters**, as well as the list at the end of the book of organizations and journals). A sample listing of some of the thousands of societies – some local, some national, some international – which operate within the humanities and social sciences is included in Box 4.5.

While there are few hard-and-fast distinctions, conferences tend to last for a day or longer. Seminars are shorter but more regular events, lasting for perhaps a couple of hours every week, month or term. Another common form of academic presentation is the workshop: these are more usually one-off and less formal events, but expect more from their participants in terms of contributions.

A typical networking strategy in this area might involve regular participation in the annual conferences of the limited number of relevant societies, plus a number of other one-off events. Box 4.6 suggests ways in which conferences and societies might be used. Different forms of participation in conferences are summarized in Box 4.7. Regular attendance at such events is likely to reap greater, long-term benefits than more spasmodic, *ad hoc*, participation, as it allows you to make new acquaintances and refresh older friendships.

Conferences may be seen as places to give papers and present some of your latest thinking to the other participants. This is probably the most common form of participation, particularly as universities and colleges have become more and more reluctant to fund conference attendance for academics who are not giving papers. This type of networking is essential to developing a reputation in a

Box 4.6: Using societies and conferences

Societies
- Join only a few societies and participate fully; don't neglect the smaller local societies.
- Present good papers; don't be persuaded that potboilers are acceptable.
- At meetings, always introduce yourself with your name and affiliation.
- Talk to people about their research, not yours . . .
- If you can join the committee, execute any task exceptionally well . . .
- Carefully study major figures . . . They are usually multi-skilled, as well as superb at their craft.

Conferences
- Plan to attend only those parts of relevance to you.
- Read the abstracts in the conference proceedings and plan which presentations you should go to.
- Do not sit through a whole session on the basis of some misguided notion that this is what you are supposed to do . . .
- When you go to listen to a speaker, do not merely sit there . . .
- Plan to attend: all keynote speeches, invited lectures, panel sessions, other special events in areas of interest.
- The luncheons and banquets are a waste of time unless you ensure that you get a table with people you want to meet.
- The gatherings for cocktails are the best bet and you should always go to these. Get there on time and have serious discussions early. Leave with friends when the venue gets packed.

(Johnson 1996: 85)

Box 4.7:   Forms of participation in conferences

- attendance
- introducing yourself to people
- introducing new friends to old friends
- giving a paper
- circulating your paper, or business cards
- giving a poster session
- giving a keynote speech or paper
- contributing to a panel session
- being a member of the organizing committee or group
- being a member of the paper selection committee
- editing the conference proceedings

particular field, to enhancing visibility and to gain useful feedback on thinking and writing.

However, many of those attending conferences are not giving papers. From their perspective, the conference is primarily a means of finding out about the latest developments in the subject, and a venue for meeting and talking with fellow academic specialists. This is particularly useful for those who are new to a field of interest, and who have yet to acquire that seasoned patina of the regular conference attendee. Networking while attending a conference means making an effort to meet people. This can be tough because not all academics are open, friendly people. Becoming more familiar with the culture and organization of conferencing, without the added anxiety of giving a paper, can be a good place to start.

Conference organizers typically advertise their plans, and invite paper contributions, at least several months in advance. Relevant disciplinary journals often carry such advertisements, and members of professional societies will be circulated with details. Some conferences are advertised in the education press, for example the *Times Higher Education Supplement*. Those wishing to submit a paper have to prepare an outline by a given deadline, which will then be considered, and accepted or rejected, by a committee of academics formed for that purpose. Conferences vary considerably in their status and popularity, so getting a paper proposal accepted will be a good deal more difficult for some conferences than for others.

Some conferences also give space to what are called *poster sessions*. These are normally less competitive than paper sessions, and involve displaying your work, and perhaps being available to answer questions, at a particular time. Poster sessions can offer an opportunity for less experienced academics to present their ideas at conferences where they might not get a paper accepted.

Another strategy for developing confidence within conference networks is to offer to organize, perhaps in collaboration with established professional friends, a 'getting to know one another' event. Those who turn up to a slot of this kind are likely to share an interest in meeting other people. For example, Stanley (1995) organized a workshop entitled 'Feeling like a working-class thicko at academic conferences' at the 1992 Women's Studies Network (UK) conference, with the aim of highlighting these aspects of inequality and of bringing together those with shared interests in the area.

The development of a reputation can lead to invitations to give a keynote paper or speech, or to sit on a panel during a discussion session. This is something of an honour, or at least a recognition that your work and opinions are known and respected within your network. Conference organizers commonly seek to structure their plans around a limited number of keynote speeches or panel sessions. These are used to draw delegates to the conference and to provide periods when all conference attenders can come together. Given the significance of publishing to academic careers, keynote papers will often be published in some form.

The discussion so far in this section has focused on conferences, seminars and workshops as networking opportunities to attend and present at. However, as some of the comments made suggest, there is another way of looking at conferences as networking events; namely from the organizational perspective. Being involved in the organization of a conference is likely to be a far more effective networking strategy than simply attending and presenting. It will bring you into contact with a much larger group of people in the field of interest, and these people will have a stronger motivation to network with you. It is also an activity which will strengthen your curriculum vitae (see the section in Chapter 3 on **Applying for a job**).

Box 4.7 identifies three related ways of being involved in conference organization: being a member of the organizing group or of the paper selection committee, and editing the proceedings. In most cases, those involved in the last two activities are also likely to be involved in the first.

There are three main ways of getting on the organizing group of a conference:

- through networking within the society or professional body running the conference;
- through networking within your department or institution, when a conference is being held there;
- by setting up your own conference, seminar or workshop.

If you haven't done anything like this before, remember you have one key resource to offer: your time and enthusiasm. Organizing a conference successfully is a complicated and very time-consuming activity. There are lots of dogsbody jobs to be done, and usually few people who want to do them. So don't be shy about offering your services to conference organizers if you are interested. You may not get much credit at first, but, if you are any good at it, your reputation is likely to spread fast. You will also learn in the process.

Clearly, the first two of the options just quoted are simpler and less stressful than the third. Joining the organizing committee of a society or association which regularly runs conferences, seminars and workshops will mean tapping into an existing body of experience. Yet the third option, of setting up your own conference, should not be dismissed without consideration, even if you are a relatively new academic and lack expertise in this area. You might, for example, want or need to do something like this in order to disseminate effectively the results of a research project or to begin to profile a developing network (see the section on **Managing research** in Chapter 6).

If you are thinking of running a first conference, seminar or workshop, you might want to start in a relatively small way: for example, with a small series of seminars or a day conference. That will involve less risk, and allow you to develop the experience needed to run something more ambitious. Running a short series of seminars can be a particularly valuable activity for new academics, as it can bring them into close contact with some important thinkers in their field, and build up some momentum. If your department or centre is looking for someone to organize its graduate seminars or visiting lectures, see this as an opportunity both to profile yourself and to gain experience.

Box 4.8 lists a sample timeline for conference organization. The timetable given is the kind that might be most appropriate for a medium-sized conference spread over a number of days. Larger, more prestigious and international conferences might well involve an even longer period of planning: two or three years is not unusual. Smaller, more local and day conferences could be organized

---

Box 4.8: Sample timeline for conference organization

18 months (and counting): recruit conference planning committee and begin regular monthly meetings.

16 months: decisions about sites, dates, type of programme and theme.

14 months: tentative confirmation of keynote speakers, approval of budget and registration fees, place advertisements and send notices with call for papers.

12 months: prepare and print brochures/registration forms, confirm general outline of programmes.

11 months: first mailing of brochures; establish submission and review process for papers.

10 months: deadline for submission of abstracts (remember that many will be late).

 8 months: confirmation of papers accepted, preparation of detailed programme, review of registrations, decision on additional publicity.

 6 months: begin recruiting local host families, tour guides, translators and other volunteers; deadline for early registration discounts; review of registration; review budget and approve changes.

 4 months: confirmation of food, housing and child-care arrangements, solicit advertising for programme from local suppliers, reconfirmation of keynote speakers, first press kit to media.

 2 months: begin (bi)weekly meetings of conference committee, review registration and adjust plans, recruit volunteers.

 2 weeks: print final programme, reconfirm all arrangements, second press kit to media, deadline for submission of papers to be included in proceedings to be distributed after conference.

 1 week: assemble registration kits, assemble all backup materials.

 1 day: registration rehearsal, walk-through of all arrangements.

 1 week after: debriefing meeting of conference committee, send thank-you letters, prepare reports to sponsors, close financial accounts and prepare for auditing; distribute proceedings.

Source: Zelmer and Zelmer (1991: 5–6)

---

within a shorter time, say several months. In each case, however, much the same stages and activities will be involved.

Box 4.8 makes clear a number of key points about conference organization. First, as just indicated, it takes a lot of time, not only in terms of forward planning but also in the amount of attention demanded over the organizational period. Meticulous attention to detail is, therefore, required. Second, as this would suggest, it is not a task to be undertaken alone: reliable coorganizers and/or assistants are needed. Third, a careful check needs to be kept on how well the conference is going throughout the organizational period: in terms of booking rooms and other facilities, paper proposals, likely attendance, and so forth. As time passes, it will be important to adjust plans to take into account both the numbers attending and their preferences.

Fourth, and perhaps most importantly, the organization of conferences requires financial planning and accounting. Before doing any detailed planning or publicity, it is necessary to estimate how many people may attend, determine what it will cost to hold a conference of this size at different possible venues, draw up a budget, and work out fee scales. Unless there is a very good reason to do otherwise, aim to make a significant profit: this will facilitate funding other activities and give more scope for inviting people who could not afford, or would not expect, to pay. Be very clear about any deposits required for booking facilities, and about the dates and sizes of any payments required for cancellations.

In running conferences, it is imperative that the financial regulations of the host institution are known and followed carefully. This may mean gaining approval from various committees or setting up specialist budget codes. In addition, the marketization of higher education means that universities and departments are seeking more and more ways of generating income, and conferences offer one way for doing this. Your university and/or department may well require that you budget for an overhead or give them a proportion of the profit. Check out who will be responsible for any loss!

Responsibility for paper selection and editing proceedings can be largely separated from other aspects of conference organization. Continuing liaison between any subgroups and the main organizing group is, however, critically important. Being part of a paper selection committee may involve only a couple of meetings in a relatively short space of time: shortly after the deadline for submissions has passed. To do the job effectively requires a clear, and shared, idea of what is sought in the paper proposals, a sense of the overall shape of the conference being aimed for, and an openness to a variety of perspectives and forms of presentation.

Editing the proceedings of a conference, either on your own or with others, can also be a fairly contained activity (the general principles involved are discussed in the section on **Writing books** in Chapter 7). Not all conferences produce proceedings, of course – some expect presenters to seek publication in existing journals – and, of those that do, not all are published commercially. Typically, the work will take place just before or after the conference, and may involve some further selection to reduce the proceedings to the desired size. In a few cases, you may find that the sponsoring organization produces precedings (a book of commissioned papers circulated before or at the conference) rather than, or perhaps as well as, proceedings.

Getting involved in the organization of conferences, seminars and societies is, then, a powerful means of networking within your discipline or subject area. It can offer a means for gaining managerial experience other than through departmental or institutional management (see the section on **Academic managerial roles** in Chapter 8). And it can also be a lot of fun, as well as hard work.

Journals and newsletters

The strategies involved in writing for journals are considered in Chapter 7. While these have an obvious role in networking, in that they help to get your name and ideas known, in this section the focus is working for and/or running journals and newsletters. As in the case of organizing conferences, seminars and

---

Box 4.9: Forms of involvement in journals or newsletters

- editor
- joint editor, coeditor, deputy editor, associate editor, section editor
- member of editorial group or board
- reviews editor
- referee of draft papers
- book reviewer
- author

---

workshops, involvement in the running of a journal or newsletter is a very powerful means of networking within your area of interest. People will seek you out, as you can offer a forum for them to publish their ideas.

Again, as with organizing conferences, there are a variety of forms of involvement possible in running journals. These range from the role of editor to that of contributing author, with many possibilities in between (see Box 4.9). A journal is a time-consuming and demanding responsibility, so it is normal to devolve or share some of the work involved. This may be done, for example, by having a number of coeditors of equal status, with perhaps each being responsible for one issue of the journal each year. Or there may be a number of assistant editors working with a general editor, perhaps with particular responsibilities for aspects or sections of the journal.

One of the most useful of these assistant editorial roles to have is that of reviews editor. Such people get to see most of the books published in their field before anyone else, and will probably keep many of them. They can also exercise a certain amount of patronage in offering books to potential reviewers, though it can be quite difficult to get otherwise busy academics to agree to review and then deliver on time.

Journals vary greatly in their practice with regard to editorial boards. In some cases, particularly international advisory boards, these are little more than lists of the great and the good to adorn inside covers. The board may meet rarely, if ever, and have virtually no influence on the journal's policy and direction. In other cases, boards meet several times a year, referee many if perhaps not all of the draft papers under consideration, and have regular contact with the editor and other members of the editorial team.

> In selecting the board members, my two associate editors and I placed a great deal of emphasis on the reviewers' past performance. We wanted not only scholars at the top of their fields, scholars with the highest academic standards, but also people who shared one of the core values of the *Academy of Management Journal* – to make the review process helpful and developmental for authors . . . About half of my initial editorial board members were ad hoc reviewers.
>
> (Tsui 1997: 7)

Box 4.10: Planning a new journal

Proposed title.
Proposed editor(s).
Proposed editorial board or advisory group.
What will be the journal's aim and scope?
Who will the journal be aimed at?
How will it differ from other journals in this field?
Will the journal be innovative in any way?
What sorts of articles will it contain?
• Length?
• Style?
• Number?
Can you provide a sample listing of possible authors and titles? This might include a list of relevant papers recently published elsewhere, plus a wish list of possible future papers yet to be written by suitable authors.
What kind of peer review system will the journal use?
Will there be a book reviews section and/or other sections?
How many issues a year? How many pages?
Who is likely to subscribe to such a journal?
How might the new journal be best promoted?
Would the journal be associated with an existing society?

If you are interested in working on a journal or newsletter, there are – as in the case of conference organization – two basic approaches: either make contact with those running the journal or start your own. To take the former first: start with one of the less renowned journals and offer your services to the editor. They are quite likely to appreciate some extra help, though they are unlikely to be able to pay you and you will get little credit. You are more likely to be successful if the journal is based within your department or institution, or in one close by. Make sure you do your tasks well and on time, build up your experience, and your reputation and responsibilities are likely to grow. As with many demanding tasks outside the immediate requirements of the job, there seem to be relatively few academics with the interest or time to devote to this important area of academic work.

The alternative approach of starting your own journal is more difficult, but by no means impossible. We live in a period when the number of academic journals is escalating, partly in response to the demands of research assessment exercises, and many publishers have become involved in this way. The first stage is to check out which publishers publish journals in your field; then approach them to gauge possible interest. To get a publisher interested in a proposed journal, as in any form of academic writing (see the section on **Writing books** in Chapter 7), you will need two things: a reasonable track record as an academic, with some previous involvement with journals, and a clear plan regarding the proposed new journal.

The main issues involved in planning a new journal are outlined in Box 4.10. If you can answer most or all of these questions, you are in a position to start presenting a proposal to prospective publishers, and to begin negotiating with them. This doesn't mean, of course, that you will be successful.

If you lack the track record to put together a new journal proposal, or have had your proposal turned down, you might like to think of publishing a journal from within your department or institution. This might start as a relatively small-circulation newsletter, carefully focused on a particular area of interest, which would serve to inform those similarly interested and do no more than cover its limited costs. If successful, this could then form the nucleus for developing something rather more ambitious and permanent. Or, if you have the interest and expertise, you might launch a journal in electronic form.

Don't ignore the possibilities for linking work on a journal or newsletter with organizing conferences, workshops or seminars, or perhaps starting a new society. These activities can be complementary, using the same specialist networks and feeding material and authors to each other. Both are demanding, take you out of your institution, and can give you a lot of pleasure.

Mentoring and partnerships

> I was aware, both through my research and through looking around me, that women were a distinct minority among academics in Britain, and very scarce in the upper ranks . . . Looking back, I see an absence of mentoring and sponsorship, although there was no shortage of friends and supportive colleagues. With no formal appraisal system until my last year in the School of Education, and a promotion system that was competitive, rested heavily on sponsorship, gave little guidance as to appropriate endeavours, and did not kick in until relatively late in one's career, I had found myself doing the work that interested me rather than satisfying a set of requirements.
>
> (Acker 1994: 60)

As this quotation suggests, personal networking arrangements such as mentoring and partnerships – as well as related ideas like coaching, sponsorship and guiding – can be of great value in developing an academic (or any other kind of) career. While networking may focus on exchange and support among a group of peers, mentoring has to do with enhancing career development. It is now becoming somewhat more common to find such arrangements formalized within universities or their component departments. However, much of the existing literature on mentoring deals with school teaching, nursing or management.

Mentoring and partnership involve the cultivation of close supportive relationships with, respectively, one colleague and a relatively small group. An individual might have more than one mentor, or be involved in more than one partnership, but multiple arrangements are relatively uncommon. The difference between the two types of relationship has to do with the status of the parties involved and the nature of exchange or work undertaken:

- Mentors are usually more experienced than, and senior to, their protégés. The mentoring relationship focuses on the personal and career development of the protégé.

Box 4.11: Potential benefits of mentoring

For the protégé
- Fast and effective learning of work demands, skills, organizational norms and values, career contingencies, and best ways to achieve work goals.
- Having an influential person to put them forward for desirable assignments, and deflect blame for mistakes.
- Having a role model to help clarify own desired future and self-concept.
- Having a confidant(e) to talk over issues of personal concern, independent of line management.
- A sense of belonging to the organization.
- Rapid career advancement.

For the mentor
- A sense of a valued role in the organization.
- The satisfaction of demonstrating and passing on his or her know-how and skills.
- Use and expansion of interpersonal skills.
- Learning new skills and perspectives from the protégé.
- Reward for effective mentoring.
- Seeing the protégé develop.
- A new challenge.

For the organization
- High levels of work performance by protégés and perhaps mentors.
- Fast progress towards effective performance by protégés.
- Speedy and complete socialization of protégés.
- High levels of motivation and commitment by protégés and perhaps mentors.
- Good communication and fostering of a culture of collaborative learning.
- Low employee turnover.

(Arnold 1997: 87)

- Partnerships involve two or more people with a shared interest in developing some aspect of their work: for example, an area of research, a teaching programme or some form of liaison between institutions. The partners may be of equal or varied experience and status. The partnership focuses on the task at least as much as the individuals involved.

Box 4.11 lists the major potential benefits of mentoring: for the protégé, for the mentor and for the organization involved. These focus on enabling all parties to perform their work roles as effectively as possible, and giving them a sense of their value to the organization. Mentorship, when carried out well, allows for the rapid induction of new members of staff, and provides them with a source of advice and support regarding all aspects of their working lives. It can be useful during all periods of a career, and offer as much to the mentor as to the protégé.

Increasingly, universities or departments are running mentoring programmes for new staff, and these can be a very important form of continuing support and coping. Regular meetings will be involved. For academics on a probationary contract, as a junior member of staff, the mentor might also be responsible for guidance through the probationary process. If the arrangement works well, the mentor can become a useful supporter, steering opportunities and information in the protégé's way, assisting their development and taking their part.

However, it is worth drawing attention to an aspect of mentoring schemes which reinforces the notion of recurrent transitions in employment careers:

> Traditional models of career development and adult development have offered interdependent relationships as a critical vehicle for addressing . . . fundamental developmental tasks. These models predict that experienced, midcareer individuals can offer guidance and support to novices and in doing so enhance their own self-esteem, self-worth, and value to their organizations. Yet it seems obvious that the stability and security once thought to be a prerequisite for enacting the mentoring role is no longer readily achieved – even by midlife. Newcomers and experienced individuals alike, in the absence of stable jobs and organizations, are that much more dependent on relationships as a vehicle for developing a sense of identity and for developing new skills and competencies.
>
> (Kram 1996: 138)

Thus, both mentor and protégé may be experiencing aspects of transition. The implications of this are that:

> We can expect individuals' reactions to this new reality to vary. Those with career concepts characterized by autonomy and excitement will not find the new context particularly disturbing, and in some instances they may thrive on it. In contrast, those with career concepts characterized by security or balance may have a difficult time coming to terms with the new reality.
>
> (Kram 1996: 138–9)

For these and other reasons, formal mentoring arrangements do not always work well. Mentors are not always adequately trained for their roles. The mentor and protégé may have little in common. The mentoring relationship may become muddied by concerns with appraisal or renewal of contract. Indeed, the term 'mentor' is now often used, inappropriately, to describe the role of members of staff who are asked to provide a variety of support and disciplinary roles which should be undertaken by separate individuals. Such 'mentors' may even be appointed and allocated to new members of staff with little or no consultation.

In seeking your own mentor, you would be well advised to take your time, and let possible relationships develop: potential mentors will make themselves known through their behaviour towards you. Though you might be hesitant to ask someone directly if they would be your mentor – it can feel a bit like asking someone to marry you, or to be your best friend – most people are likely to be flattered. You might not even need to use the term 'mentor', and thereby risk formalizing a relationship which is already developing satisfactorily. Box 4.12 offers some suggestions as to what qualities you might look for in potential mentors, and what to avoid.

Box 4.12: What to look for, and avoid, in a mentor

Qualities to look for:
• Someone with more experience in your subject or institution.
• Someone in a more senior position.
• Someone who is well connected, nationally and internationally, and who can help to network you.
• Someone who has skills which you would like to learn or develop.
• Someone whose work you respect and who is trustworthy.

Qualities to avoid:
• Someone who has a line management responsibility for you.
• Someone who may compete with you for available opportunities or positions.

Other issues to consider:
• Does it matter if your mentor is in the same department or institution?
• Would it be a help or a hindrance to have a mentor of the opposite sex?
• Would it be useful to have more than one mentor to cover different roles?

Partnerships are commoner in some disciplines or subject areas than in others, but the pressures to develop more and stronger partnerships are felt increasingly in most areas of academic life. Greater participation in higher education and larger class sizes have resulted in more team teaching arrangements. Success in acquiring anything beyond small-scale funding typically requires the development of effective research teams. A good writing profile is likely to include joint and edited, as well as single-author, publications. As departments and institutions grow in size, there has been a concomitant move away from individual leadership and line management towards team management. In all of these areas, an increased internationalism, particularly within Europe, has meant the development of partnerships between as well as within nations.

The collaboration involved in partnerships has a variety of benefits. It:

• creates a commitment to a common purpose;
• improves communication and reduces misunderstanding;
• fosters creativity in finding solutions to problems;
• enhances motivation and makes the task more enjoyable;
• prevents individuals from becoming isolated;
• generates a sense of collective achievement;
• encourages other sorts of teamwork.

(Johnson 1996: 42)

You may find, if you join a well-organized department or university, that you are invited into existing partnerships. If not, or if these partnerships prove to be inadequate, you may want or need to take a role in developing new or better arrangements. Such partnerships may be confined to your department, or perhaps just to one section of it, or may link a number of departments or institutions.

Over your career, you are likely to be involved in a range of partnerships of different kinds. As with many aspects of academic work, if you find that your skills lie in this area, using them is likely to enhance your career.

Sources of further information

In this section we list a range of materials which you may find of interest in following up in more detail some of the issues discussed in this chapter. The emphasis is on recently published books in English. In each case, brief details are given as to contents and approach.

Conway, C. (1994) *Mentoring Managers in Organizations: A Study of Mentoring and Its Application to Organizations, with Case Studies*. Berkhamsted, Ashridge Management College.

Clear review of the literature on mentoring, with suggestions on the implementation of mentoring schemes in organizations and dealing with problems which may arise. Contains six case studies illustrative of different approaches to, and reasons for, mentoring.

King, C. (ed.) (1993) *Through the Glass Ceiling: Effective Senior Management Development for Women*. Eastham, Tudor Business Publishing Ltd.

Based on the experiences of senior women in higher education networking together. Includes advice on meetings, working with men, managing the boundaries and taking the next step. Contains a useful bibliography and list of contacts.

Segerman-Peck, L. (1991) *Networking and Mentoring: A Woman's Guide*. London, Piatkus.

A guide to networking and mentoring, with the emphasis on the latter. Designed to facilitate women's career development; contains case histories.

Zelmer, A. and Zelmer, L. (1991) *Organising Academic Conferences*. Campbelltown, NSW, Higher Education Research and Development Society of Australasia.

Australian guide to getting started, programme planning, conference logistics, support services, budgets, international conferences, trade displays and evaluation.

5 | TEACHING

Introduction

This chapter considers the role of teaching in academic careers. Teaching is often regarded as being at the core of academic work. After all, if you were to ask your neighbour or someone in the street about what people who work in universities do, their initial response would probably refer to teaching. And the core activity for which governments fund universities is undoubtedly higher-level teaching. Most institutions of higher education would not exist without this funding.

As academic life is a realm of contradictions, it should not be too surprising to learn that some academics tend to be dismissive or less than enthusiastic about teaching, preferring to spend their time in other, perhaps more rewarding, activities, the most notable of which is research. It is also frequently pointed out that most academics have had little or no training for their role as teachers: or for any other role for that matter, though the possession of a PhD, for those who have it, arguably certifies some research training.

Over the years, many academics seem to have been happy with their frankly 'amateur' status as teachers. One of the enduring myths (and, like most myths, one with elements of truth) of academe has the new academic using the lecture notes they made as a student as the basis for their own lectures, and/or continuing to use the same set of lecture notes for decades with little or no change.

This anomalous state of affairs is now being remedied in most institutions, where a new interest in training and developing academics as teachers has been stimulated by the teaching quality assessment exercises. While much of this activity is being targeted at new or junior members of staff, appraisal schemes endeavour to ensure that all members of staff take at least a token interest.

These developments have underwritten the production of an extensive literature on higher education teaching during the last decade. There are now numerous 'how to' books available on most aspects of the academic teaching role, as the **Sources of further information** section at the end of this chapter makes clear. By contrast, and this is a little surprising, there is little of a practical nature published on other key academic tasks, notably researching, writing and networking. There is, as Chapter 8 makes clear, a growing literature on higher education management, together with a specialist literature for those with professional qualifications in subjects such as nursing, social work and law.

This chapter is organized into seven main sections:

- **Thinking about teaching**, which reviews the vocabulary and scope of the teaching role in higher education, and looks at the relation between teaching and other academic roles;
- **Thinking about students**, which discusses the variety and experience brought by students, and how they might be encouraged to learn;
- **Approaches to teaching**, which examines the range of methods available for teachers to use and the skills required;
- **Tutoring and supervision**, which focuses on two related, specialist forms of higher education teaching;
- **Resource-based teaching**, which focuses on the creation and use of course materials, as well as distance and open learning;
- **Assessment and evaluation**, which discusses the alternative strategies available for reviewing student, course and teacher performance;
- **Teaching as a career**, which considers the training and development opportunities available, and the option of making teaching the core of an academic career.

At the end of the chapter a selection of sources of further information is listed.

Thinking about teaching

I am an educator. I am *not* a facilitator. The act of teaching is not included in the concept of facilitation. As a teacher, I know I have things to teach. I don't need to feel ashamed . . . being different from students does not mean being authoritarian. It means being *competent* in order to get the respect and support of the students. The teacher has to struggle to transform a situation of a transfer of knowledge into a real *act of knowing*. Knowing is not just something that happens.

(Paulo Freire, quoted in Kirkwood 1991: 43)

Two things I most certainly am not is a teacher or lecturer. These terms are more or less dirty words in my department – although, as you'd expect, they do slip out from time to time. No. We don't *teach*. We *tutor* or *facilitate*.

(Stokes 1996: 2)

What does it mean to be a teacher in higher education? As the two quotations which begin this section indicate, while some are happy with the term 'teacher', there are others who reject it in favour of some other, more specific, designation, such as 'tutor' or the more industrial 'facilitator'. 'Teaching' is also seen as something indelibly associated with 'school', and, therefore, perhaps not appropriate for the higher-level and more adult educational work associated with universities.

As Box 5.1 makes clear, there is an extensive, historic and changing vocabulary associated with academic teaching. Terms like 'lecture', 'seminar' and 'tutorial', the conventional parlance of discussions about academic teaching, have, like 'college' and 'university', gained accretions of meaning and sprouted alternative interpretations over the centuries. It is not insignificant that few of the definitions quoted in Box 5.1, all of which have been taken from the second edition of the *Oxford English Dictionary*, represent the oldest usages of the terms. Nevertheless, the influence of teaching practices at Oxford and Cambridge on both our modern vocabulary and practices remains strong.

As a counterbalance to these received notions, we would suggest two, complementary or contradictory, metaphors for the teacher–student interaction that constitutes the basis of higher education:

- the teacher as *banker*, paying out knowledge in predefined units to student customers who have been accepted and are prepared to invest in a bank loan;
- the teacher as *midwife*, assisting at the birth of knowledge, which is likely to remain with students for a long time and have a major impact upon their lives.

The practice of education as a banking exercise, with students presenting themselves as empty vessels to be filled, was strongly criticized by Freire (quoted above) and others over 30 years ago, and this critique has been sustained in feminist pedagogy. That it still remains influential is shown by the continuing prevalence of course syllabuses, listing the extent of the knowledge to be covered, and written examinations, which attempt to test students on their understanding of the breadth of those syllabuses. The second metaphor, of the teacher as midwife, is also of long standing, articulating the aim of inculcating students into a mystery, and making them like the teacher, or, in the words of the dictionary definition, 'addicted to study'.

The discussion so far suggests that teaching has quite a wide scope, covering a range of different activities – such as lecturing, supervising and tutoring – as well as being subject to differing interpretations. Indeed, as the remainder of this chapter will make clear, teaching as a concept can be stretched to accommodate study situations as diverse as independent learning and distance education, mass lectures and one-to-one supervisions.

Teaching may also be thought of in relation to the other academic roles we have identified. This makes sense if you, as an academic, are expected to take on a number of those roles. There are a variety of ways in which such relationships might be developed. For example:

- With the growth in the size of student groups and classes, teaching has come to involve more and more management of the learning experience. This has

---

Box 5.1: A vocabulary of academic teaching traditions

academic: Of or belonging to an academy or institution for higher learning.

class: A division of the scholars or students of an institution, receiving the same instruction or ranked together as of the same standing.

college: A society of scholars incorporated within, or in connexion with, a university, or otherwise formed for the purposes of study or instruction.

instruction: The action of instructing or teaching; the imparting of knowledge or skill; education; information.

lecture: A discourse given before an audience upon a given subject, usually for the purpose of instruction.

lecturer: One who gives lectures or formal discourses intended for instruction, esp. in a college or university.

professor: A public teacher or instructor of the highest rank in a specific faculty or branch of learning; *spec.* one who holds an endowed or established 'chair' in a university or one of its colleges.

reader: One who reads (and expounds) to pupils or students; a teacher, lecturer; *spec.* in some universities as the title of certain instructors.

seminar: [A] select group of advanced students associated for special study and original research under the guidance of a professor. Also ... a class that meets for systematic study under the direction of a teacher.

student: A person who is engaged in or addicted to study ... A person who is undergoing a course of study and instruction at a university or other place of higher education or technical training.

supervisor: A person who exercises general direction or control; one who inspects and directs the work of others.

teacher: One who or that which teaches or instructs; an instructor; ... *spec.* one whose function is to give instruction, esp. in a school.

tutor: A graduate ... to whom the special supervision of an undergraduate ... is assigned. [A] member of the teaching staff assigned responsibility for the general well-being of a student.

university: The whole body of teachers and scholars engaged, at a particular place, in giving and receiving instruction in the higher branches of learning; such persons associated together as a society or corporate body, with definite organization and acknowledged powers and privileges (esp. that of conferring degrees), and forming an institution for the promotion of education in the higher or more important branches of learning.

(*Oxford English Dictionary*, 2nd edn, 1989)

---

led to the widespread adoption of forms of resource-based teaching (discussed later in this chapter).

• Obviously, you will need to engage in some research on the topics you teach (and, if you are fortunate, vice versa). Even if your employment contract specifies your role as 'teaching only', being researcherly and reflective about your practice is another way in which to maintain linkage. Indeed, being a 'reflective

---

Box 5.2: Ten writerly rules for teachers

1 Wait.
2 Begin early.
3 Work in brief sessions.
4 Stop.
5 Balance preliminaries with teaching.
6 Supplant self-defeating thinking.
7 Manage busyness, rushing, emotions.
8 Moderate attachments and reactions.
9 Let others, even critics, do some of the work.
10 Limit wasted effort by tolerating correction, tutoring, differences.

(Boice 1995a: 57)

---

practitioner' is a recognized stance in some subjects, such as business studies and education (see the section on **Relating research to other academic roles** in Chapter 6).
- It has also been argued that the basic strategies used for effective teaching are the same as those used in writing. Thus, Boice has identified ten writerly rules for teachers (see Box 5.2).

For many academics, regardless of whether they have had any specific training, their initial experiences of teaching are rather daunting. Box 5.3 contains a sample of quotes relating to such early experiences. They reflect a mixture of surprise, horror and loneliness. While some of this may be inevitable, as with any new experience, much of it might have been avoided with better preparation and support. In this spirit, we would offer the following two pieces of basic advice to any teacher in a university, whether visiting, new or otherwise. Much of this advice may seem obvious, but it is surprising how frequently much of it is overlooked:

- *Familiarity.* Visit the room or rooms you are going to be teaching in, when they are empty, before you first teach there. Make sure you know how to get in, how to turn the heating on and off, how to open and close any windows, and how to work the teaching equipment (particularly, but not only, those items you may yourself use). If someone else has to give you access, bring in the video equipment or unlock the overhead projector, make sure you know who and how to get hold of them.
- *Emergency kit.* Always make sure you have with you a box or bag containing chalk, whiteboard pens, overhead projector pens, drawing pins, Blu-Tack, paper, cards, ordinary pens and paper towels.

The remainder of this chapter aims to introduce the range of major activities and issues encompassed within teaching in higher education. We start this review, logically enough, by focusing on the raw material of the teaching process, the relationship with students.

Box 5.3: Initial experiences of teaching

My first term teaching was horrific. I spent the days teaching and the nights preparing lectures. An experience I do not wish to repeat.

(Quoted in Rust 1991: 17)

As a postgraduate student, not much older than the group I was teaching, my expectations were that I would have no problems creating a relaxed, open atmosphere. I had anticipated that the challenge would in fact be to be taken seriously and to assume the authority necessary to direct and structure the emerging discussion. In fact, the biggest surprise I had was the readiness with which the group handed over initiative and responsibility to me.

(Hill 1996: 48)

I dread so much the moments of silence when I've asked a question that I hardly dare look around the group. I can feel myself tightening up and I'm certain they can see it too. It's not that they're malicious or anything – in fact I think that they feel a bit sorry for me. I'm not sure which is worse!

(Quoted in Gibbs and Habeshaw 1989: 69)

It was very unnerving to find myself thrust into a classroom full of students and left to get on with it. I could have been doing anything and no one from the Poly would have known better. It was too much responsibility and I would have liked someone sitting there for just a few classes, if only to say 'yes, that was OK'.

(Quoted in Rust 1991: 21)

Fresh from finals and desperate not to bore the seventy-odd engineering students with the trivia of introductory complex analysis I prepared reams of notes from several textbooks and my own scribbled lecture notes, entered the room talking formulae, and scribbled them on the board as I went. One lucky thing happened. At the end of the lecture I asked if there were any questions, and one brave student asked a question of such breathtaking 'stupidity' that it was clear he could not have understood anything beyond my first sentence. Did anyone else have that problem? Yes, they all had that problem.

(Laurillard 1993: 1)

I can well remember being lectured by someone who ... made a complete fool of himself looking for the elusive controls to the slide projector: 'Ah ... yes ... here it is ... I think I've got it ... is anything coming on ... oh dear ... hmmm ... anything yet? ... yes? ... no ... I can't seem to get it on ... I wonder if someone could go and fetch the porter?

(Allan 1996: 41)

Thinking about students

University teachers must take the main responsibility for what and how their students learn.

(Laurillard 1993: 1)

Box 5.4: Six key principles of effective teaching in higher education

1 Interest and explanation.
2 Concern and respect for students and student learning.
3 Appropriate assessment and feedback.
4 Clear goals and intellectual challenge.
5 Independence, control and active engagement.
6 Learning from students.

Source: Ramsden (1992: 96–103).

The modern pressure upon academics to pay more attention to how they teach, and its effects upon their students' learning, can be traced partly, as has already been suggested, to the greater interest taken by the state in the quality of higher education. It is also partly due to the increased participation in higher education, and the associated decline in the unit of resource, such that it has become less and less possible to continue to deliver programmes to more (and more varied) students in tried and trusted, amateur ways. Simultaneously, students, parents and their other funders, assuming the role of customers, have become less willing to accept 'any' provision gratefully.

The burgeoning literature on teaching in higher education, based in part on good practice and in part on research, places considerable emphasis on student learning. Box 5.4, to take one example, lists six key principles of effective teaching in higher education, as identified by Ramsden. Two focus specifically on students and student learning, while the others stress interest, clarity, appropriateness and engagement. The higher educational experience is presented as an active, ordered, challenging and collaborative affair. Many of these principles and their associated practices have been borrowed or developed from the adult education literature (and amplified by feminist, postmodern and other thinking). The adult education tradition has, for a century or more, emphasized starting from where students are, acknowledging their voluntary and experienced status, and making the curriculum interesting and relevant. That these views have now become commonplace in higher education reflects in part the increased maturity and diversity of the British student body.

The remainder of this section will focus upon three key elements in thinking about students: the expectations they bring, how they learn, and the particular case of overseas students.

Students' expectations

Any group of higher education students is likely to contain a mix of experiences and expectations. Thus, at undergraduate level, they will come from a range of social backgrounds and areas, and enter with a variety of qualifications – including, for example, national vocational qualifications, access courses and overseas certificates as well as the more conventional A-level or Higher Grade

---

Box 5.5: Eleven powerful ideas in teaching

1 Students construct knowledge.
2 Students need to see the whole picture.
3 Students are selectively negligent.
4 Students are driven by assessment.
5 Students often only memorize.
6 Students' attention is limited.
7 Students can easily be overburdened.
8 Adults learn differently.
9 Students learn well by doing.
10 Students learn well when they take responsibility for their learning.
11 Students have feelings.

Source: Gibbs and Habeshaw (1989: 15–38).

---

passes. Recognizing, understanding and responding appropriately to this mix constitutes a major part of delivering a successful teaching programme.

In spite of this heterogeneity, it is possible to identify a series of common expectations likely to be shared by most of the students (and perhaps also the staff) you come into contact with. Box 5.5 represents one attempt to clarify these expectations. We would add to that list of 11 powerful ideas the following:

• Students want to learn.
• Students need time to digest, review and make sense of their learning.
• Students need regular feedback on their learning.
• Students expect staff to be available and supportive.
• Students expect staff to know most, but not all, of the answers.
• Students want to gain credit for their learning.

These listings have, of course, some similarities with the set of teaching principles set out in Box 5.4. It could not be said, however, that all of these expectations hold for all higher education students in all possible circumstances. Students' abilities and attitudes will vary to some extent. What can be said is that such basic expectations offer a reasonable basis on which to plan and deliver teaching, and/ or to begin an investigation into the expectations of a particular group of students. Where students do not share one or more of these expectations, they are likely to be in the minority.

This suggests another important point, namely the need to understand and respond to student group cultures. Even with the largest classes, there is a need to get to know students and how they expect a teacher to behave. Different disciplines and institutions may have varied practices, but much will also depend upon the students' previous and current experiences.

Anyone starting to teach a group of students for the first time could usefully give some thought to establishing some 'ground rules' which will enhance the effectiveness of the learning experience for all concerned. This might be gained in part from talking to other members of staff, particularly those who have taught the same group before, but will also involve some direct, and early, negotiation with the group itself.

Possible ground rules might cover, for example:

- arriving late, leaving early, absences;
- comfort breaks;
- not making personal criticisms;
- sharing understandings;
- encouraging all to participate;
- dealing with dominant individuals;
- dealing with prejudice;
- allowing space for discussion.

If such ground rules are not made explicit from the start, they will emerge of their own volition, and some of them may be unhelpful!

How do students learn?

The question of how children learn has fascinated psychologists and others for decades. More recently, increased attention has been given in research to youth, adolescent and adult learning processes. A wide range of competing theories – commonly summarized under the three headings of behavioural, cognitive and humanistic – have been enunciated and used as the basis for teaching strategies. The central conclusion which might be drawn from all of this activity to date is that there is no single, generally accepted, comprehensive theory which adequately explains how we learn and, therefore, offers a blueprint for planning how best to teach.

Here, we will draw attention to three popular ways in which student learning might be conceptualized: deep, surface and strategic learning; ways of knowing; and experiential learning. Many other analyses may be found in the literature on learning, which may be accessed through some of the references given in the sources of further information listed at the end of this chapter.

During the last two decades, a group of researchers from Britain and Sweden has devoted particular attention to the issue of how higher education students learn. Some of the main findings from their research have been summarized in Box 5.6. This suggests that higher education students adopt one, or sometimes a combination, of three main approaches to learning – deep, surface and strategic. Of these, the strategic approach is likely to bring the most rewards in terms of marks and recognition. The surface approach is characteristic of the student trying to get through without really engaging with the course or subject by doing the minimum amount of work required to pass. The deep approach is taken by the kind of student many lecturers admire, though it may not lead to as good a degree as the strategic approach.

A second approach, which draws out gendered differences in students' approaches to learning, is summarized in Box 5.7. This suggests four 'ways of knowing', each characterized by a:

Box 5.6: Defining features of approaches to learning

Deep approach————————————————————Transforming

Intention: to understand material for oneself

Being actively interested in the course content

Relating ideas to previous knowledge and experience
Looking for patterns and underlying principles

Checking evidence and relating it to conclusions
Examining logic and argument cautiously and critically

Surface approach ————————————————Reproducing

Intention: to cope with content and tasks set

Studying without reflecting on either purpose or strategy
Treating the course as unrelated bits of knowledge

Finding difficulty in making sense of new ideas presented
Memorizing facts and procedures routinely

Feeling undue pressure and worry about work

Strategic approach————————————————— Organizing

Intention: to excel on assessed work

Being alert to assessment requirements and criteria
Gearing work to the perceived preferences of lecturers

Putting consistent effort into studying
Finding the right conditions and materials for studying
Managing time and effort effectively to maximize grades

Source: Entwistle (1994: 11).

---

core set of epistemic assumptions. Each leads to particular expectations of the learner, peers, and instructor in learning settings, as well as to an understanding of how learning should be evaluated and how educational decisions are made.

(Magolda 1992: 29)

The third approach considered here, experiential learning, was first popularized by Kolb. At the core of this formulation is the idea of learning as a never ending, cyclical or spiral process (see Box 5.8). This process may start at any point, but typically involves four elements: concrete experience, observation and reflection upon that experience, the formulation of abstract concepts and generalization as a result of that reflection, and some testing of these concepts, leading to further experience, and so on.

Box 5.7: Four 'ways of knowing' in students' intellectual development

- *Absolute*: viewing knowledge as certain and the task of the learner as to receive and master. Women were more likely to emphasize receiving knowledge and men to emphasize mastery.
- *Transitional*: accepts that some knowledge is uncertain and so understanding becomes more important than acquiring and remembering. Two patterns of transitional knowing were identified. Men were more likely to adopt an *impersonal pattern*, wanting to be forced to think, debate and resolve uncertainty with logic. Women were more likely to manifest an *interpersonal pattern*, preferring to hear the views of others and resolve uncertainty through personal judgement based on a consideration of individual differences.
- *Independent*: assumes that knowledge is mostly uncertain and that instructors provide a context in which knowledge can be explored. An interpersonal pattern involved a dual focus on thinking for oneself and engaging the views of others. The individual pattern gave greater focus to 'expanding the mind' and being challenged.
- *Contextual*: an approach associated with postgraduate students. This assumed that some knowledge claims are better than others in particular contexts and that learning requires thinking through problems, integrating and applying knowledge.

Source: adapted from Magolda (1992).

Box 5.8: An experiential learning cycle

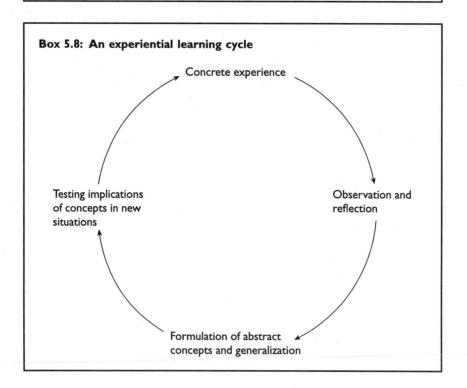

Clearly, your understanding and beliefs about how people learn will influence how you teach.

Overseas students

While students today represent a much more heterogeneous group than they did twenty or thirty years ago, it is still useful to recognize and reflect upon the particular needs of significant subgroups. Adult or mature students are still commonly singled out as a group meriting particular attention, though, arguably, general teaching and learning practices in higher education have now become more adult in their orientation and expectations. Postgraduate students represent another obvious grouping, defined in terms of level of study, and their case is considered further in the section later in this chapter on **Tutoring and supervision.**

Perhaps the most distinctive grouping within the general student body today, however, is that of overseas students. They represent a significant and growing proportion of the student body – in 1994/95 just over 10 per cent of all enrolments at United Kingdom higher education institutions were students domiciled in European Union or other overseas countries (Higher Education Statistics Agency 1996: Table 1) – and tend to stand out for a variety of reasons. The United Kingdom has successfully exploited the quality of its higher education system, its old colonial links and the primacy of English as a world language in building up the overseas student market, which attracts a substantial income to those universities involved.

While much of the impetus for developing this market has been financial, the benefits in terms of international networking and relations are not insignificant either. Nor are the costs, of course, and it has long been realized that meeting the needs of overseas students well is not a straightforward exercise. Box 5.9 details some of the findings from research regarding overseas students' expectations of British higher education. In many ways they may seem obvious, and contain much good practice which would apply to any other group of higher education students as well. The main issues relate to cultural variations, linguistic difficulties and the problems that distance creates both in ensuring adequate communication prior to study and in combating homesickness after arrival. Early contacts with academic tutors appear to be crucial.

Approaches to teaching

University teachers are now expected to be much more flexible and adapt-able in their teaching, to be proficient in a wide range of teaching methods, assessment techniques and approaches to course design, and to keep abreast of developments in all these areas.

(Supplement to *AUT Bulletin*, January 1996, p. iii)

While the language of Box 5.1 – of the lecture, seminar and tutorial – still remains dominant in discussions of teaching in higher education, these terms

---

Box 5.9: Research findings from overseas students

- Pre-arrival communications to students in their home countries were seen as a vital prerequisite to a proper understanding of, first, UK culture and higher education in general, and second, the specific institution, its expectations and academic programmes.
- On arrival, suitable permanent accommodation should be made available, as soon as students reached the universities. The vacation accommodation needs of students and their special dietary requirements should be more carefully taken into account, as should the needs of mature students with family commitments.
- Appropriate information, advice and help on arrival were important to help create favourable first impressions and to prevent a student's experiences becoming problem-centred. Pre-sessional orientation courses were especially worthwhile.
- Students generally appreciated the good quality of courses and approved of the relatively informal lecturing styles; however, the perception that this was an undirected means of teaching created difficulties for some.
- Early contacts with academic tutors seemed to be crucial.
- Many students were concerned with their inadequate English and/or study skills.
- The opportunity to meet and befriend British people, especially other students, was seen as important.

(Elsey and Kinnell 1990: 8–9)

---

have been extended, modified and supplemented in an attempt to respond to the changing realities of academic life. These changes include both an increased emphasis on preparing academics for their teaching role, and a recognition, as the quotation above indicates, that a more diversified set of teaching/learning techniques is needed to cope with a mass and heterogeneous student market.

Box 5.10 categorizes the most common types of teaching/learning activities to be found in British higher education today in terms of lecture (i.e. large group), group and independent (or individualized) strategies. Clearly, some of these approaches, such as laboratory classes, are only applicable to some subjects; while others, such as computer-assisted learning, depend upon the existence or development of appropriate software.

With larger numbers of students, and greater pressure on available staff time, more emphasis is now being placed on the third category identified, independent learning. This includes private study, always an expectation – indeed, in many ways the key aim – of higher education; and the broad area of project-based work, which has enabled higher education to remain individualized and link more closely with employment. Much time and energy has also been devoted over the last three decades to the development of, first, distance education (as in the case of the Open University), and, latterly, open learning, the wider use of specially produced course materials to support and replace direct teaching. Currently there is much discussion around the use of technology, as in the notions of the virtual college or virtual classroom. A later section in this chapter, on **Resource-based teaching**, discusses these strategies in more detail.

Box 5.10: The most common types of teaching/learning activity

Lecture
Formal lecture: 'virtually uninterrupted monologue taking occasional questions'.
Active lecture: 'lecture period including mini-sessions of student activity'.

Group
Tutorial/exercise class: 'students work through set problems, individually or together, with assistance as necessary from tutor'.
Seminar: 'presentation of a piece of prepared work by a student to his/her peers and subsequent discussion roughly structured by the tutor'.
Role play/games: 'students act out roles or play games for the purpose of learning and developing specific skills'.
Laboratory classes: 'for practical sessions required in experimental subjects or languages'.
Peer tutoring: 'the students teach each other, within a structured format provided by the tutor'.
Personal tutoring: 'one-to-one discussion of students' work and problems with a tutor'.

Independent
Open or independent learning: 'the students effectively teach themselves with the support of specially prepared courseware, frequent monitoring and feedback and maybe a small number of classroom sessions'.
Private study: 'what (we hope) the students do in their own time'.
Computer-assisted learning: 'students use dedicated teaching software, the best of which is interactive and (moderately) intelligent, to learn some of the course material'.

Source: Cox (1994: 28–9, 58).

Lectures, seminars and tutorials loom large among the remaining categories in Box 5.10, though they appear in a number of guises. Different types of lectures and tutorials are recognized, some involving more active involvement on the part of students (and less from staff), and these are supplemented by practical exercises in various forms.

The use of the lecture as a teaching method has, of course, been much criticized: Box 5.11 provides one recent summary of its perceived disadvantages. This critique has been extended to encompass the whole of the 'academic model', of which the formal lecture may be seen as the core:

First, the academic model is hierarchical. Who has power to decide the content ... is weighted heavily in favour of the tutors ... Second, the academic model rests on the notion that there are experts whose job it is to initiate students (who are ignorant) into the mysteries of their subject ... Third, the academic model denies the centrality of personal experience ... Fourth, the academic model with its emphasis on pre-established content,

---

Box 5.11: A critique of lecturing

1 Lectures are no more economical than other methods as a way of teaching students. There are efficient courses, and even institutions, that have no lectures, or very few. There are alternative methods that involve less preparation time and less contact time, or which apportion the same total time differently.

2 Lectures are no more effective than other methods at conveying information to students. Discussion and reading are as effective. Methods other than lecturing are better for helping students to apply knowledge and use it to analyse problems.

3 The idea that lectures ensure that 'the ground is covered' is false. The ground is covered for the lecturer, perhaps, but not by the students . . . Most learning in higher education goes on outside the lecture room . . . Students have to make sense of information for themselves if they are to learn anything.

4 Some lecturers are seen by students to be inspirational and stimulating. But more often students complain of poor structure, overloading and confusion. Perhaps the most compelling argument against lecturing is that few lecturers do it well, many do it just about passably, and quite a lot do it very badly indeed . . .

5 Students are usually very passive and dependent during lectures.

(Ramsden 1992: 154–5)

---

presented in a seminar style, can lead to destructive conflict-ridden group relationships; the very opposite of the kind of learning environment in which we can explore ideas, take risks, experiment with what we think and feel, challenge, and be challenged . . .

(Mahony 1988: 104)

Despite this powerful critique, however, it remains the case that many, perhaps most, of those in higher education – both staff and students – expect the lecture method to form the core of a bona fide course of higher education. In part, this reflects a continuing lack of familiarity and confidence with alternative teaching/ learning approaches, but it also has to do with the pressures of time which discourage delivery through larger numbers of smaller classes. As staffing levels have decreased relative to student numbers, the mass lecture has come to represent, for many, the only feasible and effective method for delivering courses. Hence many universities are building larger and larger lecture theatres. Simultaneously, though less visibly, the use of computer-assisted learning has also grown.

The problem of large classes and how to deal with them is not really about lectures as such, however, but has to do with the whole teaching/learning approach. As Box 5.12 indicates, strategies for coping can be seen as emphasizing either 'control' or the development of 'independence'. Control strategies typically involve greater structuring, the greater use of special course materials and more testing of students. Independence strategies, by contrast, put much more responsibility on individual students and concentrate on developing their ability to learn

Box 5.12: Problems with large classes and strategies for dealing with them

Problem	'Control' strategies	'Independence' strategies
1 Lack of clarity of purpose	(a) Use of objectives (b) Highly structured courses	(a) Use of learning contracts (b) Problem-based learning
2 Lack of knowledge of progress	(a) Objective testing (b) Programmed instruction and computer-assisted learning	(a) Development of student judgement (b) Self-assessment
3 Lack of advice on improvement	(a) Assignment attachment forms (b) Automated tutorial feedback	(a) Peer feedback and assessment
4 Inability to support reading	(a) Use of set books (b) Use of learning packages	(a) Development of students' research skills (b) More varied assignments
5 Inability to support independent study	(a) Structured projects (b) Lab guides	(a) Group work (b) Learning teams
6 Lack of opportunity for discussion	(a) Structured lectures (b) Structured seminars/ workshops	(a) Student-led seminars (b) Team assignments
7 Inability to cope with variety of students	(a) Pre-tests plus remedial material (b) Self-paced study	(a) Variety of support mechanisms (b) Negotiated goals
8 Inability to motivate students	(a) Frequent testing (b) High failure rates	(a) Engaging learning tasks (b) Cooperative learning

Source: Gibbs (1992: 44).

and support themselves. With the latter, the academic becomes more of a facilitator and adviser; with the former, more of an instructor and assessor.

The teaching/learning methods summarized in Box 5.10 constitute only a part of the process of teaching. As Box 5.13 makes clear, the teaching role is a continuing process involving elements of planning, preparation, presentation, assessment and evaluation. Of course, not all academics give all of these stages the same amount of attention; and, with more experience and practice, planning and preparation may not take up so much time.

Box 5.13: Key activities in teaching a course

- *Plan*: the content and the teaching and assessment methods to be used.
- *Prepare*: the courseware, such as notes, exercises and problems, course guides, booklists; the assessment material to be used, and the course and teaching evaluation material required.
- *Present*: the course (sometimes in parallel with the preparation), deploying skills of delivery and classroom management.
- *Assess*: the students, including possibly continuous assessment as well as a final examination requiring planning and preparation well in advance.
- *Evaluate*: the whole teaching process, possibly on a continuous, lecture by lecture, basis, providing a feedback to course planning, development and preparation.

(Cox 1994: 12–13)

A key point, however, especially for the new academic, is that the actual presentation of the course represents a small part of the total time involved. Planning and preparing a course from scratch takes a great deal of time, perhaps five to ten times as much as its presentation. Assessment, particularly where large classes are involved and regular continuous assessment is employed, will take substantially more time.

The evaluation of teaching, and the associated documentation of the whole procedure, is also becoming a major commitment with increased attention being paid to teaching quality assessment. It is here that well-established management information systems and competent administrative support are invaluable. Having a clear, documented paper trail covering everything from course approval to student assessment is of critical importance (see also the section on **Quality audit and assessment** in Chapter 8).

Tutoring and supervision

In spite of the increasing size of the teaching commitment within higher education, the more individual, or at least small-group, roles of tutoring and supervision remain of importance. This is particularly so in the older, better-resourced, more elite universities, and at higher, notably postgraduate, levels of study. While not many institutions or departments can now justify delivering much, if any, of their teaching through one-to-one tutorials, most continue to pay some attention to personal, as contrasted to academic, tutoring.

The personal tutoring role harks back to the time when students tended to be young, to have come straight from school, and the university saw itself as acting in a parental role with responsibilities for moral welfare and development. However, the more diversified student populations found in higher education institutions today also appreciate, and indeed require, the pastoral support structures associated with the personal tutor. In a more cynical vein, this remains a significant role at a time when customer care is in vogue, and when students and their sponsors are becoming increasingly litigious.

We define a personal tutor as a member of academic staff whose role and function may include responsibilities:
- to facilitate the personal development of their tutees;
- to monitor the progress of their tutees;
- to provide a link between the students and the university authorities;
- to be a responsible adult within the organization, in whom the student can confide;
- to intervene with the university authorities on behalf of their tutees.

(Wheeler and Birtle 1993: 15)

Or, in other words, being a personal tutor may involve exercising some or all of the roles of friend, adviser, referral agent, academic assessor, disciplinarian, parent, advocate, counsellor, teacher, careers adviser, referee, confidant(e) and institutional change agent!

Few academics could be said to be skilled in all of these areas. Many might not wish to spend the time involved, especially if they are not rewarded by their institution for doing so, in delivering an effective personal tutorial service. Finding out what resources are provided centrally can help to channel some student needs into one or other of the general services provided by or at most universities, such as careers advisory and counselling services, mature students' societies, health centres, specialist services for overseas students, chaplaincies and students' unions. Many of these agencies are, as a consequence, overstretched. In other cases, students' personal demands are likely to fall upon those individual, usually female, academics, who are, or appear to be, more accessible and empathetic:

Last week I had a student in my office, she was talking about how she needed me to help her to escape from home . . . because her father's been abusing her, etc., etc. Now, I'm the only person she's ever told about this, and I spent a lot of time, both talking to her, then following it up . . . I mean that's just one example, but I could multiply . . . I could tell you that over and over and over, about the ways in which women academics get involved with their students . . . I'm not saying that men don't do this, but I do think that women . . . tend to do it more, and students expect that from them more as well.

(Brooks 1997: 104, quoting a lecturer from the University of Auckland)

Indeed, there can be penalties for women academics who do not respond to students in such gender-related ways. These penalties come in the form of more critical end-of-term student assessments, as well as in their continuing relationships with students.

The roles of the supervisor, summarized in Box 5.14, may be very similar to those listed for the personal tutor. The supervisory role is critical for research students, and typically comes into play for other students when they undertake a significant project or piece of small-scale research leading to a dissertation. For some academics, this can be the most satisfactory part of the teaching role, in that it is much more individualized and likely to be close to personal research interests.

Box 5.14: The roles of the supervisor

- *Director*: determining topic and method, providing ideas.
- *Facilitator*: providing access to resources or expertise, arranging fieldwork.
- *Adviser*: helping to resolve technical problems, suggesting alternatives.
- *Teacher*: of research techniques.
- *Guide*: suggesting timetable for writing up, giving feedback on progress, identifying critical path for data collection.
- *Critic*: of design of enquiry, of draft chapters, of interpretations of data.
- *Freedom giver*: authorizes student to make decisions, supports student's decisions.
- *Supporter*: gives encouragement, shows interest, discusses student's ideas.
- *Friend*: extends interest and concern to non-academic aspects of student's life.
- *Manager*: checks progress regularly, monitors study, gives systematic feedback, plans work.
- *Examiner*: e.g. internal examiner, mock vivas, interim progress reports, supervisory board member.

(Brown and Atkins 1988: 120)

Box 5.15: What students expect of their supervisors

1 Students expect to be supervised.
2 Students expect supervisors to read their work well in advance.
3 Students expect their supervisors to be available when needed.
4 Students expect their supervisors to be friendly, open and supportive.
5 Students expect their supervisors to be constructively critical.
6 Students expect their supervisors to have a good knowledge of the research area.
7 Students expect their supervisors to structure the tutorial so that it is relatively easy to exchange ideas.
8 Students expect their supervisors to have sufficient interest in their research to put more information in the student's path.
9 Students expect supervisors to be sufficiently involved in their success to help them get a good job at the end of it all!

Source: Phillips and Pugh (1994: 147–58).

This is not to say, however, that it is unproblematic or undemanding. As Box 5.15 illustrates, research students may have heavy expectations of their supervisors. Not surprisingly, then, one of the key problems identified by research students, and at the centre of many anecdotal accounts, has to do with poor or inadequate supervision. Supervising students through to successful completion in as short a time as possible is a demanding activity, requiring at least as much management as other teaching roles.

Box 5.16: Issues in supervising research students

- How many research students can one academic handle?
- How is that number affected by the subjects they are researching? Whether they are home or overseas students? Whether they are studying full-time or part-time? Whether they need to be supervised at a distance?
- How often should you aim to meet each research student?
- Is a visit to a student undertaking fieldwork required?
- What arrangements should be made for your research students while you are on leave, on sabbatical or otherwise unavailable?
- Should you give your research students your home telephone number?
- How should the work of your research students relate to your own research interests? Is it acceptable to supervise research students outside your area of immediate expertise?
- How important is it to ensure that research students complete in the minimum possible time?
- What can you do to help your (actual or prospective) research students get funding, and get to conferences?
- How can you encourage undergraduate or taught master's students to engage in research?

In developing the skills associated with supervision, newly appointed academics may be asked to undertake supervision of undergraduate or master's dissertation students. The smaller-scale nature of such projects can, of course, bring demands of its own in terms of timing and manageability. However, it can also offer opportunities to undertake work of this kind while on a short-term contract. The supervision of MPhil or PhD students usually requires the academic responsible to have a more permanent contract. Initially, new academics may be invited or required to co-supervise such students alongside a more experienced colleague. This kind of on-the-job learning can be viewed in a similar way to the PhD studentship: as an apprenticeship.

Some of the other issues commonly encountered in the supervision of research students are summarized in Box 5.16. This is clearly an area of teaching which can lend itself to specialization, and where it can be relatively easy to build links with one's own research interests and activities.

Resource-based teaching

University teachers have always, of course, made some use of written and other resources in their work with their students. Initially much of this was based on a limited number of standard textbooks. With the mushrooming of print-based forms of media in the nineteenth and twentieth centuries, students have been expected, particularly at higher levels of study, to spend more and more time on their own and in libraries reading books, journals and other forms of publication.

Box 5.17: Ten reasons for moving towards flexible learning

1 Increasing competition between institutions of higher education and training means that we have to be able to *cater more flexibly* for a wide variety of learner needs and expectations.

2 Resource-based learning provides an easier basis for *collaboration*.

3 The availability of a substantial proportion of curricula in *packaged* form significantly helps progress towards a modular structure, and allows learners increased choice.

4 Increased pressure on funding will mean we need to be able to cater both for *larger class numbers* and for new *target groups* of part-time and distant learners.

5 As the proportion of *mature and non-traditional entry learners* increases, we need to replace entirely some traditional approaches.

6 With increasing use of supported self-study in secondary education, *learners' expectations* are likely to move away from being taught mostly in lectures or direct training sessions.

7 With the increased franchising of university programmes ... the availability of flexible learning resource materials provides an excellent means of ensuring that the *quality of learning* is maintained and controlled.

8 In *commerce and industry*, open and flexible learning is becoming much more attractive than traditional training.

9 In many disciplines higher education learners are *seriously 'over-taught'*.

10 Perhaps the most important outcome of higher education should be the development of *the ability to manage one's own learning*.

(Race 1994: 36–7)

These trends, coupled with modern communications networks, also enabled the successive development of correspondence, distance and open forms of learning. Such approaches were designed to exploit successive technologies (print, radio, television, video, computers) to reach out to those who were unable to spend much time within educational institutions. While the Open University, established in 1969, may be seen as a highly significant innovation from this perspective, its approach to teaching and learning has now been copied and further developed by many other universities in the United Kingdom and overseas.

The greatly increased participation in higher education, and the larger class sizes, have also pressurized academics into making increased use of distance teaching techniques within primarily face-to-face forms of provision. Resource-based teaching, involving the use of a range of materials or media, is now a commonplace throughout higher education. Box 5.17 offers ten reasons for extending its use throughout higher education, and making learning more flexible.

A reasonably comprehensive list of the various types of instructional materials used within higher education is given in Box 5.18. Most of these types are more or less familiar, though in practice most academics will probably use relatively few of them. Some, such as dioramas, posters or radio broadcasts, seem a little old-fashioned. Some, such as models or database systems, seem mainly applicable to particular forms of teaching or subjects. Others, such as computer-managed

---

Box 5.18: Types of instructional materials

- Printed and duplicated materials:
  handouts, assignment sheets, individualized study materials, resource materials for group exercises.
- Non-projected display materials:
  chalkboard, markerboard, feltboard, hook-and-loop board, magnetic board and flipchart displays, charts and wallcharts, posters, photographic prints, mobiles, models, dioramas, realia.
- Still projected display materials:
  overhead projector transparencies, slides, filmstrips, microforms.
- Audio materials:
  radio broadcasts, audio discs, audiotapes.
- Linked audio and still visual materials:
  tape–slide programmes, tape–photograph programmes, filmstrips with sound, radio–vision programmes, tape–text, tape–model, tape–realia.
- Video materials:
  television broadcasts, videotape recordings, videodisc recordings.
- Computer-mediated materials:
  'number-crunching' and data-processing packages, 'substitute tutor' packages, 'substitute laboratory' packages, database systems, computer-managed learning systems, interactive video systems, multimedia interactive systems.

Source: Ellington and Race (1993: 24–34).

---

learning systems, offer potential for large-scale development and usage if adequate support, in terms of funding, staff resourcing and expertise, is available.

Box 5.19 presents a different kind of summary of the main kinds of teaching media which may be found in use within higher education, one which focuses on the relation between the media and the user. Simple forms of audio-visual media, such as print and broadcast television, have been supplemented by multimedia and hypermedia (multimedia stored in non-linear form) resources held on computers or CD-ROMs. In addition, a range of media has been developed to enable individual or group interaction with program simulations or models, the use of programs to tutor students on particular topics, and audio and visual conferencing of individual and groups separated from each other.

Experience suggests three key points to be borne in mind when using, or considering the use of, different teaching media:

- Even the simplest of them take time and expertise to develop. It is far simpler to use a package, program or system which is already available 'off the shelf', adding whatever contextualization may be necessary.
- Because of their development time, and the equipment needed, anything beyond the simplest media tends to be relatively expensive. Their use is difficult to justify, therefore, except with relatively large student groups or those able to pay relatively high fees.

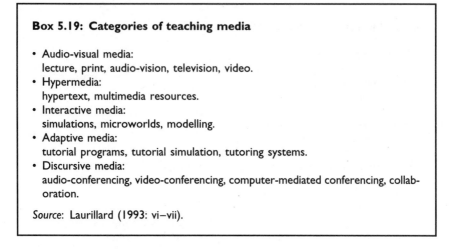

Box 5.19: Categories of teaching media

- Audio-visual media:
  lecture, print, audio-vision, television, video.
- Hypermedia:
  hypertext, multimedia resources.
- Interactive media:
  simulations, microworlds, modelling.
- Adaptive media:
  tutorial programs, tutorial simulation, tutoring systems.
- Discursive media:
  audio-conferencing, video-conferencing, computer-mediated conferencing, collaboration.

Source: Laurillard (1993: vi–vii).

- Those applying relatively new and/or complex teaching media for teaching purposes need to be well versed and practised in their use. Other staff and students will need some training, and possibly a good deal of specialist support, at least initially.

In conclusion, therefore, there is much to be said, unless there are compelling reasons otherwise, in favour of using the simple and the available wherever possible. This may run counter to national policies and publicity which emphasizes the development of information technology skills, but the issues for university teachers have to do with availability and support (for both teachers and learners). Newer teaching media need institutional support from librarians, technicians, staff development services and others, which are themselves facing cutbacks in an underfunded and overstretched sector.

Assessment and evaluation

Assessment and evaluation are key elements of the processes of teaching and learning in higher education, though they are still sometimes accorded relatively little attention. Assessment is concerned with judging what and how well students have learnt, while evaluation may involve students, teachers and others in reflecting upon the effectiveness of the learning experience and how it might be developed further.

The most conventional method of assessing courses of higher education remains the unseen, written, final examination, though various forms of continuous assessment, again usually written, have become more popular in recent years. Examinations may be modified to allow for the use of particular texts, equipment or other materials, and prior notice may be given of the areas to be covered or even the specific questions to be set. The extent of choice the student has over

---

Box 5.20: Ten principles of assessment

1 The purposes of assessment need to be clear.
2 Assessment needs to be an integral part of course design, not something to be bolted on afterwards.
3 Assessment methodology needs to be valid.
4 Assessment processes and instruments need to be reliable.
5 Assessment methodology needs to be feasible.
6 Assessment needs to be transparent to students, staff and employers.
7 Assessment needs to be a means of delivering feedback.
8 The overall assessment strategy needs to employ a wide range of techniques and processes.
9 The amount of assessment should be appropriate.
10 Assessment should be free of bias.

(Race 1995a: 67–8)

---

which question or questions to answer may also be varied. In some cases, multiple-choice questions may be appropriate, perhaps administered and marked by computer.

The attractions of continuous assessment are that it spreads the load on both staff and students, may put less stress on students, and enables an assessment of each student's performance throughout the course as a whole, rather than at just one point. It can also be used to enable students to choose or negotiate some at least of the topics they work on for their assessment. This might, for example, involve project work leading to a dissertation. One key disadvantage is that staff and students may never feel free from assessment, and that the overall load of work on both parties may be significantly increased. In continuous assessment systems it may also be harder to carry out 'blind' marking of students' work, and thus guard against marker bias, unless the teaching team is sufficiently large.

Other forms of assessment are possible, though their use may be largely confined to particular subject areas or restricted to relatively few, perhaps more innovative, practitioners or departments. They include student attendance and contribution in class, group activities, vivas and various forms of performance (e.g. artwork, conversation, design).

A number of principles can be recognized as governing the various forms of assessment used, conventional or otherwise. Box 5.20 summarizes ten of these. Clearly, assessment needs to be accurate, appropriate, relevant and valid; but it also should be clearly linked to what is being studied and well understood by all involved.

In practice, of course, actual assessment procedures can fall down in one or more of these areas. Box 5.21 identifies some of the most common failings. They include the problems associated with having too much assessment, too much variability in practices, a poor understanding of what is being done and why (on the part of both staff and students), and a lack of integration of the assessment with the course as a whole.

Box 5.21: Some common weaknesses in assessment systems

1 Overload of students and staff.
2 Too many assignments with the same deadline set in the department/school.
3 Insufficient time for students to complete the assignments.
4 Insufficient time for staff to mark the assignments before the next semester.
5 Inadequate or superficial feedback provided to students.
6 Wide variations in assessment demands of different modules.
7 Wide variations in marking across modules.
8 Wide variations in marking within a module.
9 Wide variations in marking by demonstrators.
10 Fuzzy or non-existent criteria.
11 Undue precision and specificity of marking schemes or criteria.
12 Students do not know what is expected of them.
13 Students do not know what counts as a good or bad assignment/project.
14 Assessment viewed by some departments/schools as an extra rather than a recognised use of staff time.
15 Project supervision seen as an extra or the real time involved is not recognised.

(Brown *et al.* 1997: 9)

Variability between courses, departments and institutions in assessment practices is, to some extent, inevitable and desirable. To take the issue of how assessment is graded, for example, this may vary from a simple pass/fail judgement through a finite set of grades and percentages to complex numerical marking systems. All may be justified, but the reasons for them need to be clear and shared, and the grading system needs then to be consistently applied by all of those involved in grading.

For new academics, and for those moving to a new department, grading students' work and participating in 'blind' marking systems can be extremely daunting. How do you gauge the level? What constitutes a bare pass or fail, or a distinction? These craft skills of academic work have to be learnt on the job, hopefully with the support of more experienced colleagues. Marking schemas, such as criterion-referenced and competency-based approaches, are designed to limit some of the mystique associated with this process. Box 5.22 gives some examples of such schemas, which help to make explicit performance expectations for students and staff. With practice, these methods can also speed up assessment. Whatever assessment methods are used in your department, it is obviously important to discuss the processes and expectations involved with your colleagues.

Evaluation is a more far-reaching process, and is now firmly established as a key part of teaching quality assessment. Regular evaluation of all higher education programmes by the staff and students involved, as well as (less frequently) the university concerned and external agencies, is now accepted as an essential, if burdensome, duty (see also the section on **Quality audit and assessment** in

---

Box 5.22: Examples of marking schemas

A

Objective: write clearly, concisely and logically (up to 4 marks out of total)

Exceptional (4 marks) – beautifully written, a model of clarity, doesn't waste words, makes convincing sense.

Impressive (3.5) – expressed with fluency and sophistication, logically planned and thought through.

Good (3) – quite accurately and clearly written, planned and relatively efficient.

Average (2.5) – the typical candidate, adequately written, a few mistakes of spelling and expression, tolerably organized.

Low average (2) – mistakes of spelling and expression are not uncommon, but meaning is not obscured; could be better organized but understandable.

Mediocre (1.5) – spelling or expression clearly worse than average, perhaps rather disordered.

Unacceptable (1) – spelling or expression beyond acceptable limits, no idea of logical order, incoherent and almost unreadable.

Almost worthless (0.5) – can almost understand some of it: a consolation mark.

Worthless (0) – unredeemed illiterate ramble.

B

Tick one box for each criterion:

1 Presentation of work:
   Work is legible, very neat and very well set out. ☐
   Work is legible, reasonably neat and fairly well set out. ☐
   Work sometimes illegible or poorly presented. ☐

2 Referencing and bibliography:
   Appropriately selected and presented in strict accordance with standard
      conventions. ☐
   Appropriately selected in the main and presented broadly in line with
      standard academic conventions. ☐
   Incomplete or inaccurate, with little or no awareness of standard
      conventions. ☐

Chapter 8). It carries with it the expectation that any necessary changes identified will be acted upon, with subsequent performance checked in the following review.

Box 5.23 details some of the issues involved in evaluating the quality of teaching and learning. It makes clear that the methods adopted and the judgements produced are highly debatable. It also confirms the necessary linkage between regular evaluation and development work if the process is to be meaningful.

As in the case of assessment, the methods used for evaluating teaching programmes vary. The most common is probably the student questionnaire, issued during or at the end of the course concerned. In the past, these have often been dismissed as 'happy sheets', where they have been structured in such a way as to

---

Box 5.23: Quality and standards in teaching and learning

Views of quality and standards in teaching and learning are:
• related to purposes;
• often derived from authoritative sources;
• dependent on viewpoint and are contestable; and
• related to subject or discipline specific concerns.

Judging quality in teaching may involve:
• evaluating the quality of student learning;
• evaluating qualities of educational thinking, planning and course design;
• evaluating classroom interaction, communication and management skills;
• evaluating published work on teaching and learning;
• personal qualities, such as friendliness, enthusiasm;
• giving students choice over course content;
• adequate and suitable resources; and
• well-designed activities, assignments and feedback designed to promote learning.

Judging quality in learning may involve:
• variety in assessments calling for appropriate learning strategies;
• the opportunity to question and debate; and
• assessments calling for higher-order thinking, creativity, initiative and collaboration.

Assuring the quality of teaching and learning may involve:
• student feedback;
• appraisal;
• a developmental teaching profile; and
• an institutional climate that fosters and rewards excellence in teaching.
(Ashcroft and Foreman-Peck 1995: 57)

---

produce positive results. Some universities have standardized these forms, while others encourage more varied, experimental or innovative approaches. Course meetings, or staff–student liaison committees, are also commonly used as an ongoing, representative form of feedback, which can feed into future development. Institutions and external agencies tend to use more formalized forms of evaluation, involving reports, statistics, visits and interviews.

Teaching as a career

Teaching part-time often means doing a full-time teaching load but being paid by the hour, this makes finding time and resources for research hard. Part-timers have limited pension rights, if they have any at all. More irritatingly, although academics and administrators are aware of part-timers' difficulties, salary departments don't seem to be . . . Finally, of course, being enforced part-time staff is just not the same as having a proper job.

(Eaglestone 1996: vi)

Anyone who has read this far, or has some experience of higher education as a workplace, will have received contradictory messages about the importance of the teaching role. It is still, perhaps unfortunately, the case that advancement in the old universities is largely down to research and publication, while in the former polytechnics it is more closely linked to administration and management. Teaching may be a core function of the university, but it is still viewed as something anyone with a postgraduate degree can do, so that gaps in the teaching profile may readily be filled by the appointment of part-time and/or short-term members of staff.

At the same time, it is clear that much more attention is now being given to ensuring the quality of what is taught. As noted in Chapter 3, staff development programmes for new and experienced university teachers are also expanding. A national higher education teacher accreditation scheme has been developed by the Staff and Educational Development Association (see the list of organizations and journals at the back of this book), a voluntary body within the higher education sector. The Association of University Teachers has also taken an interest, and such schemes have also been endorsed by the report of the Dearing Committee of Inquiry into Higher Education (National Committee of Inquiry into Higher Education 1997). Further developments in this area are to be expected.

Opportunities for the production of teaching materials are also growing. These have been facilitated by the expansion of desktop publishing, enabling the production of ever more sophisticated visual aids and course materials. Students increasingly expect course materials to be of high quality in terms of their production. Becoming skilled in these areas is another way in which a teaching career may be developed, and a direction which may also offer interesting opportunities for writing and publishing.

Nevertheless, few academics would now publicly aspire to a career based wholly or largely upon the teaching role. This is partly because of the continuing significance attached to research: it is significant that while the research assessment exercise is linked directly to institutional funding, this is not the case for teaching quality assessment. It is also partly because of the lack, in many institutions, of permanent teaching-only posts. Teaching is still too often seen either as a way into the profession, as an activity which may safely be contracted out to less qualified staff on poorer contracts, or as an activity to be indulged in by those who no longer have active research interests.

The tasks associated with teaching, however, have the potential to expand and become more than full-time. Becoming and remaining an effective lecturer, embodying the qualities summarized in Box 5.24, is a demanding and valuable goal. This is particularly so when teaching is seen more in terms of the management of mass higher education (see also Chapter 8, particularly the section entitled **We are all managers now**). The instructional component brings with it a whole range of associated administrative procedures and activities, including:

- course approval;
- promotion and publicity;
- recruitment and admissions;

Box 5.24: Characteristics of effective teaching: the lecturer

- Subject expertise.
- Awareness of developments in the teaching of their subject.
- Understanding of how students learn.
- The systematic use of a wide variety of teaching materials.
- A capacity to reflect upon his or her own practice.
- A willingness to develop him/herself.
- Effective planning of teaching sessions, materials and courses:
  - Clarity of explanations.
  - Effective use of oral questioning.
  - Stimulation of student interest.
  - Encouragement of student interest.
  - Encouragement of student involvement and participation.
- Course review and evaluation of student learning.
- Expertise in a variety of assessment methods.
- Awareness of the diversity of the student population.
- Understanding of equitable practice.
- Providing examples of learning for students.

Source: UK Universities' Staff Development Unit (1994: 7).

- the monitoring of student progress;
- the maintenance of records;
- liaison with external examiners;
- convening of examination boards;
- writing student references; and
- alumni relations.

Every university or college department needs at least one member of staff who is proficient in these areas.

Sources of further information

In this section we list a range of materials which you may find of interest in following up in more detail some of the issues discussed in this chapter. The emphasis is on recently published books in English. In each case, brief details are given as to contents and approach.

Writing on teaching in higher education has blossomed in the last decade or two, particularly the area of 'how to' guides. The list given here, while reasonably extensive, is not, therefore, wholly comprehensive.

Allan, D. (ed.) (1996) *In at the Deep End: First Experiences of University Teaching.* Lancaster, Lancaster University Unit for Innovation in Higher Education.
A series of revealing accounts by new university teachers: supportive, amusing, despairing.

Ashcroft, K. and Foreman-Peck, L. (1994) *Managing Teaching and Learning in Further and Higher Education*. London, Falmer Press.
Presents the teacher as a reflective practitioner, and as the manager of the teaching/ learning process rather than a subject expert. Chapters are interspersed with 'enquiry tasks' to encourage an action research perspective.

Ashcroft, K. and Palacio, D. (1996) *Researching into Assessment and Evaluation in Colleges and Universities*. London, Kogan Page.
Discusses changing practices in assessment and evaluation, promoting a researchly perspective to their understanding.

Barnett, L., Brunner, D., Maier, P. and Warren, A. (1996) *Technology in Teaching and Learning: A Guide for Academics*, 2 vols. Southampton, University of Southampton Interactive Learning Centre.
Considers the use of computers to deliver teaching and learning resources, and for communication with and between students. How to get material into and out of your computer, getting connected to and using the Internet, using the World Wide Web.

Bell, E. (1996) *Counselling in Further and Higher Education*. Buckingham, Open University Press.
Study of a developing specialist role.

Bennett, C., Foreman-Peck, L. and Higgins, C. (1996) *Researching into Teaching Methods in Colleges and Universities*. London, Kogan Page.
A companion volume to that by Ashcroft and Foreman-Peck, this book reviews existing research and discusses ideas for small-scale research projects on interactive teaching methods, small- and large-group teaching, and the institutional environment.

Bianco-Mathis, V. and Chalofsky, N. (eds) (1996) *The Adjunct Faculty Handbook*. Thousand Oaks, Calif., Sage.
An American collection targeted specifically at part-time lecturers with other employment or responsibilities, offering concise guidance, with examples, on planning, delivering and evaluating teaching.

Brown, G. and Atkins, M. (1988) *Effective Teaching in Higher Education*. London, Methuen.
A comprehensive guide to lecturing, small-group teaching, laboratory teaching and supervision, full of useful summaries, examples and illustrations.

Brown, G., Bull, J. and Pendlebury, M. (1997) *Assessing Student Learning in Higher Education*. London, Routledge.
Full of practical guidance, suggestions and questions. Considers the assessment of essays, multiple-choice questions, practical work, projects, problem-solving and oral communication, as well as peer and self-assessment, the use of computers, reliability and validity, quality and standards.

Brown, S. and Knight, P. (1994) *Assessing Learners in Higher Education*. London, Kogan Page.
Straightforward discussion of assessment principles, purposes, methods, issues and systems.

Brown, S. and Race, P. (1995) *Assess Your Own Teaching Quality*. London, Kogan Page.
Contains sets of checklists designed to enable the reader to assess their teaching abilities in relation to large groups, resource use, independent and group tasks, tutoring and supervision, as well as their personal and professional qualities.

Cox, B. (1994) *Practical Pointers for University Teachers*. London, Kogan Page.
Takes a process-oriented approach, following the teaching activity from planning through preparation, teaching/learning and assessment to evaluation. The final chapters consider the need to improve efficiency while maintaining quality, and other teaching issues of our time.

Delamont, S., Atkinson, P. and Parry, O. (1997) *Supervising the PhD: A Guide to Success*. Buckingham, Open University Press.
A handbook guiding the supervisor through all the stages of the research student supervision process. Contains examples from the humanities, sciences and social sciences, and offers advice and suggestions for more experienced as well as novice supervisors.

Ellington, H. and Race, P. (1993) *Producing Teaching Materials: A Handbook for Teachers and Trainers*, 2nd edn. London, Kogan Page.
Detailed practical guide to the variety, production and use of instructional materials.

Gibbs, G. and Habeshaw, T. (1995) *253 Ideas for Your Teaching*, 3rd edn. Bristol, Technical and Educational Services Ltd.
Full of suggestions for enlivening lectures, seminars, laboratory work, assessment, independent study and language teaching. Also includes ideas for helping students to learn effectively, communication skills, evaluating for change, and giving students more control.

Gibbs, G. and Jenkins, A. (eds) (1992) *Teaching Large Classes in Higher Education: How to Maintain Quality with Reduced Resources*. London, Kogan Page.
Largely based on experience at Oxford Polytechnic (now Oxford Brookes University), this book contains advice from practitioners in a range of disciplines coping with the creation of a mass higher education system.

Higher Education Quality Council (1996) *Guidelines on Quality Assurance*. London, HEQC.
Eleven sections deal with a framework for quality, entry to higher education, programme design, approval and review, teaching and learning, student development and support, student assessment, external examiners, staffing, research degree students, collaborative provision. Each section considers principles, policy considerations, practical implications, examples of current practice and sources of further information.

Higher Education Quality Council (1996) *Guidelines on the Quality Assurance of Research Degrees*. London, HEQC.
Packed with useful guidance on the research environment, the regulatory framework, admissions procedures, institutional responsibilities, student and supervisor roles, monitoring progress, skills training, communication of research outputs, assessment and appeals.

Laurillard, D. (1993) *Rethinking University Teaching: A Framework for the Effective Use of Educational Technology*. London, Routledge.
Views teaching as 'mediating learning'. Considers the roles of teachers and students, what happens in learning, the use of alternative teaching media (audio-visual, hypermedia, interactive, adaptive and discursive) and the design of teaching and learning.

Morgan, A. (1993) *Improving Your Students' Learning: Reflections on the Experience of Study*. London, Kogan Page.
Focuses on understanding students' experience, and their perceptions of that experience, as fundamental to developing their learning.

Newble, D. and Cannon, R. (1991) *A Handbook for Teachers in Universities and Colleges: A Guide to Improving Teaching Methods*, revised edn. London, Kogan Page.
Based on Australian experience and packed with illustrations and cartoons. Covers the stages and processes involved in teaching large groups, small groups, practical and laboratory classes, as well as curriculum planning, student assessment, teaching materials and conference presentations.

Partington, J., Brown, G. and Gordon, G. (1993) *Handbook for External Examiners in Higher Education*. Sheffield, UK Universities' Staff Development Unit.
Covers taught courses, theses and dissertations, and institutional quality assurance systems.

Peelo, M. (1994) *Helping Students with Study Problems*. Buckingham, Open University Press.
Focuses on common problems encountered by undergraduates, and methods for overcoming them.

Phillips, E. and Pugh, D. (1994) *How to Get a PhD: A Handbook for Students and Their Supervisors*, 2nd edn. Buckingham, Open University Press.
Essentially a guide for research students, this book also reviews studies of the research process and provides useful insights for academics on the practice of supervision.

Ramsden, P. (1992) *Learning to Teach in Higher Education*. London, Routledge.
Organized in three parts which successively examine learning and teaching in higher education, designing learning, and evaluating and improving the quality of teaching and learning.

Schwartz, P. and Webb, G. (1993) *Case Studies on Teaching in Higher Education*. London, Kogan Page.
Contains 20 case studies, illustrating some of the issues and problems encountered in teaching, with suggestions as to what might be done to deal with them. The issues considered range from plagiarism to class outbursts, from student complaints to conscientious objections.

Thomas, D. (ed.) (1995) *Flexible Learning Strategies in Higher and Further Education*. London, Cassell.
Examines open learning and related strategies for expanding higher education opportunities.

UK Universities' and Colleges' Staff Development Agency (1995) *Effective Learning and Teaching in Higher Education: A Resource Guide*. Sheffield, UCoSDA.
This volume serves as a guide to a 12-module, self-instructional staff development program. The modules, separately published in folder format, cover: active learning, course design, planning teaching, large classes, small groups, practical classes, field and project work, learning on one's own, essay writing, personal and professional skills, assessment, and evaluation.

Wheeler, S. and Birtle, J. (1993) *A Handbook for Personal Tutors*. Buckingham, Open University Press.
A practical guide, with examples, to pastoral care and personal tutoring. Particular attention is given to counselling and listening skills, the institutional context, and the special problems of adolescent, mature and postgraduate students, as well as those from culturally different backgrounds.

Wilkins, M. (1995) *Learning to Teach in Higher Education*. Coventry, Warwick University Centre for Educational Development, Appraisal and Research.
Designed to assist postgraduate students who are taking on teaching responsibilities for the first time. Organized in three stages: getting started, assuming more responsibilities, and using your experience as a researcher. Includes self-assessment schedules and follow-up references.

6 | RESEARCHING

Introduction

This chapter considers the role of research in academic careers. Research, in its different forms, is an important part of most academics' working lives. For some, as with those on research contracts linked to particular projects, it is the dominant role. For many, it is the route into an academic career, moving from being a research student or a research assistant to a lecturing position. For a minority of academics in higher education, such as those in designated research centres, researching may be a lifetime career focus.

In many institutions, particularly the older universities, research remains – in association with related writing and publication (see the section on **The key importance of writing to an academic career** in the next chapter) – the principal means of gaining recognition, building a reputation, obtaining promotion and advancing one's career. It is also more widely recognized as one of the distinctive features of higher education institutions. While many other organizations engage in research, universities are seen as having a key function in advancing knowledge and understanding.

With most academics now entering the profession with some recent, direct experience of research – through their first and master's degrees as well as the now increasingly expected PhD – it might be thought that research was the role for which academics require least advice, preparation and support. We would disagree. Elsewhere in this book we have argued that until recently academics have received little training in either teaching (see Chapter 5) or management (see Chapter 8). This situation is changing, however, and there is now both increasing institutional support and a growing literature for these academic roles.

For research and writing, by contrast, while there are many books and manuals targeted at students, and a more specific literature relating to research methodologies, there is little beyond this of help to practising academics. Much that academics need to know to develop their research careers remains 'secret' or craft knowledge, understood but little shared by those with more experience.

As with the discussion of networking (see Chapter 4), we aim here to redress this balance to some extent, and open up for consideration questions of practice in academic research in the humanities and social sciences. We hope that by encouraging reflection upon practices, such craft knowledge will begin to become more explicit.

The chapter is organized into seven main sections:

- **Forms of research**, which discusses the varied kinds of research undertaken by academics, and how this fits into their careers;
- **Research funding**, which considers the range of organizations involved in funding academic research, and gives details of the most important;
- **How to get research funds**, which examines the strategies required to get funding for research from different bodies;
- **Unfunded research**, which discusses research which does not require significant funding, of major importance in many humanities and some social science subjects, and associated forms of recognition;
- **Managing research**, which considers how to run a research project, whether funded or unfunded;
- **Relating research to other academic roles**, which discusses ways of linking research to other aspects of academic work;
- **Researching as a career**, which reviews the option of focusing on the research role within an academic career.

At the end of the chapter a selection of sources of further information is listed.

Forms of research

Should the definition of what research consists of take greater account of the diversity of academic practice in universities? Should not works of art, sculptures, paintings, fashion garments, etc. be permitted to count in the same way that creative writing (novels, poems, plays) often are?

(Smith and Brown 1995: 16)

Our ideas of what constitutes research have been greatly influenced by the scientific model, in which understanding is advanced by the formulation and testing of hypotheses through data collection and analysis. Research in the social sciences and humanities may not, however, accord to this model. In this broader context, research might be defined as 'planned, cautious, systematic and reliable ways of finding out or deepening understanding' (Blaxter *et al.*, 1996: 5). Yet even this definition would not be satisfactory in some subject areas. As the quotation above indicates, some would extend the term to cover expressive or creative arts.

Box 6.1: Forms of research

applied/pure
strategic/basic
developmental/exploratory
descriptive/evaluative/comparative
reflection on practice
exploratory/problem-solving
consultancy/commissioned/sponsored
instrumental/action
scholarship
individual/group/collaborative
funded/unfunded
empirical/non-empirical
quantitative/qualitative
fieldwork/deskwork

Box 6.1 lists some of the ways in which academics and their funders think about forms of research. Some of these distinctions relate to the perceived immediacy of applicability of the research findings outside academe, as in the case of applied versus pure research, and strategic versus basic. Others indicate the stage the research is at, as with developmental, exploratory and descriptive, on the one hand, and explanatory and problem-solving, on the other. Some of the other labels identified relate to who is involved in the research (an individual or a group) or to the nature of that involvement (e.g. consultancy or collaboration). Yet others indicate the methodological position of the researchers, as in the case of qualitative or quantitative, and deskwork or fieldwork. Postgraduate training and involvement in research teams can strongly affect the research identity of junior academics. Gallos reports working with a number of respected academics with varying beliefs about research and scholarship, and notes the longer-term benefits of these associations. They enabled her to make some non-conventional career moves, which were none the less anchored by a research identity and a scholarly voice which could 'harness passion and wed it with intellect' (Gallos 1996: 15).

Research and research careers can, therefore, take many forms. Research may, as Box 6.1 indicates, be funded or unfunded; with the latter implying not that there are no costs involved, but that these are small enough to be borne by the researchers concerned or their departments without any need for specific additional funding. It may also be practised at widely differing scales.

At one extreme, particularly in the social sciences, there are major research projects of international significance, involving the full-time efforts of teams of experienced researchers over a period of several years, and with budgets running into millions of pounds. More typically, at the other extreme, there are thousands of small-scale, usually individual, research projects, normally of only local or limited significance, requiring short-term, intermittent or part-time commitment, and with negligible costs. The latter can be fitted into almost any academic career, and nearly all academics engage in them, whether they dignify them with the label 'research' or not. The former constitute careers in themselves.

The dominant discourse of academic research emphasizes its scale, and the time and money involved. There is, however, a counter-discourse which challenges this as idealizing the standards of a patriarchal scholarship which cannot enable fundamental change. As Daly (1979: 23) remarked, such research does not embrace 'thinking that is vigorous, informed, multi-dimensional, independent, creative, tough'.

In between the extremes of scale, there is a wide range of levels of research engagement, requiring more or less adjustment in the balance of roles and responsibilities held by the academics concerned. Much of this will involve some degree of funding, though usually relatively small in scale. The next two sections in this chapter (**Research funding** and **How to get research funds**) focus on funded forms of research and the particular issues it raises. They are followed by a section on **Unfunded research** and related forms of recognition. The remainder of the chapter then looks at issues common to funded and unfunded research. Some suggestions on ways to profile vigorous, unconventional and creative scholarship have been included.

Research funding

There are a number of available sources of funding for supporting research in the humanities and social sciences. They vary in what they are prepared to fund and in how much support they will give. Some will specify the nature of the research to be undertaken, while others will consider any research proposals in their areas of interest. Broadly speaking, you stand more chance of getting research funding if you focus on areas in which you have, and are recognized as having, interest and expertise.

In most cases, the competition for the funds available is intense. For example, of 338 applications considered by the Economic and Social Research Council's Research Grants Board in March 1997, 237 were assessed as meriting awards but only 59 were funded, a 17 per cent overall success rate (ESRC 1997: 8). Applicants need, therefore, carefully to prepare and target their proposals if they are to have a reasonable chance of success (see the following section on **How to get research funds**). As with writing and publishing (see Chapter 7), don't be put off by rejections and critical reviews: these happen to all of us at some time.

The most obvious, and perhaps easiest, source of funding for research projects, particularly if they are small-scale, is probably your own university or college. Most higher education institutions, and many departments, have small funds available to pump-prime research initiatives or contribute to travel, secretarial or other costs. These are particularly useful for library-based research, or for developing research projects for submission to external funding bodies. In some cases, these funds exist specifically to encourage younger (e.g. under 35) researchers.

As with many other aspects of academic employment, newly appointed staff might be informed during their interview or induction about the opportunities for applying for such funds. This may, however, be overlooked, or you may forget the details under the barrage of new information. New academics would be well advised, therefore, to make their own enquiries about such opportunities.

Similarly, the degree of publicity given to external research-funding opportunities is variable, and researchers have to learn where and how to look. In some cases, as with one-off opportunities or new programmes, advertisements may be placed in the press – either in general sources such as the *Times Higher Education Supplement* (Box 6.2 gives a sample of such announcements) or in specialist magazines or journals.

It is significant that each of the examples included in Box 6.2 specifies the topic of the research to be funded to a greater or lesser extent. Such announcements may be made at any time of the year, requiring continual monitoring of likely publications, and often have short deadlines for response. Those who are well networked, and hear of likely opportunities before they are publicized, will have longer lead-in times for preparation and stand a better chance of success.

Those funders which support continuing programmes of research, year after year, tend not to advertise so much. Researchers need to familiarize themselves with the potential funders in their areas of interest, and keep up-to-date information on current funding opportunities. Many universities and colleges have research offices which are in contact with funders and can do much of this work for you. Cultivate their staff, let them know of your interests and make sure you are on their circulation list. They will probably produce a regular newsletter; they may also subscribe to a research funding information service like Refund.

Otherwise, you will need to keep track of funding opportunities yourself: you will probably want to do this to some extent anyway. Contact likely funding bodies, or check out their Web sites, and get them to send you details and put you on their newsletter mailing list.

Box 6.3 lists seven major funders of research in the humanities and social sciences in the United Kingdom. The first three are state-funded, the fourth is funded by the European Community, while the last three are independent charitable trusts set up many years ago by wealthy industrialists. Researchers in the humanities have fewer funders to turn to, while much funding for social science research emphasizes economic and policy concerns.

As Box 6.3 indicates, the kinds of research activity which these organizations are prepared to fund vary, but all offer research grants and travel awards. The amounts of money they are able and prepared to grant, and the kinds of subject and project they will fund, also vary. Most do not offer funds for all subjects in the humanities and social sciences, with some quite focused in terms of their subject interests. More details are given for each of these seven funders in Boxes 6.4 to 6.10, but full details should be sought from any funder before a proposal is prepared.

There are, of course, many other organizations which fund research carried out by academics. They include government departments and agencies, private companies, other charitable trusts and learned societies.

Government departments and agencies regularly fund reviews and evaluations of policy options. Those with a particular relevance to the humanities and social

---

Box 6.2: Announcements of research grant opportunities

The School Curriculum and Assessment Authority, Invitation to Tender, The Use of Dictionaries in GCSE Modern Foreign Language Examinations
The project involves preparing examination questions and mark schemes, and evaluating the effect of using different types of dictionaries on pupils' attainment in written tests ... The contract is expected to run from 1 September 1997 to 28 February 1998.

BT University Development Awards 1996/97
BT invited over 150 Higher Education Institutions to bid on a competitive basis for awards of up to £100,000 each to support curriculum development projects using communication technologies ... The award scheme is part of BT's programme of partnership with the education sector.

Economic and Social Research Council, Health Variations Research Programme, Phase 2
Applications are invited from researchers based at UK Higher Education Institutions and other Research Institutions recognised by the ESRC. Phase 2 of the Programme will seek to advance understanding of why there are persisting and widening socio-economic variations in health in advanced societies. Particular emphasis will be placed on five key research areas ... :
• Mental health ...
• Psychological factors ...
• Workplace influences on health ...
• The role of lifestyles ...
• The relationships between wealth and health ...

The Local Government Management Board, Central Research Programme 1997/98
Each year the LGMB commissions a number of research projects on issues of strategic importance to local government. Three major projects are planned as part of the 1997/98 programme.
• Professionalism and the Management of the Local Authority ...
• Local Governance: the community perspective ...
• Local Government and the Voluntary Sector ...
Proposals will be welcome from organisations and individuals who can demonstrate the necessary expertise and experience to undertake any of these projects.

Source: advertisements in the *Times Higher Education Supplement*, 11/4/97 and 13/6/97.

---

sciences include the Departments of Education and Employment, Health, Social Security, and Trade and Industry, as well as the Scottish, Welsh and Northern Ireland Offices. Agencies directly funded by and responsible to the government, such as the Training Agency and the Further and Higher Education Funding Councils, also fund a variety of research projects. In all of these cases, the projects concerned are likely to be closely specified, involve tendering and have multiple deadlines.

Box 6.3: Major research funders in the humanities and social sciences

| Funder | Types of award | | | | |
	Studentships	Postdoctoral fellowships	Senior fellowships	Research grants	Travel awards
British Academy	Yes	Yes	Yes	Yes	Yes
British Council	No	No	No	Yes	Yes
Economic and Social Research Council	Yes	Yes	Yes	Yes	Yes
European Commission	Yes	Yes	Yes	Yes	Yes
Leverhulme Trust	Yes	Yes	Yes	Yes	Yes
Nuffield Foundation	No	Yes	Yes	Yes	Yes
Joseph Rowntree Foundation	No	No	No	Yes	Yes

While most private companies conduct much of their own research themselves, many, particularly larger organizations, employ academic researchers to investigate particular topics of interest. Projects may be developed and carried out in collaboration. Both the nature of the topics and their outputs are likely to be determined by the company concerned. Strong emphasis will probably be placed on application of the results.

There are many other charitable trusts than those few listed in Box 6.3, but most have more specialist interests or more limited funds. Examples include the Esmée Fairbain Charitable Trust, the Royal Society for the Encouragement of Arts, Manufactures and Commerce, the Anglo-German Foundation for the Study of Industrial Society, the Fulbright Commission and the Calouste Gulbenkian Foundation. A comprehensive list is included in the *Directory of Grant-making Trusts*, details of which are given in the list of sources of further information at the end of this chapter. Not all of these trusts will fund academic research.

A final source of financial support for research and scholarship is from the learned societies. They often administer prizes as well, which can help in building a research reputation.

From the details given so far, it should be clear that there are a range of research activities which are commonly funded. The most common are the following:

Box 6.4: The British Academy

20–21 Cornwall Terrace, London NW1 4QP
Tel: 0171-487-5966   Fax: 0171-224-3807
E-mail: basec@britac.ac.uk
Web: http://britac3.britac.ac.uk

The British Academy offers a range of awards for scholars in the arts and humanities: the latter are distributed through its Humanities Research Board (HRB).

The main types of award are:

Research grants. Most are awarded to individuals, but some awards are also made to learned bodies and other groups.

Conference grants. To contribute to the expenses of scholars invited to deliver papers overseas, and to bring overseas scholars to Britain.

Overseas exchanges. Agreements with overseas institutions to provide for exchange visits of scholars.

Research posts. Postdoctoral fellowships for younger scholars and readerships or fellowships for more experienced scholars.

Research leave. Enabling scholars in the humanities to complete a sustained period of research during a term or semester of leave.

Institutional fellowships. To support research of a collaborative and interdisciplinary nature within the humanities.

Postgraduate studentships. The HRB runs the national scheme for the humanities.

The funds available to the Academy and the HRB are very limited, and the demand for them is high. In many cases, your first recourse for funds should be to your own institution.

The subjects covered (at least in part) by the British Academy include English and American studies, other languages and literatures, history, archaeology, philosophy, law, theology, linguistics, history of art, music, drama and theatre studies, performing arts, cultural studies, economics, politics, sociology, anthropology, human geography and psychology.

Source: British Academy Web site.

- Research projects, where you, as the researcher, are largely responsible for determining what and how to research, within the broad guidelines given by the funder, and for carrying out, completing and reporting upon the project.
- Consultancy, where the research brief is largely determined by the funder, and you, as the researcher, work within close guidelines, to tight deadlines and may only ever report back to the funder.
- Development projects, where funds are given to develop, for example, facilities or curricula, within or across institutions and countries.

Box 6.5: The British Council

Bridgewater House, 55 Whitworth Street, Manchester M1 6BB
Tel: 0161 957 7000   Fax: 0161 957 7111
Web: http://www.britcoun.org/

The purpose of the British Council is to promote a wider knowledge of the United Kingdom and the English language, and to encourage cultural, scientific, technological and educational cooperation. In 1995/96 the British Council funded over 9000 scientific visits and more than 1300 research links. It plays a key role in securing Britain's share of the global education and training market.

Most grants relate to specific programmes and priorities. The schemes administered by the British Council include:

Higher education links. This programme establishes contacts between departments in United Kingdom and overseas institutions of higher education, usually on a one-to-one basis.

Travel grants. These are awarded to, for example, arts professionals to set up conferences or joint programmes, establish links or undertake research.

Research programmes. A joint programme is managed with the French Ministère des Affaires Étrangères to promote bilateral cooperation between universities and research institutes. Projects are selected which fit into defined programme areas, and which show potential for subsequent funding (e.g. by industry or the European Commission).

Consultancies. The Council maintains a register of experts and appoints advisers.

Source: British Council Web site.

- Research leave, where funds are given to allow you to be released from your teaching, administrative and other duties, so that you can focus exclusively on research for a given period.
- Research travel, where funds are given to enable you to attend conferences or visit institutions or sites, perhaps as part of a reciprocal or wider arrangement, either nationally or internationally.

As an active researcher you might wish to obtain any or all of these types of funding at different points in your career. Some of these opportunities, such as research leave and research travel, will probably be easier to get than others. All five types should be seen as interlinked, however, and as relating to other academic roles and activities. All research endeavour necessitates balancing the discipline of management with creativity and adaptability.

How to get research funds

The ESRC Research Grants board distributes grants under – to use ESRC jargon – the 'responsive' mode: simply, it responds to grant proposals from

Box 6.6: The Economic and Social Research Council

Polaris House, North Star Avenue, Swindon SN2 1UJ
Tel: 01793-413000   Fax: 01793-413001
E-mail: xrel@esrc.ac.uk
Web: http://www.esrc.ac.uk/

The ESRC currently has an annual budget of around £65 million. Two-thirds is allocated to research, one-third to postgraduate training. Each year, nearly 1000 researchers throughout the UK receive funding. Research is funded through open competition, with grants awarded on the basis of excellence. Increasing emphasis has been placed on the concerns of policy-makers, businesses and other end-users of social research.

The ESRC has nine broad themes to focus its work, to which approximately 80 per cent of funds are devoted. The current themes are: economic performance and development; environment and sustainability; globalization, regions and emerging markets; governance and regulation; human communication and the social shaping of technology; innovation, organizations and business processes; knowledge and skill; life-span, lifestyles and health; and social integration and exclusion.

There are three main types of funding:

Research centres: these investigate major long-term issues, typically over a ten-year period, employing a team of researchers.

Research programmes: these address medium-term issues that often have a pressing social, commercial or political dimension. Programmes are composed of individual projects at different institutions.

Research grants: these are for stand-alone projects suggested by academics, often exploring new areas and providing the seedcorn for larger studies. Grants are awarded up to the value of £750,000.

The ESRC also runs a Research Seminar competition.

The subjects covered (at least in part) by the ESRC include anthropology, area studies, business and management, economics, education, human geography, politics, psychology, social history and sociology.

Source: ESRC Web site.

researchers in the social sciences. Membership of the Board is drawn mostly from practising social scientists, including two political scientists (ourselves). Since the Board is the single biggest source of support for the sort of 'blue skies' research which is the heart of political studies, it is important that the discipline maximises both applications and successes in those applications . . . (Incidentally, one thing will not change. Contrary to the still widespread impression in the research community, the Board's decisions are made entirely independently of the ESRC's thematic priorities: what is funded depends on what the social science community makes a case for) . . . The fact that the discipline is competing for grants with the other social sciences has a particularly

---

Box 6.7: European Commission funds

Rue de la Loi 200, 1049 Brussels
Tel: +32 2 235 1111

8 Storey's Gate, London SW1P 3AT
Tel: 0171 973 1992   Fax: 0171 973 1910

The European Commission operates a complex and changing range of funding schemes, many of which are directed towards structural or regional aid, business and industry, or cultural or social issues. There are a variety of initiatives focusing on research and development, education, training and exchange. These tend to be large-scale.

Most European funding schemes stress collaboration between partners in a number of different European countries. They may also require collaboration with industrial or professional partners, and matching funds may need to be obtained from other sources. Long-term planning is necessary for success. Initial advice should be sought from your university's research or European office. Early contact with the relevant European Commission office is also advisable: much may be gained from a visit to Brussels.

The following are just examples of some of the funding schemes of relevance to the humanities and social sciences:

Cedefop: the European Centre for the Development of Vocational Training funds research and studies concerning vocational training. The *Leonardo da Vinci* programme also funds work in this area.

Esprit: a scheme supporting research into the development and application of information technologies.

Socrates: transnational educational projects involving staff and students. Socrates incorporates *Erasmus* (for higher education) and *Lingua* (for language learning).

Training and mobility of researchers: grants to create research networks, and to support training and access to large-scale facilities.

Transport: research for a trans-European multi-modal network and for network optimisation.

Source: Finance from Europe.

---

important implication for the way applications are written. We believe many substantively good applications are failing because they *pay insufficient attention to research methodology – or, more simply, to the nuts and bolts of how the research will be done* . . . To appreciate the significance of this, it is important to understand how the Board works. All 'large grants' (in excess of £40K) are sent to external referees for grading. But all applications graded in categories likely to make them eligible for success are considered by the full Board, and it is the full Board which makes the final decision. The discussions in the Board turn heavily on issues of methodology.

(Seyd and Moran 1997: 5, emphasis in original)

Box 6.8: The Leverhulme Trust

1 Pemberton Row, London EC4A 3EX
Tel: 0171 822 6938
E-mail: josbourne@leverhulme.org.uk
Web: http://www.leverhulme.org.uk/

The Trust was established in 1925 under the will of the first Lord Leverhulme. It has up to 1000 grants current at any one time. It runs the following schemes:

Grants to institutions for research: to cover the salary costs of those working on a specific project, plus limited support costs.

Research fellowships and grants: for research expenses over and above normal living costs and/or a contribution towards replacement teaching or loss of earnings.

Emeritus fellowships: for incidental research costs to assist recently retired scholars.

Study abroad studentships: for holders of UK first degrees, or their equivalent, to enable them to study or research abroad for one or two years.

Special research fellowships: for experienced postdoctoral researchers normally under the age of 35, splitting salary costs between the Trust and the employing university.

Grants for academic interchange: the scheme is structured to enable successful institutions to award two visiting fellowships over a three-year period.

Grants for education: One-off schemes currently under way include Personal Research Fellowships, Teaching Posts in Innovative Subjects, the Literacy and Numeracy Programme, and the Business/Socio-economic Programme.

Source: Leverhulme Trust Web site.

As Seyd and Moran's comments indicate, getting funding for research activities requires not only careful planning, attention to detail and a long-term perspective, but also knowledge of how the funding process works. In the case of the ESRC, one of the messages here is that it is the shared language of methodology which enables discussion across the disciplinary boundaries. Time given up to researching the politics of the funding process is likely, therefore, to be time well spent.

Given the level of competition, most requests for funding will be rejected. You have to accept this (even if it seems to you that one of your better proposals was rejected while a less worthy one was funded), learn wherever possible from your failures, and keep submitting more, and hopefully even better, proposals. With some funders, the competition can be so intense that the outcome can almost seem like a lottery: but if you haven't got a ticket (or preferably tickets) you can't win!

Box 6.11 gives some basic advice on how to land your first big research grant, but most of the advice given applies to almost any academic activity where

Box 6.9: The Nuffield Foundation

28 Bedford Square, London, WCIB 3EG
Tel: 0171 631 0566   Fax: 0171 323 4877

Subject areas covered are education, child protection, family law, ageing and disability, access to justice, public services research, mental health, science and medicine, social sciences.
The Foundation runs the following schemes:

Project Grants: mostly for between £5000 and £75,000, usually involving the development of new ideas and methods, and leading to outcomes that will be widely applicable.

Social Science Research Fellowships.

Small Grants in the Social Sciences: upper limit £5000.

Travel Awards.

Source: Nuffield Foundation.

Box 6.10: The Joseph Rowntree Foundation

Research Department, The Homestead, 40 Water End, York YO3 6LP
Tel: 01904 615911/2/3   Fax: 01904 620072
E-mail: resdept@jrfound.org.uk
Web: http://www.jrf.org. uk/jrf.html

The Foundation emphasizes that it does not give grants for research, but sees itself as a full partner in the research work.

Current priorities for funding are:
* *housing research*;
* *work, income and social policy* (work and opportunity, work and family life, income and wealth);
* *young people and families* (preventing family breakdown, conflict and dispute resolution, young people in transition, patterns of vulnerability and exclusion, young people's perceptions of the world);
* *social care and disability* (choice, independence and quality of life, disabled children and young people, promoting change and improving practice, race equality).

A number of interests run through the Foundation's work: the importance of service users' perspectives, international comparisons, racism and the issues confronting ethnic minorities, the rural dimension, volunteering, supporting local communities, equal opportunities.

Source: Joseph Rowntree Foundation Web site.

Box 6.11: How to land your first big research grant

- Start small. Plan ahead. Aim to develop a track record.
- Establish reputation through academic publications, conference attendance and networking, newspaper articles and book reviews, and involvement in journals
- Match source of funding with type of project. Start considering funding as early as possible.
- Use the expertise of more experienced colleagues. Develop partnerships – essential for much European funding and for other larger-scale projects.
- Pay careful attention to eligibility criteria.
- Allow plenty of time for the development, drafting, costing, checking and approval of proposals within your institution.
- Produce proposals to the formats specified.
- Do not be discouraged if applications are turned down: most successful researchers have many failed applications. Use feedback constructively. Persistence is required.
- Keep project ideas flowing. Have several projects developing at different stages at any given time.
- Seek advice from your university's research office.

Source: Annabel Eccles, Research and Development Services Office, University of Warwick.

---

recognition is being sought. You need to have a strategy for building up your reputation, so that those who judge your proposals will have heard of you and have an opinion about your worth. Bigger successes have to be built on the backs of smaller ones. Hence the need for a long-term perspective.

You should seek advice wherever you can get it, and act upon it. Senior colleagues may welcome a junior partner who is prepared to do more than their fair share of the donkey work, and they are likely to be much better networked than you. The people who staff your university's research office and/or European office are there to be used, and rely upon people like you to keep them in work.

You must pay attention to detail. It is pointless submitting proposals at the wrong time, in an incorrect format, or on a topic outside the scope of the funder. And yet plenty of people do. If you fail to meet the funder's age criteria, or are not in a recognized institution or department, or do not satisfy the specification in some other way, you are wasting your time in making an application: it is likely to be rejected immediately without any consideration of its academic merits. So you will need to allow plenty of time to get your application into the right shape before the deadline for submission: it is never too early to start drafting and discussing.

Get yourself known, keep applying, don't be too downhearted when you are rejected, and you will be successful in time. After that, you have to keep going, as it does not really get that much easier. Larger proposals and European initiatives require a great deal more preparatory and development work.

Box 6.12: Common reasons why grant proposals are rejected

Mechanical reasons

1 Deadline for submission was not met.
2 Guidelines for proposal content, format and length were not followed exactly.
3 The proposal was not absolutely clear in describing one or several elements of the study.
4 The proposal was not absolutely complete in describing one or several elements of the study.
5 The author(s) took highly partisan positions on issues and thus became vulnerable to the prejudices of the reviewers.
6 The quality of writing was poor – for example, sweeping and grandiose claims, convoluted reasoning, excessive repetition, or unreasonable length.
7 The proposal document contained an unreasonable number of mechanical defects that reflected carelessness and the author's unwillingness to attend to detail. The risk that the same attitude might attend execution of the proposed study was not acceptable to the reviewers.

Methodological reasons

8 The proposed question, design, and method were completely traditional, with nothing that could strike a reviewer as unusual, intriguing or clever.
9 The proposed method of study was unsuited to the purpose of the research.

Personnel reasons

10 As revealed in the review of the literature, the author(s) simply did not know the territory.
11 The proposed study appeared to be beyond the capacity of the author(s) in terms of training, experience, and available resources.

Cost–benefit reasons

12 The proposed study was not an agency priority for this year.
13 The budget was unrealistic in terms of estimated requirements for equipment, supplies and personnel.
14 The cost of the proposed project appeared to be greater than any possible benefit to be derived from its completion.

(Locke *et al.* 1993: 163)

Box 6.12 provides the converse view to Box 6.11, in outlining the main reasons why research grant proposals are rejected. Those categorized as mechanical may seem obvious and readily avoidable, but it is surprising just how frequently proposals fail because they are late, incomplete, poorly organized or vague. Funders' specifications should be read carefully before you develop a proposal, and again before you submit it. If you don't believe your proposal is ready for submission you will do yourself less harm if you don't submit it.

The other reasons given are not so easy to control, and it is here that your growing experience of seeking funding for research will stand you in good stead. Most subjects or disciplines have fairly established methodologies and methods for research. While it should not be too difficult to identify appropriate methods for a project, the challenge is to appear innovative or original, so that the proposal will be noticed. Be warned, though, it also needs to be sufficiently comprehensible to be positively reviewed and approved by your peers.

The personnel reasons identified in Box 6.12 point up the key importance of having a track record in the topic you wish to study. A proposal is likely to be reviewed by one or more experts in the field. They may not have heard of you, but if your proposal reveals an ignorance of key studies or methods, or a highly partisan view, you will have no chance.

Budgeting is probably the aspect of producing a research proposal where academic researchers may feel most ill at ease. It should not, however, be too complex an exercise, particularly if the proposal is small-scale, and you should be able to get advice within your university or college. After all, if you cannot draft a reasonable budget, how are you going to manage one if you are successful (and when the cash rolls in, everyone will be after it)?

While it is good sense to keep your proposals tightly costed, and to keep below psychologically important monetary break points where possible, it is foolish to ask for less than you need to do the job efficiently and well. It is not uncommon for research budgets to underestimate the time required by research assistants to, for example, transcribe tapes or learn new skills. It is still common to find that research funds run out before the writing up is finished or the dissemination has really begun.

Remember that your department and institution will also wish to build into your proposal, where the funder allows this, an allowance to cover overheads such as accommodation, heating and lighting, maintenance, administrative and other support costs. These may be expressed simply as a percentage or set out in detail. Either way, they will add significantly to your overall budget, so make allowance for these additions early on.

With these suggestions and strictures in mind, what then might a research proposal look like? Box 6.13 provides some general guidance as to contents. Different funders will specify different headings, of course, and may have forms for applications, and you should modify your proposal accordingly. Similarly, some sections will not be required for some kinds of research funding, though most, if not all, will be needed if you are seeking a grant for a research project.

Without doubt, the most important part of any research proposal, assuming that you satisfy the criteria for application, is the first part, the introduction. This might take the form of a covering letter or might be the first section of a proposal document. It is here that you have to grab the attention of your funders and their reviewers, by persuading them that this research has to be done now and that you are the most suitable person to do it. If you can do this, half the battle is won; if not, your proposal may be rejected straight away.

The aims and objectives should appear clear and achievable: neither unambitious nor over-ambitious. They should then be traceable throughout the rest of the proposal, so that the design has clarity. In this section you may have to reconcile what you would like to do with what you think a funder will be interested in funding:

Box 6.13: Typical contents of a grant proposal

Introduction
Briefly summarizes the proposal, placing it in its disciplinary and policy context. States succinctly why the research needs doing, why it should be done now, why you are the person(s) to do it, what will be achieved and why it should be funded.

Aims and Objectives
Specifies what the project will achieve and how it will contribute to a broader understanding of the issues and area concerned. Relates your aims and objectives to those of your funder.

Methods
Describes how you will carry out the research, detailing what data will be collected, from where or from whom, and how it will be collected (e.g. through documents, interviews, observations and/or questionnaires).

Analysis
Sets out how the data collected will be checked, coded, transcribed and/or entered into a computer, and the forms of analysis which will then be carried out (e.g. textual analysis, simple statistical analysis, multivariate analysis).

Timetable
Provides an overall schedule for the project, details what will be done when, and sets out stages for the work.

Dissemination
Describes plans for reporting on the results of the research, both during the project and after it has been completed. Reports may be produced for the funders and for other interested parties inside and outside academe. Other kinds of dissemination, such as through workshops or conferences, may also be specified.

Budget
A detailed summary of the funding needed for the project, broken down year by year and in terms of staffing, travel, equipment, consumables and other costs.

Curriculum Vitae
An outline of the career, publications and achievements of all those involved in the project.

Referees
The names and addresses of key figures in your field who can advise on the appropriateness and worthwhileness of your project.

When it comes to research aims, I think I have always worked with double sets of aims – one for the sponsor and one for myself! . . . The whole art of the business in funded research is to find scope for your own aims within and alongside the sponsor's aims – and without costing the sponsor anything.

(Stenhouse 1984: 213)

There are few, if any, sponsors who are completely open regarding the subject and content of proposals, and some have very tightly defined interests. On the other hand, sponsors may not be that clear about what they want, or about its feasibility, necessitating some discreet and careful negotiation about what will actually be done:

> Although its aims seemed most consistent with the empowering type of action research, the research brief was something of a 'mish mash' in that the sponsors seemed to be wanting one thing and yet asking another.
>
> (Hart and Bond 1995: 63)

Your description of the methods you will use for collecting and analysing data needs, again, to be feasible. There is no sense in suggesting, for example, that you will carry out more interviews or administer more questionnaires than you need to or have the resources for. This section should also demonstrate your familiarity with the techniques you propose to use, and with their application in similar projects in your subject area. Where possible, attention should be drawn to their innovative nature.

The research timetable, like the budget, is a critical section for demonstrating that you will be able to do what you propose. Research can be a very labour-intensive activity, and you will need to show that you have allowed enough, but not too much, time to carry out each element effectively. The ordering should also be logical, with each activity carefully related and appropriately timed. Make sure you have allowed sufficient time, for example, for data analysis, report writing and dissemination.

The two final headings listed in Box 6.13 are also important. Your curriculum vitae, and those of any collaborators in the project, should demonstrate your experience, skills and ability to carry out the research in question. Some funders also ask you to suggest possible referees to comment on your proposal, though most also use, or rely upon, their own. If this is the case, you will need to be able to suggest referees of sufficient repute, and who you might reasonably expect to be supportive of your proposal.

Unfunded research

As noted already, in discussions of research in higher education institutions most attention is given to funded research. Research income is an important element in the budgets of many universities and departments, and individual academics may be given income targets against which their research performance will be appraised. The quality of the research carried out in departments is also regularly reviewed through the research assessment exercises – taking into account factors such as research income and publications produced – and this has major consequences for the basic funding of all universities and colleges.

The focus on funded research places particular emphasis on the experimental sciences, and, to a lesser extent, on those social sciences which mount large-scale research projects (e.g. economics). In other disciplines, however, there is a long

---

Box 6.14: Academic awards: the case of social anthropology

The *Leach/RAI Fellowship* was established by the Esperanza Trust and the Royal Anthropological Institute in 1990 to honour the memory of Sir Edmund Leach. Its intention is to enable recently qualified anthropologists (within five years of being awarded a PhD) to devote time to writing, and will be offered annually on a competitive basis.

The *Jean-Marie Delwart Foundation* will support a fundamental original research project in the field of cultural anthropology and human ethnology by awarding, for the first time, a prize to a study dealing with a European society considered in its ethical dimensions apart from any ideological consideration.

The *Curl Lecturer* is elected by the Council of the Royal Anthropological Institute every other year, with preference given to topics outside the field of social anthropology strictly defined, and the lecturer must be under 40 years of age.

The *Michaelis-Jena Ratcliff Prize*: applications are invited from persons interested in folklore to enter their contributions for this prestigious prize. The Prize will be £4000.

The *Curl Essay Prize* of £1100 will be awarded to the author of the best essay, of not more than 10,000 words, relating to the results of anthropological work.

Sources: announcements in *Anthropology Today*, June 1993 and August 1993; *European Association of Social Anthropologists Newsletter*, October 1992.

---

history of independent, often individual, philosophical, literary or theoretical research, requiring little or no funding beyond the support given to the academic through their employment. In some of these disciplines, these forms of research are the most prestigious. Here, as in other areas of academic work, there is, of course, a hierarchy of achievement, with scholarly endeavour recognized and rewarded through a series of grants, fellowships, prizes or honours.

Box 6.14 contains a series of examples of such awards, all drawn from one sample discipline, social anthropology. Honours and prizes of these kinds are commonly administered by professional associations or learned societies. Some may be applied for, and applicants are then judged through a process of peer review. Other honours may not be directly sought, or even lobbied for, but are bestowed through a process of nomination and election. As with some research grant awards, age may be an important qualifying factor. Gaining awards of the kind listed in Box 6.14 brings recognition and honour, which can enhance an academic's career in the same way that successfully obtaining research funds may in other disciplines.

Whether research is funded or unfunded, much the same issues are involved in its management – the subject of the next section – though clearly the scale of the exercise may vary a great deal. Most research activities or projects are, of course, relatively small-scale, and require little or no additional funding. In these cases, it can be both useful and important to use the language of research to structure and add credibility to the work involved. Thus, much library-based work and some of the preparatory work involved in teaching may be seen as research. Viewing your academic activities in this way may help you to think creatively about your skills and career, as well as to restructure your curriculum vitae (see Chapter 3, especially the section on **Applying for a job**).

Managing research

Once you have been successful in gaining research funding, or have set up a project which does not require significant funding, the business of managing the work begins (the role of managing in academic careers is considered more generally in Chapter 8). There are a number of related elements involved here:

- ensuring that the proposed research is done more or less on the lines, and within the time-scale, proposed, or responding appropriately when the project throws up unanticipated lines of enquiry;
- endeavouring to keep the project within budget;
- maintaining good working relationships with others involved in the project; and
- towards and after the end of the project, reporting back and disseminating the findings.

Each of these elements will now be considered in turn.

While you may have produced a precise and carefully considered research plan, in practice few research projects proceed exactly according to plan. In most cases, many small-scale changes need to be made as the project progresses – in terms, for example, of what documentation is accessed, which institutions or people are studied, and, especially, how the texts and other data collected are analysed and interpreted. In some cases – for example, where access is refused or the researcher becomes seriously ill – major changes may need to be made to the research strategy; and, if the project is funded, some renegotiation with the sponsor may be required.

Doing research involves being flexible and adaptive, paying attention to detail and trying to ensure that you keep roughly on course. It is a pragmatic business. If you have a detailed plan and timetable, you will know where you are at any given time and whether you are on schedule or not. This is essential for most funded projects, particularly when you have other tasks and responsibilities, and when your funder expects regular progress reports. Monitoring your progress is a valuable discipline, and helps you to identify when you come across the unexpected and have to respond imaginatively. It makes sense, wherever possible, to maintain at least two copies of your research records, and of all of the data you collect. Keep these copies in different places, to reduce the risk of losing crucial information.

Budgeting is another key element of project delivery. If you are the fundholder, make sure your institution provides you with regular statements of expenditure, but keep your own accounts as well. Higher education institutions are complex organizations, typically with thousands of budget codes: mistakes in allocations are commonly made, and need to be corrected quickly. You may also find that other people are deliberately charging expenditures to your budgets which you will need to correct or challenge.

The key to managing research (and other) budgets is to make sure that all of the money allocated, or almost all, is spent, but no more. If you overspend, you will have to find other sources for supplementing your funds, and you are likely to be unpopular within your department or centre. If you underspend, you will probably have to return the balance to your funder, who might then have doubts about your financial acumen. Where underspending seems likely, carefully review all that is being charged to project budgets. Don't forget to charge for the use of existing services like printing, secretarial support and computing facilities.

If you are undertaking research as part of a team, possibly across different departments, institutions or countries, maintaining good relations with your co-researchers is clearly critical for the success of the project:

> Research projects are rarely pleasant and cooperative endeavours. It is also far from unusual for funds to be allocated on joint projects which prove less productive than they might have been because the participants are unable to collaborate. Shared theoretical perspectives and research aims are frequently little more than paper constructions, abandoned as soon as the project is underway. Stimulating intellectual discussions are a scarce commodity in most academic contexts where the adversarial model reigns supreme.
>
> (Davis 1997: 191)

Obviously, it helps if you know your collaborators well and have worked with them before. There is little point in constructing research teams – though you may have little choice in this – if you cannot be confident that they are going to work. Those managing such teams should normally have considerable experience of leading smaller-scale research projects, be able to devote a substantial portion of their time to the task, and have administrative support.

Reporting back and dissemination are features of research which tend to be given relatively little attention in humanities or social science research, yet are ethical matters to some scholars and a matter in which research funders are also becoming more interested. Many sponsors require reports at different stages of the project, as well as a substantial final report. These reports may be carefully reviewed, and funding may be withheld or delayed if they are deemed to be unsatisfactory.

In the case of consultancy, dissemination may only be to the sponsor. Most research projects, however, may be written up and reported on to two or three different audiences:

- the sponsor, in the form of a project report and perhaps workshops;
- the academic audience, in the form of journal articles, books and conference contributions; and
- a more general, popular audience of policy-makers and others, who may be interested in the research topic and can be reached through the mass media.

Much relevant guidance is given in Chapter 7, which focuses on writing.

There are good social and career reasons for disseminating the results of research carefully and thoroughly. The process may lead to useful contacts and sources of further funding. There is also continuing pressure on researchers to be 'relevant' and to contribute to the creation of a common culture of learning. Yet, the popular audience is perhaps the easiest for academics to neglect, as many of them feel uncomfortable or out of their depth talking to the media or writing in plain English. It is also in many ways the most difficult to satisfy, as the research findings will need to be carefully angled to gain attention. For example, in the area of economics:

> The research that seems to generate most media attention tends to have at least one of the following characteristics: it covers subjects high on the domestic economic policy agenda, such as job security and fat cats; it comes up with distinct and easily quantifiable results; it has clear policy implications for government and/or the private sector; it provides novel perspectives on industries of general public interest, such as Hollywood and horse racing; or it offers an overarching theory on matters of broad *fin de siècle* concern, such as the impact of globalisation and new technology.
>
> (Vaitilingam 1997)

It is still worth trying to address wider audiences, however, particularly if you bear in mind the underlying purpose of higher education in developing and sharing understanding.

Relating research to other academic roles

The pressures on academics to research, to teach, to write, to manage and to network – in short, to carry out a range of academic tasks – are so great that it makes sense to relate these closely together wherever possible. This helps to make the job a little easier and more interesting. There is an obvious linkage between research and writing, since there is little point in carrying out the former unless it leads, at some stage and in some form, to the latter. Other relationships might be usefully made, for example, between your research and teaching, through using your research in your teaching, or carrying out research on the topics you teach. Or you might link your research to your management responsibilities, by studying management in higher education; or to your networking activities, by specializing in collaborative or comparative work.

The relationship, actual or potential, between research and teaching has been much examined, but remains contentious. Some claim that this relationship is necessary and inviolable; that it is impossible to be a good teacher unless one is engaged in frontline research. In professional areas, such as teacher and nurse education, this view underlies the concept of the 'reflective practitioner', which stresses the linkages between theory and practice, and between research and action. Similarly, the idea of reflexivity – used, for example, in feminist and participative research – has encouraged attention to be paid to the impact on research of the researchers' values and identity.

The connection between research and teaching would seem to be supported by the results of the recent research and teaching quality assessment exercises, where departments which were highly rated for their research also tended to score well for the quality of their teaching. The reasons for this association have been disputed, however, and the relationship as a whole has also been questioned (Hughes and Tight 1995).

Clearly not all – in fact, probably relatively few – academics teach only those things they research, and vice versa. Where research and teaching are linked, the relationship may be direct or indirect, one-way or two-way, immediate or with time-lags. If indirect, the linkage may be through general scholarship rather than specific projects, or it may be through the department, discipline or profession rather than individual academics.

Taking a more positive and proactive perspective, one strategy would be to think about deliberately seeking linkages between research work and teaching responsibilities, as well as other academic activities. Research and teaching might then be seen as linked through development. Among the possible strategies here might be:

- acknowledging the contribution which students make to academics' work through their understandings and responses to text, literature searches, field data, dissertations, and work and life experience;
- being more strategic in organizing student project work around existing or developing staff research interests;
- seeking and valuing the contributions of students in developing research methodology and analysis through their involvement in work-in-progress seminars;
- considering how research and teaching might be linked through external organizations, such as through students' actual or potential employers, who could provide venues for developing research skills.

These strategies would suggest a particular engagement between postgraduate teaching and research, but other approaches could also be possible.

Researching as a career

If you have enjoyed your time as a research student, or perhaps have successfully completed one or two small-scale research projects or consultancies, you may be attracted to the idea of a career in academic research. This may be where you feel your skills and interests lie, with teaching and management perhaps seeming mundane or boring by comparison. As the first two quotations in Box 6.15 indicate, it is certainly possible to pursue this kind of specialist career. However, as the third quotation suggests, the road is long and hard, and your chances of emulating Ann Oakley or Cynthia Cockburn are slim. Broadly speaking, three main kinds of academic research career may be recognized:

- the research assistant;
- the more senior and permanent research fellow; and
- the more independent contract researcher.

Box 6.15: Alternative perspectives on research careers

In juggling the dual responsibilities of part-time work and child-care,
[Ann] Oakley took the route many of her generation chose – research
projects, consultancy work and novel writing, all of which could be conducted
from home and dovetailed with looking after the children … Although she
has written movingly about the frustration of years spent on short-term
research contracts, Ann Oakley avoided the typical traps that ensnare
part-timers, gaining her own research unit at the University of London
as well as a personal chair.

(Griffiths 1996a: 180)

For most of her research career, [Cynthia] Cockburn has been a member of
the School of Social Sciences at the City University, London, though her
residence there has depended on obtaining research grants to fund her projects
– from the ESRC, the Equal Opportunities Commission and the European
Commission, among others. 'The advantage is that I've had no teaching or
administrative responsibilities. That's been great, because dealing with a
university, as far as I can see, is as time-consuming as a marriage.'

(Vines 1996: 47)

The problems of contract research staff – disproportionately women – have
long been known. They include difficulties of building a career across a series
of short term contracts; the lack of time allocated within the contract to
develop the academic publications that are needed for this; their treatment in
the university policy process as second-class citizens. The effects of focusing on
the RAE [research assessment exercise] will vary across disciplinary areas, but
in the main it will be likely to encourage greater dependence on contract
income and hence will promote a rise in contract staff. Furthermore, incentive
monies for research are already in some cases encouraging staff to bid for very
small sums to employ researchers for a matter of weeks or hours to get the
work done. Again, women are likely to be the ones available for this casualized
form of academic labour.

(Davies and Holloway 1995: 15)

The majority of those specializing in academic research are *research assistants*, typically in the earlier stages of their working careers and on the lower levels of academic salary scales. They may be employed on a project for anything from a few weeks, or its equivalent, up to several years, and may work on a series of projects, end to end, within one department or centre. They will be the junior partner in the research activity, under the direction of the fund-holder; and are likely to do most of the work and get the least credit (perhaps with only an acknowledgement, rather than joint authorship, in any publications).

At its best, working as a research assistant can be a great preparation for a career in academic research or elsewhere. Your manager may have excellent connections and be able and willing to help you to a more permanent position. At its worst, it can be very exploitative, leading nowhere, with no guarantees of continuation at the end of the current contract.

Research fund-holders and managers do not always know what is currently considered good practice in working with assistants, or may assume that the university personnel department is responsible for all staff issues, including career development. While the Committee of Vice-Chancellors and Principals and other parties have recently signed up to a Concordat on Contract Research Staff Career Management (CVCP *et al.* 1996), the terms and conditions of research assistants and their career prospects typically remain inferior to those of staff on permanent contracts. The employer may require research staff to waive any legal rights to redundancy payments before agreeing a contract, and will normally write in an expectation that some teaching duties will be undertaken in addition to the research tasks associated with the project.

Senior *research fellows* may come up through the research assistant grade, be employed directly as research fellows, or be on secondment from lecturing positions. Such a role means more involvement in getting research funding and managing projects. It is likely to be longer-term, perhaps on a rolling contract, perhaps even permanent. It may even lead to a research professorship, though these are rare.

The *independent researcher* may be self-employed, and work outside higher education wholly or partly. Here, you have much more responsibility for organizing your own career, subject to the availability of funds and success in gaining contracts. What you have to offer are proven skills in carrying out and completing research to tight deadlines, almost regardless of the subject being researched. Accordingly, both your reputation and your networks are of key importance in securing work. Such a job can be rewarding, and may be combined with caring or other responsibilities, or with writing, if it can be done from home and the planning of tasks is open to negotiation. It can be difficult to combine with other work or responsibilities, however, if it involves working away from home for unpredictable or extended periods.

Before accepting a research post you should seek information on these matters. It would be wise to explore options and to make a careful appraisal of the possibilities. You may, of course, have little choice of career move. Remember then that it is possible to have a successful academic research career, but that you will need to be well organized, well networked and good at research and delivery, as well as having some luck. Box 6.16 suggests some of the strategies you might use, and some of the potential results.

Sources of further information

In this section we list a range of materials which you may find of interest in following up in more detail some of the issues discussed in this chapter. The emphasis is on recently published books in English. In each case, brief details are given as to contents and approach.

There is a vast literature on academic research, but it is mostly specialized or geared to the needs of particular audiences. Thus, there are many 'how to' guides, but these are targeted at undergraduate or postgraduate students. Many more detailed analyses of particular research methods and methodologies also exist, at least in some subject areas, but

---

Box 6.16: Factors associated with research productivity

1 Obtaining research funds provides one with resources such as a secretary, a research assistant and travel opportunities which can facilitate the research and writing process.
2 Spending less time advising students and serving on committees allows one to spend more time on research and writing.
3 Consulting and being in a selective and prestigious university brings greater visibility, more resources, and contacts with more eminent scholars – which often bring offers for publications.
4 Being driven – that is, wanting to advance rapidly or having strong status or achievement needs – can motivate one to become more productive.
5 Having reached a higher rank (i.e. full professor) also allows one to be more productive, mainly because the privilege of rank can exclude academics from unwanted departmental responsibilities, and because professors of higher rank generally teach less and choose to teach seminars with graduate students rather than large undergraduate introductory courses ...
6 At the same time, higher rank does not necessarily mean older age influences productivity; younger female academics who now may face less sex discrimination (and who also may be more driven precisely because opportunities are now opening in academia) also tend to be highly productive.

(Davis and Astin 1990: 98–9)

---

these focus on the interests of the disciplines concerned (a useful bibliography is to be found in our book, *How to Research*, detailed below). More general considerations of research processes and strategies in the humanities or social sciences are less common. The listing here, therefore, is short.

Ashcroft, K. and Foreman-Peck, L. (1996) *Researching into Assessment and Evaluation in Colleges and Universities*. London, Falmer Press.
The first volume of a 'Researching into' series, focusing on current issues, with ideas for small-scale research projects.

Blaxter, L., Hughes, C. and Tight, M. (1996) *How to Research*. Buckingham, Open University Press.
A guide to the processes involved in doing research as much as the methods. Includes chapters on thinking about research, getting started, thinking about methods, reading for research, managing your project, collecting data, analysing data, writing up and finishing off. Also includes extensive annotated bibliographies.

Goldsworthy, J. (ed.) (1997) *Directory of Grant-making Trusts*, 15th edn. Tonbridge, Charities Aid Foundation.
Provides details of thousands of trusts and foundations, and what they give grants for, with separate geographical and subject indexes.

Locke, L., Spirduso, W. and Silverman, S. (1993) *Proposals that Work: A Guide for Planning Dissertations and Grant Proposals*, 3rd edn. Newbury Park, Calif., Sage.
American text aimed at graduate students and new staff. Includes chapters on the function of the proposal, ethics, proposal content and preparation, writing style and form. Appendices include four complete sample proposals.

Whiston, T. and Geiger, R. (eds) (1992) *Research and Higher Education: The United Kingdom and the United States*. Buckingham, Open University Press.
Includes comparative papers by British and American authors dealing with trends, issues, industrial collaboration, the institutional environment, linkages with teaching, and prospects.

7 | WRITING

Introduction

This chapter considers the role of writing in academic careers. Writing is something that all academics engage in regularly: from writing notes and references on students, through committee papers, to reviews, articles and books. It is a role which many academics find hard, particularly when sustained pieces of writing are called for, but also one which can give great pleasure and a sense of achievement. It is the role, particularly when connected with research and leading to publication, which, alongside managing (see Chapter 8), tends to have the most influence in terms of career development and promotion.

The aims of this chapter are to introduce some of the variety of forms of writing which academics engage in, give some practical tips for improving and placing your writing, and develop the sense of academic writing as a worthwhile and enjoyable experience.

The chapter is organized into seven main sections:

- **The key importance of writing to an academic career**, which discusses why you need to write, and how writing can relate to other work roles;
- **How to write**, which considers alternative writing strategies, the benefits of writing with others as well as on your own, the importance of knowing your purpose and audience, of finding a voice, and organizing your writing;
- **Writing for journals**, which indicates the different kinds of journal published, and suggests strategies for placing your papers in journals;
- **Writing books**, which looks at types of book and publisher, and advises on the production of both the book proposal and the finished book itself;
- **Other forms of writing**, which considers alternatives to journals and books, such as reports and course materials;

- **How to avoid getting stale**, which offers some suggestions for keeping writing both fresh and varied;
- **Writing as a career**, which considers the option of making writing the core of an academic career.

At the end of the chapter a selection of sources of further information is listed.

The key importance of writing to an academic career

> While publication constitutes the formal and explicit criterion for recognition, there is (here as elsewhere) an informal and tacit dimension which also has to be taken into account. However important quality may be, it is not only what you write but who you are and where you come from that counts.
>
> (Becher 1989: 54)

> So long as busy, tiring days persist, procrastination dominates; most new faculty manage little writing during their first few years on campus. Without the self-efficacy born of reasonable mastery in both teaching and writing, new faculty remain doubtful and inefficient, rushing but never quite catching up, rarely meeting their career plans or potentials. Promise shown at hiring can soon deteriorate into a pattern of uninvolvement that persists through midcareer, where neither teaching nor writing are matters of pride.
>
> (Boice 1995b: 415)

Why write?

There are many related reasons for writing as an academic. The phrase 'publish or perish' is often thought of as being the underlying motivation. It is also common to read newspaper or magazine articles which deride the quality and significance of much academic writing. The reality is rather more complicated and varied, however, than either of these positions would suggest. Writing is simply of key importance to all academic roles and an academic career.

There are, of course, a range of reasons, some political, some value-led, for trying to get work published. Box 7.1 identifies ten career-related reasons for publishing, and hence writing. Some of these are clearly closely related, and you may be able to think of others. More practically, you might write and publish in order:

- to get your views across;
- to see your name in print;
- to change the world;
- to get tenure;
- to get promoted; or
- to make money.

Box 7.1: Ten good reasons for publishing

1 Publication demands highly disciplined writing, and therefore clear and precise thinking.
2 Publication places your work under open professional scrutiny.
3 Publication contributes to the scholarly literature in a field.
4 Publication reaches a wide international audience.
5 Quality journals are usually widely and professionally indexed and abstracted.
6 Publication identifies you with a domain of research or scholarship, and facilitates contact with other professionals working in the same area.
7 Publication in journals is economical.
8 Publications improve your academic credibility with students.
9 Publication enhances your academic reputation.
10 Publication is *fun*; you can get a lot of personal satisfaction out of it.

Source: Sadler (1990: 2–3).

You might not be able to realize some of these aims, particularly perhaps those connected with changing the world and making money, but you will develop yourself and your standing as an academic. And, as the final reason in the box suggests, it should also be satisfying and fun.

Writing in relation to other roles

There are many forms in which academics write. While the emphasis in this chapter is on writing for publication, Box 7.2 draws out the potential relationships between types of writing and different stages in an academic's career. This serves as a reminder that writing includes professional tasks associated with everyday work as well as developing professional and intellectual interests.

Writing may also be closely related to the other academic roles which are considered in this book: networking, teaching, researching and managing. You may find it useful deliberately to build upon these relations, emphasizing and developing strengths and experience. This may seem obvious practice in the case of research – after all, researchers are expected to write up and publish their findings – but it can also be fruitfully applied to other roles. For example, an academic might publish articles about teaching practices or innovations, textbooks for use in teaching their subject to students, or accounts of management or networking experiences. Not all of this writing would necessarily be for publication in the conventional sense, of course. Some of it might serve to help self-reflection, or be shared with only a limited number of people. There are, however, a number of potential outlets for biographical, confessional or developmental writing of this kind.

Academic writing can also be seen as closely related to other activities, such as reading and general scholarship. We may seek to set out our thoughts in writing in order better to understand, reflect upon or criticize what we have been

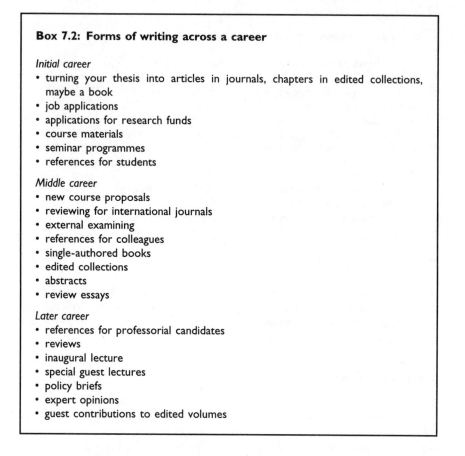

Box 7.2: Forms of writing across a career

Initial career
- turning your thesis into articles in journals, chapters in edited collections, maybe a book
- job applications
- applications for research funds
- course materials
- seminar programmes
- references for students

Middle career
- new course proposals
- reviewing for international journals
- external examining
- references for colleagues
- single-authored books
- edited collections
- abstracts
- review essays

Later career
- references for professorial candidates
- reviews
- inaugural lecture
- special guest lectures
- policy briefs
- expert opinions
- guest contributions to edited volumes

reading. Thus, literature reviews are an important aspect of academic writing, whether they form one section or the entirety of a piece of work.

Finally, the importance of correspondence in initiating and maintaining contacts across networks should not be underestimated. In short, writing of various kinds may be seen as forming an important element of all academic activities.

Building writing into your everyday life

Some people prefer their scholarly writing to be done with passion, when the spirit moves them. Some prefer, and need, the discipline of deadlines, and the intensity of their attention is directly related to the closeness of these. For others, writing has to be fitted in with other significant employment and caring responsibilities.

Writing is, however, so central to academic life that one obvious response is to try and build writing into everyday life as a regular and continuing activity. Like most skills, your writing abilities are likely to improve with practice. You will find it easier to write and, perhaps more importantly, to write effectively and quickly, the more you write. The next section contains advice and suggestions on how you might do this.

How to write

This section considers a range of related topics concerning writing:
- the different writing strategies which may be adopted;
- the issues involved in writing collaboratively;
- the importance of purpose in writing;
- the need to relate writing to its audience;
- the question of voice; and
- organizing the writing product.

Writing strategies

You may have heard of authors who get up at a certain time, and aim to write so many thousand words before breakfast or lunch. They might do this every day, or so many days a week, and then have the rest of their time free for other activities. Some of this time might be used, of course, for editing and refining what they have written. Not all of us are able to write what we want straight off, though with practice this too becomes more feasible. Writing strategies vary greatly: Box 7.3 gives some examples, ranging from those who subscribe to the work ethic to those whose practices reflect the task at hand or the stage of the project. Basically, you should use whatever strategy or strategies will work for you, but you may need some experience to find out what these are.

Two basic writing strategies are:

- writing every day, or as often as is possible, and fitting it within or around other activities; and
- writing in defined, set-aside periods.

In practice, of course, these strategies may not be so readily distinguishable, and individuals may use both at different times or for different tasks.

You may be able to identify certain regular periods in your daily or weekly schedule which can be used for writing. You may already be writing a personal diary. This will inevitably involve some sacrifice, if only in terms of time that might otherwise be spent in relaxing or doing nothing in particular. With practice, you may be able to pick up and continue a piece of writing using, say, half an hour a day, though having more time would obviously be preferable. Even if you know that you need sustained periods of time for thinking creatively, some writing tasks could still be broken up into small pieces in this way.

The alternative strategy involves blocking off larger chunks of time for writing every so often. For example, it might be possible to clear a whole day, or a weekend, once a month, or perhaps a week every three months or so. The initial part of this block of time may not be the most productive, as you may have to work yourself into writing again each time, but you should become more effective as time goes on.

Box 7.3: Writing strategies

As an academic, management of time is more personal, but I find I am still governed by protestant ethic standards. The ritual of sitting down to work at 9.00 am and working through to 12.00 or 12.30 pm, and then a further two hours in the afternoon, is a good mental discipline. Without this moral impulsion behind the ritual I doubt whether I would ever get round to writing at all. However, it is a curious thing that while I keep to the ritual, 'off-duty' hours can be vastly more productive. Thus, winter evenings, weekends, late at night and occasionally early morning are all comparatively high productivity times. Protestant ethic standards dictate that these are 'free time', and the psychology of it is that I cannot make a mess of them, or it does not matter if I do. I am consequently more relaxed, and usually therefore more productive. Periods before holidays are also useful. Holidays must be earned, and if a project is unfinished, will not be enjoyed.

(Woods 1985: 94)

When I came to write, there were very few material obstacles in my way. Writing was a reputable and harmless occupation. The family peace was not broken by the scratching of a pen. No demand was made upon the family purse ... You have only got to figure to yourselves a girl in a bedroom with a pen in her hand. She had only to move that pen from left to right – from ten o'clock to one.

(Woolf 1995: 1–2)

It occurs to me that for half of our jobs we are really novelists (the research, writing and publishing parts) and for half we are talk-show hosts (the teaching and executive teaching parts) ... When I am in a heavy research mode, I let myself sleep in if that is what I need, I work all hours (and odd hours) ... I do things that spur my creativity ... I do my worst writing (coming up with responses to reviewers and so on) when I try to shoehorn that activity into the work mould of a professional. I do my best thinking while lying down ... I am happiest when I take advantage of my flexible career and live my life this way when I am focused on writing ... Once I am engaged in the task and the task is broken into small pieces ... it allows me, in very busy times, to keep going, finding small things that I can tackle in the few minutes that I can squeeze out of a day for research.

(Ashford 1996: 123–5)

In the later stages I began to feel like an amalgamated version of the research participants' accounts of tiredness. I was beavering away inside the project, but became concerned that I had lost my sense of perspective. I had set aside all the life activities I could, to give the writing priority. But my life became flat and dull, and this affected my writing. There were times when I seemed to have a very limited vocabulary; words with texture did not come readily. I noticed all this and allowed myself a little more activity, leisure and reading fiction. A new academic term began, and provided some alternative views of the work – and duties, delights and pressures. I took a final break away from home to review the draft book in its entirety, and complete the project.

(Marshall 1995: 38)

Dr Brock was dressed in a bright red jacket, looking vaguely bohemian, as authors are supposed to do, and the first question went to him. What was it like to be a writer? He said it was tremendous fun. Going home from an arduous day at the hospital, he would go straight to his yellow pad and write his tensions away. The words just flowed. It was easy. I then said that writing wasn't easy and it wasn't fun. It was hard and lonely, and the words seldom just flowed. Next Dr Brock was asked if it was important to rewrite. Absolutely not, he said. 'Let it all hang out', and whatever form the sentences take will reflect the writer at his [sic] most natural. I then said that rewriting is the essence of writing. I pointed out that professional writers rewrite their sentences repeatedly and then rewrite what they have rewritten ... 'What do you do on days when it isn't going well?' Dr Brock was asked. He said he just stopped writing and put the work aside for a day when it would go better. I then said that a professional writer must establish a daily schedule and stick to it. I said that writing is a craft, not an art ... If your job is to write every day, you learn to do it like any other job.

(Zimmer 1990: 3–4)

Writing on your own and with others

> Collaboration is inseparable from conversation and commentary ... Conversation as an activity of the mind can generate writing ... Collaboration, then, is less an effort to share writing than a function of conversation that renews writing, keeping it supple, reflective and lively.
>
> (Burns *et al.* 1996: xxii)

Writing is, of course, not only or not necessarily a solitary activity, though that is how it is usually conceived. It is also common to write with others. As the quotation above indicates, such collaboration can extend the boundaries of intellectual thinking through the conversations shared with colleagues. It can also be a useful means of sharing expertise, spreading the load, or gaining experience. And it can be fun, as the present authors can testify.

There are, obviously, both advantages and disadvantages in writing together. The issues to be considered include the following:

- Do you get on well with the people you will be writing with?
- Do you share much the same values and ideas?
- Do their interests and skills mesh with and complement yours?
- Will the relationship be fairly balanced?
- Will you be credited fairly for your share of the work?

If the answer to any of these questions is negative, or you are unsure, you would be well advised not to commit yourself to too large or lengthy a joint writing project. Try something limited and small-scale first, and try working with a number of different collaborators.

If you are engaging in writing with others for the first time, and if you have the option, consider agreeing some ground rules before you start. Don't assume that you are thinking on the same lines, or that you can work it out as you go along. For example, if you are seeking to publish what you are writing, consider the following questions:

- Whose name will go first?
- Who will have responsibility for drafting which sections?
- Who will produce the final version?
- Who will pick the publisher or publication?
- Who will decide the title?
- How will any disagreements between you be resolved?

You may think that you have sufficient confidence or a good enough relationship not to need to address these questions in advance. You may also, however, be surprised later at the simmering discontent that can arise when your colleagues think their views are being overlooked or they are being exploited.

For less experienced academics, challenging entrenched hierarchies and associated power plays, and insisting on alphabetical ordering of authors may be impractical. It could be more detrimental to a career not to be listed than to come last in the list. It can, however, also be problematic to be only ever viewed as a member of a team. Those without sole publications are not rewarded for their team-playing skills.

There is another aspect to collaborative writing, though it will probably only become significant for those with more experience. This is your role in helping others to write. You could see this as a kind of responsibility or duty, particularly if you have been helped in this way by someone else in your own career, or just a pleasurable aspect of the job. Whichever way you view it, if you have had some success in writing and getting published, think about the possibility of helping to develop others' skills and strategies in this area.

Writing for specific purposes

As Box 7.1 suggests, there are many reasons for writing. Throughout the process of writing, it is necessary to be aware of the purpose(s) of a given piece as well as of the target audience.

For example, you may be writing a document or a report to meet a contractual requirement (e.g. from the organization funding your research). In such circumstances, it would be foolish to do anything other than follow the specifications you have been given. Where these have not been set out in any detail, it may be necessary to tease out the expectations of the contractors through discussion. In such circumstances, it is sensible to do no less, but also no more, than what the contract specifies.

Another common reason for academic writing is to help make out a case for tenure or promotion. Here, it makes sense to take advice from the kinds of people who will judge the case about the sorts of writing which they value. This would probably include articles in respected refereed journals and single-authored books with reputable publishers, but might also extend to a wish to see a range of kinds of publication. Getting this advice well in advance should help in orienting your writing plans.

Writing to meet the demands of research selectivity exercises offers a third example. Here, the concern is likely to be to ensure that you produce, and get published, a certain number of articles or books of particular kinds within a given period. As in the case of writing for tenure or promotion, early awareness of the rules of the game, even if these are not formally published, and a willingness to alter one's writing plans to fit, are of key importance. Remember also that the rules of games like this do change from time to time.

In each of these examples, and in many others that could be imagined, the critical points have to do with knowing what you are about, taking advice from those who are well placed to give it – because they have already done it themselves, or will be in a position to judge you – and proceeding accordingly. If this seems to be unduly restrictive or instrumental, bear in mind two points. First, writing as an academic is a job of work like any other, and as such subject to rules and restrictions, and with safe and risky strategies. Second, you may be able to extend yourself in other forms of writing as well.

Knowing your audience(s)

Closely linked to the purpose of writing is the question of who you are writing for. The answer might, of course, be primarily yourself. More probably, however, you will be writing with the aim of informing or influencing other academics and/or practitioners in your field, and/or a more general audience. If this is the intention, then it will clearly help to know something about what these audiences might expect and to keep this in mind while writing.

For example, when writing for other academics in your field, it may be expected that you use a particular shared specialist language, or jargon, and make detailed reference to existing writing. If, on the other hand, you are writing for a non-specialist audience, you will want to write in a generally intelligible style, explaining any specialist terms, and may not include any references at all. Or, to take a third example, if you are writing a student textbook, the text might be carefully organized in short sections and include items like exercises, summaries, glossaries and reading lists. It is sensible, therefore, to research the publishing genre first to get an indication of appropriate formats and styles.

Whichever audience you are writing for, there are other, general guidelines regarding language to bear in mind. The most important of these have to do with the use of non-sexist and non-oppressive forms of language. While some might see this as an unwarranted intrusion of doctrines of political correctness, such practices are increasingly accepted as the norm for academic writing in the social sciences and humanities.

Finding your voice

I worried then and wondered about the codes and conventions of academic literacy. In fact I encouraged students to adopt an experiential, autobiographical approach but was constantly concerned about what I was doing and whether they might be penalized by examiners. Certain colleagues were more mainstream than me and had different even disparaging attitudes towards the role and relevance of the personal in written work. I felt I was taking risks with others let alone myself. Gradually, I found some resolution to these tensions and, in the process, more of my own voice. The literature on life history/biographical research provided a crucial conceptual and methodological link between the personal and cultural, the psychological and social, the academic and experiential for students as well as myself. I began to understand how I might relate some more recent psychotherapeutic interests to teaching, research and academic writing.

(West 1996: 24)

A key part of the writing experience, particularly in the early part of an academic career, is finding your own voice. How you choose to write is, of course, closely linked to self-identity and reasons for writing. What should be understood is that there are alternative ways of writing and different voices which you might adopt, and that these may be safer or riskier to pursue, depending on your position.

Clearly it is safer, particularly if you are a relatively new or junior academic, to couch your writing within established styles or traditions. Such writing is likely to be written in the third person, qualified, respectful of existing authorities and carefully referenced, and your personality and experience will be little in evidence to the reader.

Other kinds of writing may give you more scope to develop your voice, but are likely to be riskier. Such writing could, for example, lay much more stress on your personal experience and be written in the first person (e.g. confessional, evaluative or reflective writing). It could be more challenging of received wisdom and accepted forms of expression or presentation. It could state a definite point of view, arguing for desired actions or changes.

The degree of risk associated with different forms of writing is, of course, linked to who your audience is and what the accepted conventions of your discipline, or sub-discipline, are. Many of the more recently established journals (see the following section on **Writing for journals**) allow for and even encourage less conventional kinds of writing. Such journals may be divided into a number of sections, with space given over not just for conventional academic articles but also research notes, viewpoints, work in progress, responses to previously published articles, review articles, autobiographical pieces and poems.

As part of your role as a writer, in developing your voice, you will need to decide how safe or risky your writing will be. You can, of course, use a number of different styles and voices. You might also use different names, as some academics do, for different kinds of writing.

Organizing writing

This subsection is rather more mundane, and serves to emphasize the need to organize writing, not in the sense of finding times or places to do it but in terms of its structure. Two key points will be made:

Box 7.4: What's in a title?

Training Matters
Academic Discourse
The Empire Strikes Back
Teaching Well and Liking it
Women's Ways of Knowing
Managing Effectively
The Wheels Used to Talk to Us
The English Language
Images of Organization
Health and Well-being: A Reader
The Erotics of Instruction
A History of the Swedish People
The Joy of Stress
The Politics of Poverty
The Audit of War
Feminist Praxis
The Private Life of Plants

- the role of titles; and
- the importance of internal structure.

Titles, whether for articles or books, are a key factor in attracting and drawing in readers. They should also indicate the focus of a piece of writing. To achieve both of these aims calls for some skill. In the case of books, the publisher will have some say as to whether the proposed title is appropriate, and will also help to formulate it if the author is unsure.

Much academic writing opts for the safety of the carefully descriptive title, often with a lengthy subtitle as well. However, more readers are likely to be attracted, particularly non-specialist ones, if a more attractive title can be devised. Some examples of book titles are given in Box 7.4. They include a mixture of the ambiguous, like *Training Matters*, the seriously humorous, like *The Erotics of Instruction*, and the deadpan, like *Academic Discourse*. What they share in common is their brevity and ambiguity. They make the potential reader question what the book is about, and then pick it up to find out. Once you have your audience's attention in this way, the battle is half over.

The relationship between title, content and audience is the most usual concern in a writer's mind. As indicated in Chapter 3 (see the discussion of curricula vitae in the section on **Applying for a job**), the titles of published papers also help to frame an academic's public identity. Thus, the titles listed in Box 7.4 say something about the authors' scholarly interests. Consequently, in deciding upon a title it is worth giving some attention to the ways they may contribute to creating a sense of cohesion across, for example, several research projects or teaching jobs, as well as to building a reputation in a particular area.

The importance of the internal structure of what you are writing may seem obvious, but it is surprising how many academics seem to ignore it. We used to be taught at school that the key to essay writing was to 'say what you're going to say, say it, and then say what you've said'. In other words, a piece of formal writing requires some kind of introduction and conclusion, in which you might summarize your argument or highlight key findings or recommendations. As pieces of writing become longer, they require more careful organization as well, so that successive sections and chapters are effectively and purposefully linked.

One way of ensuring that this internal structure is provided is, of course, to build it in from the start. You may find it helpful to start a piece of writing with a section-by-section plan on one side of paper, or on your word processor, and then work from there. Alternatively, you might simply start writing, let your work evolve, and then clarify the structure, signposting and linkages once the piece has been fully drafted. Either way, a final check through to make sure that the internal structure is clear is usually a good idea.

Box 7.5 offers some further advice for academic writers from another author, in the form of nine maxims to write and publish by. These both confirm and extend the points made in this section. They also demonstrate the somewhat conflictual nature of advice, noting the importance of quality as well as the need to 'crank papers out'. At root, however, as the ninth maxim indicates, 'It's only business' – a craft to be learned, practised and, hopefully, enjoyed.

Writing for journals

Academic writing comes in a variety of lengths. Shorter pieces of writing, which are typically called articles or papers, are usually less than 10,000 words in length, and are published in journals. These are the subject of this section. Longer pieces of writing, say 40,000 words or more, are normally published as monographs or books and are discussed in the next section. Other kinds of writing, such as reports and course materials, are considered in the section following that.

In this section, we will focus on two main aspects of writing for journals: the different kinds of journal that are published, and the strategies which you might use to help you to place your writing in them.

Distinctions between journals

There are a variety of kinds of journal within which academic writing may be placed. Understanding these distinctions, and planning and directing writing accordingly, is an important part of the writing craft.

From the perspective of their intended audiences, three main types of journal may be recognized in many subject areas:

- *academic* journals, which are clearly both written by and directed towards academics;
- *professional* or *practitioner* journals, which include articles by academics alongside others by people working in the field;

Box 7.5: Nine maxims to write and publish by

1 *Nobody cares* ... In writing ... it is critical to remember that problems, questions, and the like that strike you as fascinating are likely to bore other readers ... your first task in writing a paper is to make them care ...
2 *No one ever went broke in underestimating the American public* ... You have to present your research in such a way that readers can understand with a minimum of effort what you did, why it is important, what you found, and what it means ...
3 *Add simplicity and lightness* ... Always look for the simplest and most direct way of getting at the question.
4 *Ask Aunt Clara* ... your papers should be written in such a way that any reasonably intelligent person would be both willing and able to understand what you say.
5 *Who needs paper?* ... the acid test of a paper is the feeling that I could stand up in front of an audience and read it to them without feeling stupid, and without confusing them ...
6 *The importance of the information on a written page is inversely proportional to the page number* ... The farther you are from the first sentence of a paper, the less important the material is likely to be ...
7 *The quality of your work counts, but you also need quantity* ... assuming that you can identify reasonably interesting research questions and apply reasonably sensible methods to the problem, my advice is to crank papers out at a pretty regular pace.
8 *The quality of the journal probably counts more than the quality of the paper* ... You can always find some journal that will publish your work, but unless some of that work gets into the journals that someone reads, you might as well not bother publishing.
9 *It's only business* ... Anyone who hasn't been called a fool by reviewers hasn't submitted enough papers to the journals. It comes with the territory.

(Murphy 1996: 133–4)

- *newspapers, magazines* and other forms of journalism, including television and radio programmes, which frequently carry shorter and less technical pieces by academics.

In some cases, these distinctions are not so straightforward: academics may also be practitioners, and journals may seek to accommodate a variety of kinds of writing. The recent, rapid development of electronic communications and journals has also added a further dimension. Some examples of different kinds of journal are given in Box 7.6.

Another distinction which is commonly made in academic circles is that between *refereed* and other journals. Refereed journals are those to which you are expected to submit a draft paper, which will usually then be read and evaluated by two or more 'independent' referees: experienced academics with some expertise in the area which you are writing about. After a sometimes rather protracted period, you will receive a report back from the journal editor, summarizing

---

Box 7.6: Examples of types of journals

- Popular:
  The Economist, Education, Psychology Today, New Scientist, Red Pepper, Times Higher Education Supplement.
- Professional:
  AUT Bulletin, Journal of Advanced Nursing, NATFHE Journal, New Law Journal, Operational Research Letters, Social Work Today, Trade Union News.
- Applied:
  Inquiry, Journal of Applied Social Psychology.
- Academic:
  British Journal of Educational Studies, Daedalus, Journal of Aesthetics and Art Criticism, Journal of European Public Policy, Mind, Modern Law Review, Philosophy, Psychological Research, Studies in Higher Education.
- Multi-disciplinary:
  Cultural Studies.
- Electronic:
  Journal of Information, Law and Technology.

---

or including the referees' comments, and recommending publication, redrafting or rejection on that basis. Non-refereed journals, by contrast, will accept or reject drafts more quickly on the basis of the judgement of the editor or their representative.

Refereed journals, by being more selective and careful about what they publish, have higher status, at least within their particular field of study. Here, as in other aspects of academic life, there is a clear pecking order. Where you publish has implications for who reads you and how seriously your writing is regarded.

Some refereed journals practise blind refereeing: that is, the authorship of manuscripts is withheld from the refereees. In the words of one journal editor:

> the *Academy of Management Journal*'s double-blind review policy . . . is important to ensure objectivity in the review process and to maintain high quality reviews. Knowledge of a manuscript's authorship inevitably introduces bias – positive or negative – into the review process (and slows the process down). You can help by avoiding the use of obvious self-citations.
>
> (Tsui 1997: 8)

The last sentence is a discrete jab at the propensity of some authors to encourage their developing reputations through self-citation.

One other important distinction is that between international and other journals (though there are many journals which claim to be international but carry few articles from outside their country of publication). Here, the general view is that publishing in truly international journals carries more status, because it brings exposure to the range of thinking of scholars in a number of different countries.

How to place your writing in journals

I began, as advised, spinning off articles from my dissertation. I sent out three pieces within 4 months of receiving my degree. I was feeling good and right on track, especially in light of the fact that I also carried a full teaching load, was still nursing my infant son, and shared care for my mother, who now lived with us and was dying of cancer. I worked on additional articles while I waited for word on my initial submissions. Three letters came. I quickly interpreted them as three flat rejections – letters that I now realize, years later and a journal editor myself, were encouraging, complimentary and much more suggestions for refocusing and revising than recommendations to throw in the towel. But, inexperienced and too quickly discouraged, I stopped writing articles.

(Gallos 1996: 11)

There are no particular secrets to getting writing published in journals: you need practice and experience. So long as you can construct a reasonable and well-presented argument of some relevance, you ought to be able to get it published in a journal. This will probably not, if you are new to the game, be one of the leading journals in the field. It is also likely to be the case, as the quotation above indicates, that your draft will be sent back with some suggestions for further development or changes. Publishing in journals is an ongoing, and long-term, process.

If this seems a little off-putting, remember that journals need both readers and writers. Most are published a number of times a year, with each issue containing several substantial articles. While some may have waiting lists for publication of two or three years, and turn away much potentially publishable material (indeed, they may reject the great majority of the draft papers submitted), others cannot be so choosy. Some may, indeed, be short of acceptable material.

Box 7.7 contains ten suggestions which should help you in placing your writing in journals. If you follow these guidelines, you should, with a bit of luck – and providing that you have the ideas and time required – be able to build up a substantial list of publications within a few years.

Writing books

Many writers of theses think of their job as merely the presentation of research and the results therefrom. Writers of books must get beyond the mere public display of data: they must chew the material well, digest it, and turn it into something of their own.

(Holmes 1976: 65)

Writing books is a rather more complex process than writing papers for journals. Not only is the product bigger, but also more people are likely to be involved in gaining its acceptance and publication. Not surprisingly, therefore, books are regarded rather more highly than journal articles in most disciplinary assessments, though, as with journals, there are also hierarchies of esteem in this area.

Box 7.7: Ten suggestions for placing your writing in journals

1 It can be a good idea to approach journal editors in advance, particularly if this is suggested in the journal, to inform them of what you have in mind to write, and to check whether this would, in principle, fit in their journal. This may save you time later, and may yield some useful advice regarding other, perhaps more relevant, journals, or about forthcoming special issues of relevance. If the editor doesn't reply, don't be offended, as they may simply be too busy.

2 Write to the format, style and length suggested. Most journals normally contain detailed instructions as to the format and length of papers published. If not, such guidance should be available from the editor. Follow this guidance scrupulously, unless you have an agreement to the contrary. There is nothing more irritating to a journal editor than to receive submissions from authors who have either not taken the trouble to read their guidelines, or who have patently ignored them. If you do this, which a surprising number of academics do, your writing may be rejected before its quality has even been considered.

3 Write on the subjects suggested either in the journal guidelines or by the existing selection of articles published. Responding to, or building upon, previously published papers offers one way of doing this. Another is to pick a topic from within a journal's remit on which it has published little. Box 7.8 contains some examples of the guidance which journals give, usually inside their covers, on format and subjects.

4 Write in good-quality, accessible English. Both deliberately complicated and sloppy writing are likely to put off reviewers and readers. Jargon should only be used where it forms part of a disciplinary understanding. Include sufficient references to support your argument, but no more than that, and don't refer to everything you've ever written before. If you are writing in a foreign language, get a native speaker with an understanding of your field to read through your draft before you send it off.

5 Start modest, and build up a track record. Choose less prestigious journals for your initial publications, and develop a strategy for steadily building up the numbers of journals you have published in. This will help to ensure that potential editors and referees are aware of your work, and its strengths, in advance.

6 Take careful note, and revise your papers in the light of, comments received. While you may be fortunate to get some papers published without any alteration, it is more normal for referees and editors to make more or less critical comments on your work. To some extent, this is simply going through the process: after all, what would be the point of editors and referees if they did not criticize your work? Your work is likely to be read more closely at this stage than any other, so it is wise to take notice and benefit from the reviewing process.

7 Unless you are incredibly fortunate, some of your papers will be rejected by one or more journals. This does not mean, however, that they are worthless. It may be that you have simply chosen the wrong journal, and that another will accept your paper with or without some alteration. So don't give up at the first rejection. Bear in mind any comments received from the rejecting journal, do some more work on the paper, and try your luck elsewhere. If the same, or a similar, paper gets rejected a few times, put it on the back burner and move on to something else.

8 Make use of your networks. It may be that a journal is published from your department, or from another in the same institution. You may know some-body on the editorial group or board. Such contacts can be very useful for getting advice, opinions and support, and usually relatively quickly.

9 Work for a journal. Offer your services in some capacity to journals that interest and engage you: as a reviewer, associate editor, reviews editor or general dogsbody. Journals are usually poorly staffed and produced at the margins of busy people's time: offers of help are quite likely to be gratefully received. Once you are involved in this way you will have the benefits of an insider's view, and can learn more about journals as well as build up contacts.

10 Start your own journal. While this may not be an option open to someone just starting an academic career, it could become so, particularly if you have built up a good network. The numbers and kinds of journals are increasing all the time, and many publishers are looking for good ideas for journals to add to their portfolios. (See also the section on **Journals and newsletters** in Chapter 4.) You should then find yourself very well placed for placing your own future papers (and not just in your own journal).

This section starts by considering the different kinds of book published, and the different kinds of publisher that publish them. It then goes on to discuss the critical issue of the book proposal and the techniques involved in actually writing a book.

If there is one key piece of advice for any academic thinking of writing a book, however, it is this: *don't do any more than the minimum until you have a proposal accepted by a publisher.* You should certainly do no more than produce a couple of draft chapters. To get any further risks potential heartache, for you may find you have put a great deal of time and effort into something which proves to be unpublishable.

Books and publishers

As in the case of journals, there are various kinds of book written by academics. The most obvious is probably the *single-author* book, for which one academic takes on sole responsibility. This is shared in the case of *multi-author* books, which may also involve senior and junior partners, with each perhaps having specific responsibility for a number of chapters or sections.

Edited books, by definition, involve several authors, and one or more editors. While they may be viewed as less original than the single-author or coauthored text, they can involve at least as much work to put together, especially if the contributions are original. Liaison with authors, and getting them to deliver acceptable drafts on time, can be very demanding.

Alternatively, as when they are designed as course readers, edited books may consist wholly or largely of previously published pieces. In such cases, much of the editorial work concerns the selection, abridgement, introduction and linking together of the papers. In some cases, the editor may also be responsible for contacting the original authors and getting their permission for republication, though this task may be undertaken by the book's publisher.

Box 7.8: Guidance on journal back covers

The Editors are particularly keen to publish work by younger sociologists on current developments in research and analysis.

(British Journal of Sociology)

The Journal encourages debate on contemporary pedagogic issues and professional concerns within the UK and abroad.

(Journal of Further and Higher Education)

Contributions may encompass critical discussions, accounts of new methods, developments and controversial issues as well as research reports. Analytical contributions from those actually involved in the practical management and administration of education . . . are particularly welcome.

(Educational Management and Administration)

There are two main sections of the journal. The first section includes longer articles with references (normally from 2000 to 6000 words). The second section includes issues for debate, grass roots observations, research notes, conference reports and reviews (normally from 800 to 2000 words).

(Open Learning)

People Management welcomes ideas for articles. It would be helpful if writers could send a short written proposal first, with a telephone number where they can be contacted. A note on our preferred format and style is available on request.

Organization Studies aims to promote the understanding of organizations, organizing and the organized, and the social relevance of that understanding. It encourages the interplay between theorizing and empirical research, in the belief that they should be mutually informative.

The *Asian and Pacific Migration Journal* is published quarterly . . . to encourage and facilitate the study of socio-demographic, economic, political, psychological, historical, legislative and religious aspects of human migration and refugee movements from and within Asia.

Books are typically written and published as a one-off exercise; unless, that is, they prove popular enough to merit producing a further edition some years after original publication. They may also be conceived as part of a series. Where a publisher has a relevant series, placing a book proposal is a different sort of exercise.

Books may also be categorized in terms of their content and approach. Thus, *textbooks* aim to summarize or synthesize existing understandings within a particular field of study, providing an introductory overview for the student and novice academic. Such books tend to sell better as the market is larger, and may require a new edition every few years. They can help to get your name known more widely, though they may not be as highly regarded by your peers in promotional and research assessments. Other books tend to have a smaller potential readership and to be more focused in their coverage, often making use of the personal research undertaken by the author(s) concerned. They may take the form of a research *monograph* or report, or may be much more polemical in character.

The distinction between *hardback* and *paperback* books rests more on the perceived marketability of the book than on any other factor. The latter are cheaper and, unlike most academic monographs, are expected to sell by the thousand over a continuous period of a number of years. Most hardback-only publications produced by academics are relatively expensive, and designed primarily for the shelves of university libraries.

Book publishers also vary considerably in character, not least in terms of their relative status. Broadly speaking, the longer-established *general publishers* based in or around capital cities carry the most credibility. However, some newer, specialist or regional publishers are also highly regarded. The recent upheavals in the ownership of publishing firms have complicated the position considerably, with many amalgamating or going out of business.

Some *university presses* – those associated with high-status universities (especially Oxford and Cambridge) – are also of relatively high status. The status of other forms of *in-house* publication, such as by a department or centre, and some of the newer university presses, is largely dependent upon the perceived status of the university, department or centre concerned. *Vanity presses* and *self-publication* are rarely accorded much credibility, though there are some exceptions, and these may serve as a stage towards other forms of publication.

How to produce a good book proposal

The key to producing a good book, or at least to getting a book published, is the development of a well-considered book proposal. It cannot be stressed too strongly that writing the book first, and then seeking a publisher, is the wrong way to go about the process. Secure a contract from a publisher first.

The first stage in producing a book proposal is the initial formulation of your ideas. Once this is done, it is time to make some contacts with publishers. Much of the advice given in the preceding section on **Writing for journals** also applies here. Approach publishers who publish in your field, and any with whom you have contacts, for advice on your initial ideas. Large conferences can be a good meeting place, as relevant publishers often send representatives and stands, and are usually on the lookout for new authors and books.

Don't be afraid to approach a number of potential publishers, though not simultaneously: most will turn you down. Generally speaking, book publication is a rather more competitive business than placing your papers in journals. Publishers need to make money, and can have very particular ideas about the kinds of book and author they publish, so finding the right one for your book can take some time.

Once you have some initial leads, you need to spend some time researching the market for your book and any potential competitors it may have. Prospective publishers will want to be able to estimate how many copies your book is likely to sell, and to whom, so that they know how many to print and what sort of profit they might make. They will be particularly interested in whether your book will become recommended reading for a range of university courses. They will also want to know what other books have been published on your topic in recent years, and by whom.

Perhaps surprisingly, publishers who already have a number of closely associated titles in their catalogues are likely to be interested in publishing others in the same or similar fields. It is easier to market a group of related titles, and the purchaser of one may buy others as well. Conversely, publishers may also be interested in building up a list in an area in which rival publishers have done good business.

The key point in producing a saleable book proposal, however, is knowing your major theme(s) and selling point(s). You need to be able to distinguish your book from others, state what is original about it and show what will make it either a popular purchase in academic and student circles or an important work that will have a more limited but enduring market.

Most publishers, if they are interested in your initial idea, will give you some guidance and help in producing your book proposal. Be as succinct and punchy as you can. Your proposal will likely be reviewed by both the publisher and one or more academic referees. They will be looking for reasons not to proceed as much as for reasons to go ahead. You need to be able to impress and sell your idea quickly and attractively.

The writing process

Once you have your book contract, what then? Writing a book is clearly a different exercise, at least in terms of magnitude, from writing an article. As such, it is likely to take a good deal longer and require much more in the way of planning and organization. Seeing a book through from proposal acceptance to publication will typically take a year or more, during which period you will, of course, have many other things to do. It involves both determination and patience.

One way of making this process more manageable is to treat a book as a series of connected articles. You can then focus on the chapters one at a time, and later seek to pull them together when all have been drafted. Some of your chapters may, indeed, be at least partly based on articles you have already written (or subsequently become the basis for further articles). If you have produced a reasonably detailed and accurate outline for the proposal, you should be able to start drafting almost any chapter. You may want to do them in order – though perhaps leaving shorter introductory or concluding chapters until last – or prefer to start with the most appealing, and progress more quickly from there. Having a timetable, with periods set out in advance for working on the book, is likely to be helpful.

Producing an edited book is a rather different process, particularly if it involves putting together new pieces of writing from several authors. Here, while more of the work devolves upon other writers, the editorial responsibility for organizing and linking it all together is critical. Book editors need to build up good working relationships, and keep in regular contact, with all of the contributing authors if the process is to come to a successful conclusion. The ability to put together an edited book relies not only on your knowledge of the field but also on your networks.

Writing books jointly with others is another activity requiring good mutual understanding. It may be the case, for example, that there are senior and junior authors, with the former essentially directing the work of the latter. Or, where the authors have more or less equal status, the writing responsibilities might be divided up, with each author then working on all of the draft materials. It is also possible for the authors literally to write jointly, sitting down together for periods and thrashing out drafts sentence by sentence, or to write together at a distance using the Internet.

If you are engaged in any form of writing with one or more people, it is sensible, if not essential, to work out and agree how the authorship will be presented before you start work. Will the authors appear in strict alphabetical order? If not, why not? Such discussions can usefully reveal your own, and your coauthors', assumptions.

There are two other key factors in writing books which should not be over-looked: writing to length and writing to deadlines. Publishers are unlikely to be pleased if a promised book is delayed without warning, or is presented signifi-cantly over or under the agreed length. Keep to the terms of your contract if you can, and let your publisher know of any likely problems as they occur. They, like you, will want you to produce the best product you can, and are likely to be sympathetic and helpful unless you really try their patience.

Other forms of writing

We believe it is time to review the hierarchies: to look again at the relative value of letters in the press, in-house publications (often effectively vanity presses), conference presentations, workshops and keynote speeches. How can we compare the relative merits of writing and editing publications? Can we find ways of breaking down the old boys' networks (sadly there is often a gender division) which control access to publication in many disciplines? What constitutes an international publication and are some countries of publication more reputable than others? Frequently co-authored texts are seen as being inferior to those that have single authors: is this necessarily the case?

(Smith and Brown 1995: 16–17)

While books and journals are the major, and the most prestigious, outlets for academic writing, there are many other forms of writing. An academic's career strategy might involve publishing work in diverse forms across a wide range of outlets. These other forms of writing and publication, which should not be seen as mutually exclusive or unrelated, are summarized in Box 7.9.

The most obvious British producer of *course materials* is, of course, the Open University, which is a publishing and production house as much as it is a uni-versity. However, many departments in other higher education institutions now also produce high-quality packs or volumes of course materials for sale, both internally and externally. As in the case of basic textbooks, these can be a useful source of income. Producing such materials is a demanding activity, not to be entered into lightly or without adequate support (see also the section in Chapter 5 on **Resource-based teaching**). Box 7.10 offers some tips for those involved.

Research projects, whether funded or unfunded, are typically written up in the form of a *report*. Indeed, this will normally be expected for funded research,

---

Box 7.9: Other forms of publication

course materials
reports
internal publications
newsletters
briefing papers
conference papers or presentations
newspaper and magazine articles
television and radio appearances
reviews
abstracts
research proposals

Box 7.10: Tips for writers of open learning materials

* Set yourself stage deadlines ... Work on small manageable jobs – don't try to work on the whole package at once.
* Show your writing to other people long before it is ready. Critical feedback on an early draft is easier to swallow than criticism of your completed master-piece.
* Keep the tone relatively informal. Use 'you' for your learners, 'I' as the author ...
* ... Don't stand on your professional dignity in your writing.
* ... Leave room for your learners to write in their answers to your questions, and their own notes and comments ...
* Use short words rather than long words where possible ...
* Use short, simple sentences rather than long, complex ones ...
* Include headings and sub-headings so that learners can see at a glance what each page is doing ...
* Include illustrations whenever they help learners to understand things.

(Race 1994: 55–6)

---

with a particular format often specified and some form of evaluation likely (see the section in Chapter 6 on **Managing research**). Research reports, and other work in progress, may also be published by departments or centres in the form of *internal publications*. Such publications can serve as the basis for more public documents. Longer-term research projects, research centres and interest groups frequently disseminate news, opinions and findings to specialist networks by means of *newsletters* or *briefing papers*. These may be the first outlet for pub-lication of new material or findings relating to work in progress.

Conference papers and *presentations* serve both as a means of networking and as another stage towards publication in book or journal form. They have varying status, in terms of the location, size, sponsorship and composition of the conference, and in relation to the nature of the contribution made. Being invited to give a keynote speech is a notable accolade, while contributing a paper in a parallel session is more standard fare. Workshops and poster sessions tend to be less highly regarded (see also the section in Chapter 4 on **Conferences, seminars and societies**). Much of the advice given in the section above on **Writing for journals** also applies to getting papers accepted for conferences. Such presentations may, of course, lead directly to wider publication, as when papers appear in conference proceedings, edited books or special journal issues.

For those who are interested in a wider and more popular dissemination of their ideas, submitting shorter and jargon-free pieces to quality *newspapers* and specialist *magazines* is an important option. This may help to get you noticed, but it is unlikely to earn much money. If your research or thinking is particularly topical, or you make a name for yourself within a specialist field, this may attract the attention of *television* or *radio programmes*. Most universities or colleges now have publicity officers or departments, and they can be extremely helpful in this respect: make sure they know of you, your interests and expertise.

Writing *book reviews* for journals can be a particularly helpful form of publication. Reviewers get to see new books as soon as they are published, and get them free. The review pages of journals and magazines are often also the most widely read sections as well. *Abstracts* are similarly useful, but less widely known about. There are many journals published which consist entirely of abstracts (i.e. summaries) of recently published books and articles. They function as up-to-date literature reviews in particular subjects. Abstracting services use academics to produce many of the abstracts included, for which service they receive the books or journals concerned.

Publishing your work in different forms and outlets can help to get you better known and to further your career. Reports or course materials can be converted into papers. Papers may be summarized in the form of newspaper or magazine articles. Everything you write, even unsuccessful *research proposals*, might be published in another form. It is, however, important not to overdo this. Recent research assessment exercises have encouraged academics to adopt the salami strategy. Academics thereby seek to publish their books as a series of articles, and vice versa, and to pare each publication down to the minimal acceptable length and content, with the aim of ensuring the maximum number of separate publications. Taken to an extreme, the results are likely to irritate publishers, readers, reviewers and assessors.

It is also important to be aware of your priorities. In the enthusiasm to disseminate and popularize your ideas, don't overlook single-author books and refereed articles. Whatever the past publishing conventions of your discipline may have been, you are likely to need to keep turning these out if you wish to have a successful academic career.

How to avoid getting stale

Most people, whether in academic or other walks of life, are likely to feel that they are 'getting stale' or 'going off the boil' at some point. This affects writing at least as much as other academic roles. As we have argued elsewhere, being an academic is a way of life: it can at times seem like a never ending commitment. For most academics, particularly in the humanities and social sciences, it doesn't really matter where they are in a physical sense – in the office, the lecture room, at home, at a conference, walking the dog or shopping – they are still at work. Since writing is a part of academic life which usually has to be fitted around other roles, it may be done at times and in places when you may feel least like working. So, if you begin to lose motivation, your writing may suffer most.

How can you cope when staleness hits you? One strategy is to keep your writing varied, so as to avoid, as far as possible, the possibility of staleness creeping up on you. This can be done by:

- writing on a range of topics;
- writing on your own and with others;
- writing popular and academic pieces;
- writing several things at once;
- keeping a writing journal to record and progress your ideas.

By placing diversity at the core of the writing activity, you should be able to shift from one writing project to another as you lose interest. You should also be able to keep your writing fresh by engaging in smaller-scale pieces of work, while waiting for time and inspiration to develop bigger writing projects.

The other obvious strategy is to have or develop other creative interests. It can be very stultifying to have only academic pursuits. Take up and/or maintain an interest in walking, painting, dancing, dog breeding or whatever. Make sure that you have regular holidays and 'get away from it all'. As well as clearing your mind, such breaks away from academic life can give you the space to think more creatively and clearly.

Writing as a career

Like each of the other academic roles considered in this book, writing can be seen as, or develop into, a career in its own right. This need not mean that you give up other roles or activities entirely, of course, or that you cannot continue to be employed within a university. In practice, however, it is probably less easy to make a living out of academic writing on its own than it is from the other academic roles. This is chiefly because for much academic writing the market is limited. There are only so many sociologists or philosophers, staff and students, particularly if you are restricted to the United Kingdom, who might buy your books.

Nevertheless, you might well get to the point where writing becomes your second or supplementary career. The key here is not to focus your writing on purely academic audiences, but to identify continuing mass markets or niches and devote some of your writing activity to them. For the aspiring writer, *The Writer's Handbook* (see the list of sources of further information at the end of this chapter) and the writers' professional associations, such as The Society of Authors and the Writer's Guild (see the list of organizations and journals at the end of the book) can provide invaluable advice on contracts, royalties, agents, publishers and the media.

There are at least three ways of making academic writing the core of your career:

- *Writing textbooks or course materials.* If you are good at this, and your potential audience is large enough – e.g. all A-level geography students, all new social science postgraduates – you might be able to make a living out of writing. This would mean cornering a significant part of the market, and producing texts which were regularly updated through new editions.
- *Popular books, journals and broadcast media.* Beyond the academic world, there are a large number of people who are interested in developing ideas about a range of subjects. They buy and read paperbacks and magazines, and listen to radio and television programmes, which popularize current trends in academic thinking. If you are prepared and able to adapt your skills to write for these large audiences, the financial rewards can be significant.
- *Becoming a sage or guru.* This is probably the most respectable academic strategy for making writing your career. To achieve this status, you will need, however, to publish at least one highly influential book or article, the kind to be given a prominent position on the airport bookstall and spread your reputation internationally. Once you have succeeded in gaining sagehood or gurudom, your employer is likely to be happy to let you do more of the same.

For most academics, however, regardless of how much you may enjoy writing, it is unlikely that you will be able to base your career upon it. So don't give up the day job.

Sources of further information

In this section we list a range of materials which you may find of interest in following up in more detail some of the issues discussed in this chapter. The emphasis is on recently published books in English. In each case, brief details are given as to contents and approach.

As the selection indicates, writing, like research, is one of the skills which it is assumed academics develop as postgraduate students, and which needs no further subsequent development. Thus, while there is a small, specialist, linguistic literature devoted to the nature of academic writing, comparatively little of a practical or general nature has been written about academic writing.

Becker, H. and Richards, P. (1986) *Writing for Social Scientists: How to Start and Finish Your Thesis, Book or Article.* Chicago, Chicago University Press.
  This book discusses persona and authority, editing by ear, learning to write as a professional, and getting your work out of the door.
Berry, R. (1994) *The Research Project: How to Write It*, 3rd edn. London, Routledge.
  A concise guide to the elements of writing a dissertation, research project or paper. The chapters include discussion on using a library, preparing a bibliography, taking notes and composing the paper. The text contains as an appendix the 'Guidelines for Non-sexist Language in Journals of the American Psychological Association'.
Butcher, J. (1992) *Copy-editing: The Cambridge Handbook for Editors, Authors and Publishers*, 3rd edn. Cambridge, Cambridge University Press.
  A reference guide used by editors and others preparing text for publication.

Cassell and the Publishers Association (1996) *Directory of Publishing: United Kingdom, Commonwealth and Overseas*, 22nd edn. London, Cassell.
Details of publishers, agents, associations, services and fields of activity. A separate volume covers continental Europe.

Day, A. (1996) *How to Get Research Published in Journals*. Aldershot, Gower.
Discusses your motivations, making sense of the literature, and the need to focus on your audience. Offers a guide to the process from planning to finished paper.

Dorner, J. (1992) *Writing on Disk: An A–Z Handbook of Terms, Tips and Techniques for Authors and Publishers*. Hatfield, John Taylor Book Ventures.
Covers the 'new writing techniques' opened up by computer technologies.

Hamack, A. and Kleppinger, E. (1997) *Online! A Reference Guide to Using Internet Sources*. New York, St Martin's Press.
A guide to academic writing and its relation to the internet including citation styles and hints on writing for electronic publication.

Hamack, A. and Kleppiger, G. (1997) *Beyond the MLA Handbook: Documenting Electronic Sources on the Internet*. New York, St Martin's Press.
This text gives models for citation from electronic sources using all the leading styles (Chicago, Modern Language Association, American Psychological Association, Conference of Biological Educators).

Kellogg, R. (1994) *The Psychology of Writing*. New York, Oxford University Press.
An academic study that examines issues of anxiety, motivation and knowledge and the variety of approaches and different stages of writing.

Luey, B. (1995) *Handbook for Academic Authors*, 3rd edn. New York, Cambridge University Press.
A comprehensive American guide, including chapters on the publishing partnership, journal articles, revising a dissertation, finding publishers for scholarly books and textbooks, multi-author books and books for general readers, the mechanics of authorship, electronic publishing, costs and prices, plus a useful annotated bibliography.

Modern Humanities Research Association (1991) *MHRA Style Book: Notes for Authors, Editors and Writers of Theses*, 4th edn. London, MHRA.
Useful guide to typescript preparation, spelling, abbreviations, punctuation, capitals, italics, quotations, references, indexes and much more.

Sadler, D. (1990) *Up the Publication Road: A Guide to Publishing in Scholarly Journals for Academics, Researchers and Graduate Students*, 2nd edn. Campbelltown, NSW, Higher Education Research and Development Society of Australasia, second edition.
Australian book giving general guidance on what to write, how to write and the publication process.

Schwartz, M. (1995) *Guidelines for Bias-free Writing*. Bloomington, Indiana University Press.
This text gives advice on bias-free writing in relation to gender, 'race', ethnicity, citizenship, nationality, religion, disabilities, medical conditions, sexual orientation and age.

Turner, B. (ed.) (1997) *The Writer's Handbook 1998*. London, Macmillan.
Published annually, and an invaluable resource for the serious writer. This is a vast directory of guidance, contacts and information on publishers, agents, newspapers, magazines, news agencies, television, radio, film, theatre, associations, societies, services and much more.

Zimmer, W. (1990) *On Writing Well: An Informal Guide to Writing Nonfiction*. New York, HarperCollins.
Three sections cover principles, forms and attitudes. Discusses style, audience, interviews, business writing, criticism and humour, and writing with a word processor.

8 | MANAGING

Introduction

This chapter considers the role of managing in academic careers. Historically, the cult of the amateur has been as influential in higher education management as in teaching. Until comparatively recently, there were relatively few professional managers working in British universities and colleges. Most academics who took on managerial roles could do so part-time or in the latter part of their careers.

Nowadays, however, universities and colleges are seen as complex, multi-million-pound businesses, subject to numerous external checks and constraints. It is considered that the operation of a mass higher education system can no longer be safely left to the academics, but requires the close involvement and (increasingly) direction of a growing cadre of managers, both within and outside institutions of higher education.

Three trends may be identified as a result of this development:

1 There are growing numbers of opportunities – for younger and more experienced staff, academics and non-academics – to pursue interesting and demanding careers within academic management.
2 There are rising concerns among academic staff about the increasing managerialism apparent within higher education. Many feel that their institutions are now run by managers rather than led by academics.
3 These opportunities and concerns are reflected in an expanding literature concerning higher education management, focusing in particular on how to manage, the experience of management, and critiques of management practices. Some of this literature is referred to in this chapter or listed in the **Sources of further information** section at the end.

This chapter assumes that most, if not all, academics are likely to assume some managerial responsibility at any one time. Some may wish to enter higher education management early in their careers, while for others this may become a major role later on or for discrete periods. At the same time, all academics share the experience of being managed, so it is doubly important to understand and feel able to respond appropriately to the process of managing.

The chapter is organized into eight main sections:

- **We are all managers now**, which discusses the increasing importance of management in academic life, and indicates how it relates to other academic roles;
- **Academic managerial roles**, which outlines the range of managerial tasks undertaken by academics;
- **Committee work**, which looks at the different tasks involved in the most common institutional or inter-institutional management role;
- **Running a department**, which discusses the varied duties of heads of department or centre, from the mundane to the visionary;
- **Quality audit and assessment**, which examines the increasing involvement of external agents in monitoring the work of academics, and responses to this;
- **Working with support staff**, which talks about the work of secretaries and technicians, and academics' relations with these crucial members of staff;
- **Legal matters**, which outlines some of the legal issues involved in working in academe, whether as manager or managed;
- **Managing as a career**, which considers the option of making management the core of an academic career.

At the end of the chapter a selection of sources of further information is listed.

We are all managers now

> The management of the curriculum, if this is taken to mean that decisions about its aims and objectives, content, teaching methods and patterns of assessment are taken by others than those intimately engaged in its delivery, is seen by many teachers in higher education, especially in the traditional universities, potentially as a threat to academic freedom, an invasion of student–teacher intimacy, a denial of professional expertise and an assault on collegiality ... Such criticisms are certainly exaggerated.
>
> (Scott and Watson 1994: 33)

The new management discourses of the 1990s have emerged in a context that seeks economy and efficiency, whatever the rhetoric of quality and choice may claim. Human resource management and total quality management are two particularly powerful forms of this discourse, but although they seem to stress groupwork, cohesiveness and collaboration, their origins do not lie in any recognition of disempowerment, but in the entrepreneurialism of the 1980s. These new discourses are linked to the reassertion of management's right to manage, and emerge against a context of significant unemployment and diminished trade union power. As a consequence they may be understood as representing more effective management tools, producing internalised controls that serve to ensure that performance indicators and other targets are met.

(Ozga and Walker 1995: 37)

Higher education is undoubtedly a large and complex sector, in receipt of substantial funding from external sources, and with integral links to many economic and other activities throughout society. It is also subject to increasingly close scrutiny from a range of governmental and other bodies. This climate of intervention has buttressed the view, indicated in the first quotation above, that institutions, departments and individual academics can only survive and prosper by regularly demonstrating their fitness to manage. Yet, as the second quotation indicates, this view is highly contested, and regarded by others as enabling management to assert greater power and control.

One of the key places where this contest takes place is over the relation between hierarchy and collegiality:

Hierarchy assumes that the individuals in designated roles possess authority to affect the behaviour of others. Collegium designates a structure in which members have equal authority to participate in decisions which are binding on each of them. It usually implies the individuals have discretion to perform their main operations in their own way, subject only to minimal collegial controls (on, for example, the use of resources and the observance of proper procedures in the admission, teaching and assessing of students). As a consequence of the duality of hierarchy and collegium, academic institutions contain systems of executive roles and systems of committees. They seldom resolve the overlaps and conflicts between them in any logical way.

(Becher and Kogan 1992: 72)

Universities, in Becher and Kogan's terms, operate through a mixture of hierarchy and collegium. As they suggest, these modes of operation may be contradictory, or they may rub along more or less successfully. In the latter case, universities may be seen as relatively benign, if rationally inefficient, semi-democratic organizations.

Those who subscribe to a belief in the existence at some time in the past of a golden age of universities may argue that some, at least, were originally established as self-governing, independent corporations of scholars. A glance back at Box 5.1 confirms this as a historic interpretation. Whether or not many universities ever operated for any length of time in this way, however, it has to be doubted that there is any higher education institution in existence today in which all members of staff are valued and treated equally.

Many regret the extent to which managerialism has come to dominate the operation of universities, and, in particular, the increase in the size, scope and degree of control exercised by central university staff and external agencies.

These are seen as displacing what were more 'traditional' academic values and professionalism. Yet, if most academics are, in some sense, managers now, it has to be recognized that some are more so than others. The 1996 Commission on University Career Opportunity (CUCO) survey of senior staff on gender, ethnicity and disability found that only 1 per cent of respondents were from ethnic minorities, that only 1 per cent of disabled people held senior positions, and that the number of women in senior posts in higher education was 18 per cent (CUCO 1997).

In delineating management as an all-encompassing feature of academic employment we would suggest that it can be viewed as a form of simultaneous internal and external control. There are, for example, the subjective and objective elements involved in managing oneself. It is also likely that, in working with a number of others (students, staff, external partners) over a range of different activities, attention has to be paid to how these relationships are enacted.

More formalized management responsibilities include directly managing others as a module leader, as the leader of a teaching team, or as the fund-holder for a research grant. Further on in a career, one may become involved in leading a department or centre, chairing a faculty or university committee, an inter-university working party, a professional association, or a national or international group. Finally, there are those senior career positions associated with running an institution, a research council, a funding agency or an international body.

This simple reiteration of increasingly senior managerial roles within universities suggests one important motivation for being an academic manager. This is that it is a critical, possibly now the most critical, means for gaining promotion and advancement in an academic career. It is still possible, of course, to rise through the academic ranks on the basis of the quality of one's research, teaching, writing and/or networking, though to do so is likely to involve taking on an increasing management load. For these careerist reasons, an interest in academic management may enhance employability and promotion prospects. Indeed, as Spurling (1997) indicates, insufficient management experience and limited knowledge of formal committee work, and the informal work that underpins it, were among the drawbacks of accelerated promotion schemes.

Yet it is the case that many academics shy away from or disdain management, or simply prefer to focus their attention on teaching, research, writing or networking. Initial academic selection is, after all, largely on the basis of the latter skills, and few have received, or subsequently receive, much in the way of management training. So, if your skills and interests include managing the activities of your colleagues and their students, you might be well advised to emphasize this aspect in your career. This doesn't mean, though, that you should neglect other academic roles, since academics resent being managed by those whom they feel lack academic credibility in their own right.

When managing is seen in this way, as a role endemic to academic life, it can, as we have suggested, be seen as operating on at least three levels: managing yourself, managing others, and managing your manager. It behoves all academics to have some appreciation of these three levels if they are to function effectively and enjoy their working careers.

Managing yourself

There is much discussion in the contemporary management literature regarding vision and mission. The significance of this is to stress that goals and objectives need clear articulation and sharing if they are to be achieved. Covey (1992) illustrates this point by suggesting that you think about your own funeral. What would you want your family and friends to say about you and your life? What will they say? The point, of course, is not only to encourage clarity about personal ambitions but also to recognize the values at their heart. Covey argues that many of the ordinary decisions one needs to make in daily life become much simpler when they are conducted within ethically based systems of behaviour.

As an academic manager, the most basic and continuing responsibility, and one shared by all academics, is self-management. This clearly involves rather more than using the available time effectively to carry out a variety of roles and tasks – a 'simple' matter of time management. Managing yourself also involves having a sense of direction, of the alternatives available to you, and of how you might progress them. It necessitates a degree of self-knowledge, and a willingness to be accommodating and collaborative, where appropriate, in dealings with others; but also being suitably assertive in safeguarding and developing your position and career, and those of your colleagues.

Box 8.1 seeks to draw a set of distinctions between groups and teams. Underlying these distinctions are fundamental, value-led questions about those relations. Do you, for example, see organizational groupings as mainly administrative or as about mutual interdependence? Are you cautious or open and honest in your communications? How might you answer these questions as either a member of a group or team or a manager of one? Inevitably, then, managing yourself involves managing your relations with other academics and hence, to some extent, managing others.

Managing others

To enjoy some success in your academic life, or even just enjoy that life, will require the use of interpersonal skills. This applies whether your motivation is to be left alone so that you can do your own thing, or to enlist cooperation in some more collaborative endeavour. Both of these goals will require you to make a case, more or less effectively, for the course of action you prefer to take.

Many, perhaps most, academics will, at some time in their careers, also exercise a more direct responsibility for managing at least some aspects of the work of some of their colleagues. The level and extent of that responsibility may, as already indicated, vary widely, from, for example, overseeing the work of a single research assistant to running a large institution. The particular case of running a department is considered later in this chapter. However extensive your responsibility is, you are half-way to possessing the capabilities required if you are conscious of your own values in relation to styles of management and leadership. Box 8.2 offers some practical ideas for both managers and managed, and suggests one possible set of values.

Box 8.1: Groups versus teams

	Groups	Teams
Interdependence	Members think they are grouped together for administrative purposes only.	Members recognise their interdependence and understand both personal and team goals are best accomplished with mutual support.
Focus	Members tend to focus on themselves because they are not sufficiently involved in planning the unit's objectives.	Members feel a sense of ownership for their jobs and unit because they are committed to goals they helped to establish.
Objectives	Members are told what to do rather than being asked what the best approach would be.	Members contribute to the organisation's success by applying their unique talent and knowledge to team objectives.
Trust	Members distrust the motives of colleagues because they do not understand the role of other members.	Members work in a climate of trust and are encouraged to express openly ideas, opinions, disagreements and feelings.
Communication	Members are so cautious about what they say that real understanding is not possible.	Members practise open and honest communication.
Training	Members may receive good training but are limited in applying it to the job by the supervisor or other group members.	Members are encouraged to develop skills and apply what they learn on the job.
Conflict	Members find themselves in conflict situations which they do not know how to resolve.	Members recognise conflict is a normal aspect of human interaction but they view such situations as an opportunity for new ideas and creativity.
Decision-making	Members may or may not participate in decisions affecting the team.	Members participate in decisions affecting the team but understand their leader must make a final ruling whenever the team cannot decide, or an emergency exists.

Source: Maddux (1994: 10–12).

Box 8.2: Practical ideas for managers and managed

For managers:

1 Give clear, specific messages about constraints and opportunities. Avoid the sense of mystery, and/or conspiracy, about the 'management's' assessment of the strategic position of the institution.
2 Don't oversell either threats or opportunities. Resist the temptation to attempt to scare, or to bribe, colleagues into the appropriate responses.
3 Prepare step changes in practice in advance. Sudden, institution-wide edicts rarely work, and often stimulate sophisticated and effective resistance strategies.
4 Protect the academic infrastructure, even if it means hard choices. If you let a piece of the infrastructure – say, a library collection, a research group, or a curriculum area like teacher education – go, you never get it back.
5 Don't get disengaged from the operation.

For the managed:

1 Establish an agreed pattern of workload early. One of our starkest lacks, within the university, is an effective and comprehensive mutual understanding of obligations.
2 Think about the purposes of assessment. This is perhaps our biggest challenge to practise as the system expands.
3 Don't feel you have to do it all yourself: build teams. One of the major morale traps, for teachers especially, is the effect of making major changes alone, and feeling that they are 'letting go' or 'letting the side down'.
4 Welcome rather than deny responsibility. Responsibility, for budgetary control or for 'quality', can and should be an asset and not a liability; in particular, it can get you into the strategic planning debate at a different level.
5 Don't turn the department into a laager. Team building goes wider than the department.
6 Above all, think hard before you invite students (and other clients) to collude in your own frustration. Remember that they only get one shot at an experience which for us is a career-long privilege.

Source: Watson (1994: 84–5).

Managing your manager

Just as we are all managers now, so we all have managers. In addition to an ability to manage yourself and to manage others, it is also important successfully to manage relations with managers. This is particularly difficult if the values and management style of managed and manager conflict. In such cases, your life may become very difficult. You will end up 'being managed' autocratically, with little or no say in how this is done.

In our view, it is counter-productive for those exercising management responsibilities to deny conflicts or suppress diversity of values. The tensions inherent in institutional adjustment will keep being reproduced if they are ignored. Yet the skills needed to manage contradiction and mediate in conflicts are still only possessed by a minority of managers. Don't forget, however, that they can be learned or brought in.

Managing your manager will involve you in anticipating and negotiating their expectations of you, and in constructively responding to and supporting their initiatives. More proactively, it will probably involve you in actively contributing to the development of the centre, department, faculty or university you are working in, and perhaps even in taking on some of your manager's responsibilities.

A willingness voluntarily to shoulder some of the mundane, routine and time-consuming work that has to be undertaken, and to do this work well, can be an excellent means for developing a good working relationship with your manager. Since some of this work may well be delegated to you anyway, by getting in first you may have more say over which tasks you take on.

Academic managerial roles

The variety of managerial roles exercised by academics may be conceptualized in a number of ways. Two are used here: the first, from paperwork to politics, is based on the mode of managerial engagement; while the second, institutional or disciplinary focus, identifies the arena(s) in which the individual operates. Some strategies for coping with the routine endemic in many managerial (as well as other) roles are then considered.

From paperwork to politics

Political skill is crucial to success ... for all those in the organization ... Real, lasting support ... only comes with one thing – success – so an essential part of the 'politics' ... is choosing the areas of priority [which] will make the most noticeable impact on the organization's effectiveness, then succeeding in those areas and ensuring that the success is broadcast in order to build on it. In other words: *Find out what they want. Give it to them; and be seen to give it to them.*

(Harrison 1992: 106–7, emphasis in original)

Supplying an answer to the question 'what is management?' is by no means as straightforward as mainstream, or even more progressive, texts on management are inclined to suggest. Received management wisdom takes it for granted that the social divisions between managers and managed are either natural (e.g. based upon superior intelligence or education) and/or functionally necessary. Received wisdom then proceeds to concentrate upon refining the technocratic means of raising employee commitment and productivity. This philosophy, in our view, is symptomatic of a way of making sense of management that *reduces the political to the technical*, and represents the politics of management practice in terms of the development and application of formal procedures and impartial, 'professional' skills and competences ... the political quality of management is denied or trivialized ... Rarely is the darker side of management theory and practice acknowledged or considered, and then most often it is presented as an aberrant and avoidable deviation from the normal state of affairs.

(Alvesson and Willmott 1996: 37)

As these quotations indicate, there are a variety of ways, not necessarily mutually exclusive, of thinking about managerial roles. The first three managerial modes identified in this subsection – administration, execution and development – present management in technical and rational terms. The fourth and final mode identified, however, views it as inherently political.

Administration concerns the basic paperwork that has to be engaged with, whether in academic or other positions. This includes the maintenance of necessary records, such as a personal diary, files on students, names and addresses of professional contacts, statements of expenditure, research documentation and so forth. It also covers responses to requests for information, such as from prospective students, colleagues in other institutions, and those maintaining research databases or preparing quality assessment documents. The processes involved in quality audit and assessment are considered in more detail in a later section.

If you are fortunate, you may have some clerical or secretarial assistance in dealing with the steadily growing avalanche of paperwork which afflicts academics, but you are very unlikely to escape it altogether.

Execution has to do with the oversight, direction and control of the resources, both human and non-human, available to carry out particular tasks. Such tasks may include, for example, the delivery of a particular course or degree programme, running a conference, editing a journal, directing a research project, or chairing a department or research centre. The particular case of running a department is considered in more detail later in this chapter. Editing a journal and running a conference are discussed in the sections on **Journals and newsletters** and **Conferences, seminars and societies** in Chapter 4. Such responsibilities may be a limited involvement, a small part of your academic life, or an open-ended commitment. They may impact upon you during specific periods of your career, or dominate the whole of your working life.

Development is an aspect of academic work which is often overlooked. While administration and execution have to do with day-to-day tasks and existing resources, development is concerned with change and innovation. This may mean, for example, the introduction of new courses or programmes of study, bidding for research funds, setting up a new journal, or creating a department or centre from scratch. While all academics are involved in administration and most, at least to some extent, in the execution of tasks, many may only occasionally engage with developmental activities. For some, though – including all of those with staff, course or research development responsibilities, as well as many in new departments or institutions – this may be their main activity.

Politics is a term which has a variety of meanings depending on the particular context in which it is used. While it may refer to the processes involved in negotiating and agreeing strategies within and between institutions, it also, as the remarks of Alvesson and Willmott quoted above indicate, may refer to the 'darker' aspects of organizational life. As such, it is an activity both publicly disdained

---

Box 8.3: Negative politics and what to do about it

The most pernicious political operators are personally motivated to work behind the scenes, blocking proposals they do not like. They are envious and jealous and act accordingly . . . There are operators who do not know their own motives and would not recognise themselves when reading this description . . .

The signs that operators are at work . . . include the following:
* unexplained and apparently arbitrary delays in decision making
* hidden decisions
* people evading responsibility
* excessive lobbying
* the formation of orchestrated offensives against individuals and groups
* memorandum wars
* whisper campaigns
* snide comments and criticisms

When you spot this behaviour, find out who the operators are, how they are working, and what they are trying to achieve. In the early stages, direct and open confrontation can bring an end to the campaign. It is not always possible to do this; political activity can unsettle those with formal authority, who may take the easy option and suppress anything which threatens them.

The best course of action is, whenever you can, to bring the issue into the open. Do not give into the temptation to fight back with the same political weapons. Do not lie or shade the truth. When you are baited, never respond without thinking through the correct principles and only act when you are sure of them . . . Do not let negative politics sap your self-confidence and foster self-doubt. Evaluate what has happened or is happening to see what you can learn from it.

(Johnson 1996: 61)

---

and engaged in with great (private) pleasure by some. Alternatively, being 'politically astute', according to Harrison, is something which can be learnt. Presented in this way it becomes a techno-rational activity of the wise careerist.

Box 8.3 describes what can happen in an organization when politics becomes negative, and what an individual might be able to do about it. This is an all too common experience, both in academe and elsewhere. Dealing with it can be very disabling: this is another reason why it is important to be aware of, and have confidence in, your own values.

Institutional or disciplinary focus?

An alternative way of thinking about academic management is in terms of whether the focus is on the institution or the discipline. At the level of the department, these two foci might be seen as being in some sort of balance. Thus, the department is part of an institution, relies upon it for its infrastructure and other kinds of support, and is also affected by its particular nature. Yet the department may also be seen as the institution's representative of a much wider body of academics, those committed to the same discipline who are based in similar departments both nation-wide and overseas.

As indicated in Chapter 2 (see the section on **The changing nature of higher education**), for much of the twentieth century it has been common to think of individual academics' allegiance as being primarily to their discipline rather than to their institution. To use a sporting analogy, like football players, many academics seek to further their careers through successive movements or promotions between similar departments in different institutions, often with the aim of ending up in one of the leading departments in their subject area. To an extent, it doesn't matter which university or college they work for, so long as the department in which they are based is suitable (though departmental and institutional quality are, of course, linked).

This 'tribes and territories' perspective on academe, which depicts intellectuals as separate 'non-communicating cognitive groups' (Morley and Walsh 1996: 4), presents problems for academics who work in interdisciplinary areas. This is partly due to the lack of disciplinary identity, which is so important to developing a reputation, but also a result of the seemingly inherent logic in the relation between organizational structure and subject. Such logic is supported through quality assessments, audits and inspections:

> Teaching quality assessments are taking place on a rolling programme. Academic *subjects* are inspected which means that departments are the focus, and quality assurance mechanisms, linked to both the HEFCE teaching assessments and the Higher Education Quality Council quality assessment, are based on *departmental* audits. All courses have to belong to departments and when the various auditors do their inspections, they inspect departments. Ultimately, it will become almost impossible for courses not to be based in a department, which, at the University of Bristol and elsewhere, means based in a discipline. What then happens to interdisciplinary work?
>
> (Bird 1996: 153)

At the same time, the recent growth in the size of the higher education enterprise, and the consequent increase in the importance of its management, has tended to shift the balance of allegiance away from the discipline and towards the institution. Nevertheless, for the individual academic there is still some degree of choice as to whether a career emphasizes discipline or institution, or balances these elements. Those with an inclination towards management might exercise it in either or both of these arenas, seeking to take on increasing managerial responsibilities within their university or within their field of study. In the former case, the route might lead through running a department to faculty or cross-institutional roles. In the latter, it might involve taking on offices within professional bodies, associations or journals.

Balancing boredom with excitement

Box 8.4 offers two contrasting views on the individual academic's involvement in administration. These different perspectives relate to the opportunities for

---

Box 8.4: Administration: boring or exciting?

- However you look at academic management and conceive of the various roles it comprises, and almost regardless of the extent to which you are involved, it remains the case that much of management is a day-to-day, humdrum and, frankly, boring activity. Many of my tasks require more time spent on paperwork than politics: filling in forms, filing, reading memoranda and checking regulations. The truly innovative or exciting elements are few and far between for most people.

- I might be a graduate but I was really pleased to get this part-time administrative job. I have a lot of responsibility for keeping the record system, a chance for making recommendations for improvement and a chance to be proactive. I get plenty of appreciation and expect to get excellent references. The department gives me time off for lectures and I don't pay fees for my higher degree. This makes up for the rather basic pay.

---

new skills to be developed at different stages of a career, and to the pragmatics of personal circumstances. Whether boring or not, however, the minutiae of administration, marking, assessment, record keeping and so forth can too easily spread into those more precious moments when one wishes to focus on research, teaching, writing or networking. How therefore to retain a sense of control, and possibly keep some of the boredom at bay?

Those who regularly attend committee meetings may have noticed their colleagues enter with a clutch of papers, to which they intermittently give intense attention. While paying some attention to the meeting, they are working on their 'in' tray. In a similar way, advertisements encourage us to travel by train by stressing the opportunities this gives for working, something which cannot be done so easily when driving. This strategy of task simultaneity, of interleaving small amounts of routine administration into opportune moments, can, of course, be used at other times: while watching the swimming gala at school, in the doctor's waiting room, while waiting for a student, and so forth.

An alternative, or complementary, strategy is to reserve certain periods of the day for managerial tasks; and to endeavour to keep other times, and perhaps whole days, free for other roles or activities. This may not always be feasible, of course, but, without attempting such compartmentalization, you may find that managerial roles absorb more and more of your working day.

Committee work

Committee work is probably the most common way in which individual academics get involved in institutional or inter-institutional management. Indeed, it must be rare for an academic who has been in post for a few years not to be so involved, or at least to have been invited to become involved. While universities and colleges regularly prune their committee structures as managerial cycles

---

Box 8.5: Functions of the committee system

- assuring the quality of educational provision;
- defining the institution and its work;
- developing policies and procedures;
- making one level and area of work visible to another;
- bringing new areas of activity into being;
- establishing the institutional pecking order;
- legitimatizing dubious political activity; and
- tempering the power of the executive system.

(Ashcroft and Foreman-Peck 1995: 36)

---

pass, they just as regularly multiply again, while *ad hoc* working groups rise and wither (or are forgotten) at even greater speed. Every discipline or subject area also has a range of regional, national and international societies and associations, all of which come equipped with committees of various sorts.

For those who enjoy committee work – and there are some – the scope for involvement is huge. For those who don't, on the other hand, avoiding any involvement may be difficult. While we may express scorn at those who seem to spend their lives moving from one committee room to another, committees do serve important functions, as Box 8.5 indicates. They serve, in the terms employed by Becher and Kogan in the quotation used earlier, to link the collegium with the hierarchy; to allow academics and others some kind of involvement in decision-making processes, whether at departmental, university or national level. In career terms, they also offer opportunities to be institutionally visible, which matters when much of the routine associated with academic tasks is invisible. It is important, therefore, to understand the workings of relevant committees, and to be able to contribute to them appropriately and effectively when the occasion arises.

Characteristics

Most, but not all, academic committees share a number of characteristics. They usually have:

- chairs, secretaries and ordinary members;
- written agendas, established (but perhaps unwritten) procedures for discussing or debating items, and for reaching and acting upon decisions;
- written minutes, which record the discussion and, particularly, any decisions taken and who is to action them;
- set frequencies and lengths of meetings;
- reporting arrangements from or to other committees.

That said, committees also vary a great deal in terms of their mode of operation and degree of formality. Their members may, for example, be there in their own right or be acting as representatives. The intention may be to seek to network, to promote particular ideas or interests, or to resolve differences.

Box 8.6: Some tips for meetings

- be sure why you are there. Are you there representing yourself or others?
- are you prepared? Have you read the papers and do you know where you might make a comment?
- can you deal with public criticism or disagreement? If not, get some help or training?
- can you argue a point without being out of control? If not, deal with this!
- can you cope when someone steals your idea? There are strategies you can learn and practice.
- can you resist jumping to your feet to hand round the coffee?
- do you know and follow the codes of behaviour: on dress, for example (a suit means business, a suit jacket kept on gives you authority) and on the language of the meeting (is it formal or informal; do you sit or stand to make your point?)
- can you project your voice without waivering? If not, get some help.

(King 1993: 34)

Box 8.6 presents some very useful tips for those unfamiliar with committee practices, or other forms of meeting. In a number of places, it suggests that you should seek advice or help if you are unable to perform in a certain approved fashion: if you cannot cope with being publicly criticized, cannot argue a point without getting out of control, cannot cope when someone steals your idea, cannot project your voice without waivering. These are all aspects of the cultural codes of committee behaviour, which are deemed to enhance your effectiveness as a committee contributor. If you want to change committee cultures, you'll need to get networking!

Chairs

Perhaps the key member of a committee is its chair, though some committees may operate without one or with some shared arrangement. Certainly, the effectiveness of the chair has a powerful impact upon the usefulness and enjoyment of committee work for those concerned. Box 8.7 offers a series of humorous characterizations of a range of dysfunctional committee chairs. Anyone with anything beyond a basic experience of committee work should recognize some of these characters with amusement, regret and/or disdain.

Most committee chairs are probably not as bad as these stereotypes, however, and manage to deal with the necessary business more or less efficiently. Unfortunately, if the chair of a committee you are on is really ineffective, there may be little you can or (politically) should do about it. This will apply with particular strength if the chair is of superior status to you, and your views do not appear to be widely shared by other committee members. The best advice is probably to share your concerns with a senior colleague you trust, put your energies elsewhere, and/or to wait until the chair's term of office expires.

Box 8.7: Chairs I have sat under

- The *actor manager*, flamboyant, oratorical, charismatic even. Better suited for big occasions where he (it is usually a he) can stand rather than sit and can orchestrate other role players as they pop up to do their bit.
- The *philosopher king*, who believes it is better to travel enquiringly than to arrive. He or she will indulge in Socratic dialogue in a peripatetic fashion, walking all round an issue to view its many facets.
- The *flight lieutenant*, a reluctant chair who adopts flight strategies so that someone else can be in command: referral and deferral are the prime tactics.
- The *anal retentive*, tightly controlled, formal, obsessed by procedure not process, task not mission, and restricting the imagination of the group by an inability to tolerate even slight disorder. He or she may indulge in rites of personal hygiene as an obsessive action.
- The *paranoid*, for whom any comment is a criticism, any suggestion a challenge, any question a revolutionary challenge.
- The *hippy happy anarchist*, also known as *laissez-faire*, for whom time is passed, not spent, and timetables are a control device of a capitalist corporate bureaucracy . . .
- The *benevolent dictator*, who may smile and smile and be a villain. The sort in my acquaintance who, after 20 minutes' debate of an issue, would pull a paper from an inside pocket and say, 'Well, ladies and gentlemen, that's all been very interesting; now, here is what we will decide'. And the troops lined up, the hands went up and the show moved on to the next business.

(McNay 1996: 124)

If you have acted as a committee chair yourself – a role which has similarities to that of running a department, the subject of the following section – you may even, if you are honest, recognize elements of your own character in Box 8.7. Reading between the lines of these characterizations, it is also possible to identify the main qualities an effective committee chair might possess. They will include:

- an awareness of the duties and powers of the committee, and their limitations;
- an openness to contributions, and to the sharing of information, and a desire to involve all committee members in deliberations;
- a clear sense of direction, and an ability to move the committee's discussions along and see that they are translated into action.

One of the key duties usually exercised by the committee chair is setting the agenda for its meetings, though this will usually involve some consultation, most notably with that other key member of the well-found committee, its secretary. Committee agendas and minutes shape the public record of what took place and provide much of the material for ongoing discussion.

Secretary

The duties of the committee secretary consist of advising the chair and members, particularly about issues of procedure and powers, maintaining a record of its discussions and decisions (the minutes), and helping to ensure that these decisions are acted upon.

Taking minutes is an art form, though practice differs from institution to institution and committee to committee. Minutes are redolent with language conventions: items are 'discussed', documents are 'noted', decisions are 'agreed'. Their language can also be very legalistic, to guard against possible challenges. Before taking on the role of committee secretary, some training on minute-taking and other practices may be available within the institution. If not, discussion with the previous secretary and the current chair, and a careful perusal of recent sets of committee minutes, will probably prove extremely useful.

Five standard components of committee minutes may be recognized:

- a list of those present;
- a record of the items discussed;
- some indication of the nature of that discussion;
- a record of any decisions taken;
- an indication of who is responsible for actioning those decisions.

The greatest variability in practice concerns the third of these items, which may be virtually omitted or fulsome. The fifth element is also sometimes missing, though usually at least implicit.

Other committee roles

The committee chair and secretary aside, the committee may contain only a few or many other members. Some of the most commonly recognized committee types are characterized in Box 8.8 in the guise of animals. Fortunately, this box also contains some suggestions for dealing with some of these contributors, recognizing that many of them may have valuable contributions to offer.

Most academic committees seek to achieve some form of consensus, though this is not to say that they do not have heated arguments from time to time (sometimes about relatively trivial issues). They are also, however, arenas where power is exercised, and where the relative status of different members is likely to be important. Unless they are to be simply vehicles for approving decisions favoured by those with power – with papers tabled rather than read – it is critically important that all members are respected and enabled to contribute their talents.

Running a department

As already indicated, the department may be regarded as the key organizational unit in higher education, representing the conjunction of institutional and disciplinary interests. It follows, then, that the head or chair of a department is seen as a key managerial position:

Box 8.8: Committee contributors

- The *budgie*. A constant chatterer, distracting to neighbours and to the business of the meeting. Shame them into shutting up . . . or ask them for a contribution . . .
- The *starling* interrupts. Reciprocate, and go formal so that he or she waits until called.
- The *kookaburra* jokes, which can be useful to help [the] group process but needs to be limited. . . . Train kookaburras by a quiet word outside.
- The *bullfrog* speaks loud, long and often, but without substance most of the time. The Open University senate has a three-minute rule in its standing orders and time flies for bullfrogs when they are enjoying themselves, until choked off.
- The *bulldog*. An aggressive growler, somewhat slow, who needs to be given useful tasks to perform . . . and praised if he or she isn't to become . . .
- The *wolf*, who may get personal in attacks and may attract a pack if not controlled.
- The *white rabbit* is constantly late. Don't make white rabbits comfortable when they arrive.
- The *hedgehog*: prickly, reserved but with some wisdom. Prime hedgehogs before the meeting that you will seek advice and show respect for it.
- The *cat*: a loner, not interested in others' views or the business of the meeting. Decide how far the cat's self-alienation is infectious: one can be left alone without harm.
- The *monkey* thinks he or she knows all the answers . . . Accept the monkey's ideas as proposals to return to, which gives others time for more mature reflection.
- The *ferret* . . . always wants more facts and is often suspicious of . . . anything less than concrete. Useful in the secondary stages . . . : make the ferret a subgroup member with the remit to uncover the facts.
- The *fox* is there to trap the chair. Try a role reversal by asking him or her to make positive proposals, not to snipe at others.
- The *rook* is a lawyer . . . full of points of order and challenges to the chair. Use the democracy to establish process norms within the group . . .
- The *horse* is a keen, intelligent, hard worker. Public according of esteem is often a motivation stimulus, so give credit and praise, but don't overload.

(McNay 1996: 127–8)

Academic chairs occupy a pivotal position in the organisation of higher education. An estimated 80 per cent of all university decisions are made at the departmental level, and the position of department chair is the most common entry point into the hierarchy of academic administration.

(Seagren *et al*. 1993: 1)

As Box 8.9 indicates, this role should not be assumed lightly: a truly fearsome list of responsibilities comes with being head of department. Not only that, but their pivotal position means that, like middle managers generally, heads of department often feel like the meat in somebody else's sandwich. Nevertheless, there are some benefits:

Box 8.9: Responsibilities of heads of department

Governing the department
- conducting departmental meetings;
- establishing departmental committees;
- establishing and implementing departmental plans and goals in collaboration with staff;
- preparing the department for accreditation and evaluation;
- serving as an advocate for the department to higher administration.

Managing instruction
- scheduling classes;
- managing of off-campus programmes;
- supervising and scheduling examinations;
- managing space and budgets;
- keeping department curriculum and programmes vigorous and up to date.

Managing personnel issues
- selecting and recruiting staff;
- assigning responsibilities to staff;
- initiating and managing staff development activities;
- evaluating staff performance;
- supervising promotion and tenure recommendations;
- invoking termination proceedings;
- participating in grievance proceedings;
- making merit recommendations;
- dealing with unsatisfactory staff performance;
- keeping staff informed of department and college activities;
- preventing and resolving conflicts;
- promoting affirmative action.

Promoting development
- fostering good teaching;
- helping in the formulation of professional development plans;
- stimulating research and publication;
- encouraging staff participation in professional activities;
- representing the department at professional meetings.

Working with students and student issues
- recruiting, selecting, and advising students;
- working with the student government;
- encouraging student participation in department governance;
- overseeing financial aid.

Representing the department to the institution
- interpreting the discipline to rest of the institution;
- representing the department in front of the administration;
- building and maintaining departmental reputation.

Serving as link to external groups
- coordinating activities with outside groups;
- ceremonial functions;

- appearance at community functions;
- attending meetings of professional groups;
- processing departmental correspondence and requests for information;
- completing forms and surveys.

Managing the budget and resources
- preparing and proposing departmental budgets;
- seeking outside funding;
- encouraging staff to write proposals;
- administering the departmental budget;
- setting priorities for the use of travel funds;
- preparing annual reports.

Supervising the departmental office
- managing facilities and equipment;
- monitoring building security and maintenance;
- correspondence, files and paper flow;
- supervising and evaluating clerical and technical staff.

Source: Green and McDade (1991: 139–41).

It is still worth while being a head of department, for a large number of reasons. As head one can speak for the department; the head chairs meetings and thus arranges the agenda and controls the shape of the discussion; controls the distribution of funds for equipment and supplies; has first call on secretarial services; can allocate and reallocate the use of premises available to the department; influences and has a formal responsibility for the distribution of the teaching load and the course content, and certainly decides what he or she will teach at what hour of which day; influences and sometimes controls staff appointments and student admissions; chairs the board of examiners; and has a role in higher policy-making as a member of the faculty board and the Senate.

(Bland 1990: 56)

The detail of the responsibilities listed in Box 8.9 will vary from department to department and university to university, but most heads will exercise most of these, and perhaps other, roles. The period during which heads exercise their responsibilities also varies, with some elected for a few years at a time while others are appointed for an indefinite period. Heads may have considerable support, in the form of administrative, clerical, financial or technical officers, if their department is large or complex. Some of their responsibilities may be devolved to other members of the department, particularly where a number of distinct activities are carried out. Or they may just work with several staff and a single secretary.

A number of desirable or important characteristics for any head of department are suggested by Box 8.9. Clearly, they will need to be able to cope with a great deal of stress, yet still gain some enjoyment from the job. They will need to have a detailed understanding of both the department's activities and its place within

---

Box 8.10: The ten most important headship functions, as ranked by staff and heads

Ranking by staff
1 Serving as an advocate for the department
2 Considers staff's points of view
3 Developing long-range plans for the department
4 Consulting staff and encouraging them to communicate ideas on departmental matters
5 Encouraging good teaching in the department
6 Implementing long-range plans for the department
7 Trusts staff's abilities
8 Dealing with unsatisfactory staff performance effectively
9 Maintaining morale
10 Stimulating research and publications

Ranking by heads
1 Selecting staff members
2 Maintaining morale
3 Developing long-range plans for the department
4 Implementing long-range plans for the department
5 Stimulating research and publications
6 Serving as an advocate for the department
7 Evaluating staff performance
8 Supporting staff subjected to unfair criticism or treatment
9 Encouraging good teaching in the department
10 Encouraging all staff to perform at a high standard

Source: Moses and Roe (1990: 36–7, 64).

---

the university. They will need to be able to get things done on schedule. They should also have the interpersonal skills associated with getting on, listening to, involving and working with all sorts of people (students, junior and senior staff, administrators, parents, funders) within and without the department. In short, they need to have leadership qualities.

Unfortunately, it is still the case that many confuse leadership with imposing one's own ideas, and substitute bullying for management:

Heads should not be psychopaths and there are some around. One should not have a one-track mind, one should be reasonably intelligent, and should not be a reactionary like one of our deans who always says no to suggestions. One should be able to tolerate other people getting credit for things that oneself has initiated. One should have a sense of irony and humour, and should enjoy delegation.

(Quoted in Moses and Roe 1990: 53)

Of course, heads and other staff have somewhat different ideas about what are the most important aspects of running a department. Box 8.10 summarizes some of the results of an Australian research project concerned with this issue. It found that only six out of the top ten headship functions, as ranked by staff and heads, were common to both, and that there were significant differences in ranking. Thus, heads ranked 'selecting staff members' highest, yet this did not even make the top ten in their staff's estimation. Similarly, while staff ranked 'considers staff's point of view' second, and 'consulting staff' fourth, these did not feature in the heads' top ten.

Such differences of perception are likely to be most evident during that modern form of bear-baiting, the departmental meeting:

> the form [of the departmental meeting] is that colleagues meet to seek to achieve a consensus; the reality is sometimes like that, but more often there are factions and personal attractions and animosities that cause such meetings to be long and emotionally highly charged.
>
> (Bland 1990: 56)

Taken as a whole, the staff's top ten given in Box 8.10 suggests a concern with building on, safeguarding and responding to their interests, while the heads emphasize planning and meeting targets. This is not surprising, given that heads of department have two key audiences – their department and the university – which have unequal power, but which they nevertheless may try to balance. This is so regardless of how they came by their position – whether they were more or less democratically elected by the members of their department, or were appointed by the university, perhaps without any consultation.

For those who aspire to running a department, a number of preparatory activities may be suggested:

- talking to a predecessor and to other members of the department;
- talking to other heads of department in the university;
- attending some general management training;
- attending a head of department's training course, if available, and any other course concerned with financial arrangements;
- studying the university's handbook for heads of department, and any other relevant available documentation;
- gaining experience by covering for sabbatical leave or seeking delegated responsibility.

We would add to these general suggestions two others:

- work out what it is that you want to do while you are running the department;
- remember that, however much advice you take, or support you get, the buck will stop with you, so you might just as well do something you believe in.

Ten further lessons for heads of department from someone who used to have that role are outlined in Box 8.11. Many others who have tried to exercise this role with more or less success will recognize their pertinence.

Box 8.11: Ten lessons for herding cats hygienically

1 We *take good administrators for granted, and are probably too harsh on poor ones* ... when people are good administrators, we punish them with greater burdens ... anybody who is willing to try out this role deserves some slack. Those who are good at it deserve more than our thanks – they deserve to be left alone for a while.

2 *It's easier to complain than it is to fix what's wrong* ... Fixing things takes a lot of resources, planning ahead, and energy. These commodities are in short supply ...

3 *There is something to symbolic management* ... The academic world is fraught with symbols, rituals, rites of passage, and myths ... Don't ever discount the role of process in managing academics.

4 *It's far too easy to slip into Theory X/high-control mode* ... Rather than being re-sponsible for everybody, I'd rather have people feel responsible for themselves.

5 *Lamaze breathing techniques work for more situations than giving birth* ... My biggest mistakes and personal disappointments have occurred when I let my anger at particular situations talk before I put my training to work ...

6 *Communication is a daily challenge* ... Being open and honest, gaining people's trust, and keeping confidences are really very difficult goals to keep in balance.

7 *There is something to be said for setting your goals higher than simple survival* ... It's important to move forward, if only in one small area ...

8 *Keep your sense of humour* ...

9 *The lower the stakes, the more heated the battle* ... those small issues will get you every time ...

10 *Delegation and division of labour make sense.*

(Fukami 1996: 322–4)

Quality audit and assessment

All academics, whether they run departments or not, now find that they have to spend an increasing amount of their time dealing with quality issues. This is largely a consequence of previous governments' doubts about the quality of higher education provision, and their wish to make universities and colleges more open and accountable. The Further and Higher Education Act of 1992 helped to establish a set of quality audit and assessment mechanisms, which are still being developed and refined.

At present, the main quality assurance procedures affecting higher education are as outlined in Box 8.12. Academics' immediate experience of these procedures has been in terms of an avalanche of paperwork descending upon them, demanding the production of detailed responses for consideration. British higher education has been both better documented and under far closer scrutiny than ever before, even if much of this scrutiny has been by fellow academics seconded from their posts for the purpose.

Box 8.12: Quality assurance arrangements in universities and colleges

- All universities and colleges have their own procedures in place both to periodically review all departmental and other activities, and to approve new developments. For example, proposed new courses typically have to be approved by a series of committees before they are launched, while bids for research funding usually require the approval of institutional authorities before they are dispatched for consideration.
- The Quality Assurance Agency (QAA) is responsible for auditing all institutions' quality assurance mechanisms, and for providing guidance on how quality might be further enhanced. The QAA took over this role from the former Higher Education Quality Council (HEQC) during 1997.
- The Higher Education Funding Council for England (HEFCE), the main funder of universities and colleges, carries out periodic quality assessments of teaching and learning in all departments, grading their work as excellent, satisfactory or unsatisfactory.
- While the two previous arrangements apply largely to teaching, the HEFCE also organizes periodic research assessment exercises, which grade the research performance of departments on a five-point scale. These gradings are then linked to selective funding.

The details quoted apply to England. There are some differences of detail in other parts of the United Kingdom.

The main implications of this activity for academics' work have been as follows:

- A need to document all activities (e.g. course structures, teaching materials, student supervisions, staff appraisals, student assessments), and to maintain careful records of these for subsequent scrutiny.
- A tendency to standardize procedures both within and between institutions, so that perceived 'good practice' in teaching, research and managing is widely adopted.
- The likelihood that activities which are found wanting in quality assessments (e.g. teaching graded unsatisfactory, research rated as only 1 or 2 rather than 4 or 5) will be shut down, amalgamated with other units or departments, or replaced.
- The setting of performance targets, usually in simple quantitative terms, at the departmental and individual level (e.g. student enrolment, entry qualifications, dropout rates, research grants, publications).

In practice, then, individual academics have found more and more of their time taken up in meeting quality audit and assessment procedures. Even when these have been satisfied, there is little opportunity to rest on their laurels, as further improvements and progress are expected year by year. As in many occupations in this increasingly competitive world, like Alice in *Through the Looking-Glass*, one has to run just to stay in the same place, while each year the speed of the treadmill is increased a little more.

In such an environment, yet more emphasis is placed on the skills of managing. Much of this is, as we have indicated, at a fairly basic, administrative level, requiring the maintenance of detailed and appropriate records. A significant amount of the work involved is, however, at the political level, with the need regularly to justify and argue for one's activities within the institution and beyond. Good political skills, and their use through networking, can make a great difference to the external perception of your work, and consequently to the funding and support received. If we are all managers now, it can also be said that all departments need at least one good advocate if they are to survive and perhaps prosper.

Working with support staff

Another management skill which academics need to develop and exercise has to do with working with support staff. In any university or college, full-time permanent academic staff make up a minority of the total number of employees, though they loom large in terms of influence. The support staff, broadly defined, who make up the majority of the establishment, come in a variety of guises:

- short-term and or part-time contract staff, employed to teach and/or research;
- secretarial and clerical staff, employed to answer telephones and correspondence, deal with queries, file and maintain records;
- technical staff, employed to run laboratories and computer services, and to maintain the infrastructure of the institution;
- administrative and managerial staff, responsible for the central functions of the university or college (e.g. personnel, student admissions, finance, staffing committees).

It is obvious that without these staff the academic's lot would be harder than it is; indeed, it would become insupportable. Support staff of various kinds form an essential part of the complicated organization that is today's university. If you doubt this, consider Box 8.13, which poses some key support questions. If you don't know the answers to these and similar questions, then you should probably try and find out.

Our advice on working with support staff may seem obvious, yet it is surprising how often academics neglect these relationships to their cost. Support staff are human beings, and may at times – like other human beings – be awkward and difficult to deal with. Remember, however, that most of them are less well paid than 'permanent' academics and often in less secure positions.

We would suggest three key rules in working with support staff:

1 Understand their roles, and the limits on them, and what you can reasonably ask for in terms of support.
2 Seek support in good time, wherever possible, bearing in mind that many things may need to be done at the last minute.

Box 8.13: Ten key support questions for academics

1 Who do you contact if you wish to get access to a teaching room?
2 Who is responsible for approving and progressing your application for funding to attend a conference?
3 Who takes messages for you when you are not in your office?
4 Who can you turn to for advice on the qualifications held by an overseas student applicant?
5 What do you do when you cannot get access to the network through your computer terminal?
6 Who might best advise you on completing a quality assessment document?
7 Who can help if your salary does not appear to have been paid into your bank account on time?
8 Who knows where the photocopying equipment spares are kept?
9 Who is likely to have a closer day-to-day relationship with many of your students than you have?
10 Who might be prevailed upon to make your distinguished visitors a cup of tea?

---

3 Cultivate good relations. Support staff may be as clever as you, and just not so fortunate in their life chances. Discuss your work with them, keep them informed about your movements, and take an interest in their lives.

If you at least try to do these things, you are likely to enjoy better and less grudging support.

Legal matters

It would appear that Britain is becoming a more and more litigious society, and this is having an impact on academic life as well as in other areas. This may affect you from one or more directions. People (e.g. students, colleagues) and organizations (e.g. your employer) may seek to take legal action against you; or you may wish to take action against them. There is a considerable emerging case law concerning higher education (see Farrington 1994). It makes sense, therefore, to have at least a basic understanding of relevant legal processes and equal opportunities policies, so that if they affect you, a colleague or someone you are responsible for, you have some idea about what to do.

In many cases, there are parallel or successive processes for resolving issues within and without your university or college. You might be surprised, however, to discover that not all universities have identified policies for a range of equal opportunities issues. For example, a 1996 survey of universities found that only '96% of universities had equal opportunities policies; 83% had policies dealing with harassment; 79% had recruitment and selection procedures; 84% had someone at senior level with responsibility for equal opportunities' (Commission on University Career Opportunity 1997, p. 1). It is important, therefore, to remember that, whether or not you work in an institution with established procedures and policies, higher education institutions are not laws unto themselves, and that the external procedures operating through courts and tribunals are both available and overriding.

As an individual academic, the most likely legal procedures to affect you are those concerning unfair dismissal or harassment. Until recently, British academics with full-time, permanent posts enjoyed security of tenure. This meant that in practice, though it was little tested in law, they could not be dismissed except in a limited number of extreme circumstances. Since the passing of the Education Act of 1988, this security of tenure has been removed from all new appointments (including promotions), so that the job security enjoyed by most academics is that provided by standard employment law. They can be made redundant if their department or centre is closed down, or because of financial pressure on their employing institution. They can also be dismissed if they are judged to be under-performing. All such decisions are, however, challengeable, both within the institution and through external courts and tribunals.

In cases of unfair dismissal, you may be the one being dismissed or the one seeking dismissal. So, in cases of harassment, you may be the victim or may be seen as the harasser. A colleague or students may accuse you of sexually harassing them, or you may feel that they are harassing you. Increasingly, it is also likely that you may feel that your manager, or a colleague, is bullying you. Trade unions such as the Association of University Teachers (AUT), and employer organizations such as CUCO, regularly produce guidelines and reports on harassment and other equal opportunities issues. Copies of such documents can be obtained through your local representatives.

In addition to being informed in these ways, here are five possible actions to take in such situations:

1 Keep a careful, dated, written record of all the events relevant to the case. Keep copies of any relevant documents. Keep duplicates in different places.
2 Seek the support of sympathetic family, colleagues and friends. Build yourself a support group. Network with others you hear of who have been through similar experiences. It is perilous to try and cope with such cases on your own.
3 Get advice from your union, or, if you are not a member, consider joining. They will have a detailed knowledge of similar cases both within your institution and nationally, and may be able to offer practical support.
4 Check your contractual entitlements with regard to sick leave. Disputes with employers are not often quickly resolved, and the stress may build up to the point where you have little choice but to take extended sick leave.
5 Seek professional legal advice early. It won't be cheap, unless it is provided by a union, but it will probably be worth it.

All of these five points are important, and you would be foolish to ignore any of them. In any such case, however, it is unlikely that the situation will be resolved to your full satisfaction, or without exacting an emotional as well as financial cost:

In challenging the adverse decision of the Appointment Committee through a quasi-legal procedure within the University, I sought several goals. First, I was hoping that by making those whose actions and decisions victimize others hear about the effects of their actions they would positively alter their conscience and behaviour in the future ... Second, I sought to draw attention to the fact that, if we are serious about combating racism, sexism and other dehumanizing prejudices, we must make individuals accountable for the decisions they make behind closed doors. Finally, I believed that the open hearing of a case involving racism and sexism would serve an educational purpose ... The University Grievance Board, after several months of hearings, which were open to the University community, decided that I had been 'the victim of unfair treatment at the hands of the University' ... However, the Board ... refused to acknowledge the personal and moral responsibility of individual members of the Appointment Committee ... Instead, it whitewashed those responsible, made excuses for their actions and decisions, showed much consideration and sympathy for their discomfort, and tried to appease them by criticizing my conduct and praising their behaviours.

(Moghissi 1994: 224–5)

Managing as a career

Getting involved in management is probably the most common way to advance a career within academe, though it will take you away from the more common and widely valued roles of teaching and researching:

There are real personal costs and it is important to be aware of these. Like many other teachers/researchers turned managers, I have had to face losses; of students, of sabbaticals, of 'serious' research and of a large cohort of colleagues. Pursuit of my 'subject' has become my hobby. The benefits are that it is possible to effect change on a much wider scale than before and that I can introduce what I believe are real benefits for the work of students and teachers.

(King 1995: 42)

There is a certain amount of happenstance involved in pursuing a successful career in academic management. You have to be in the right place at the right time, and have some luck:

I stumbled unintentionally into senior management ... like almost all academics, I have received no systematic training in management and, initially, I viewed management as alien to the whole academic enterprise ... That the first reluctant foot on the managerial ladder led to my present post is explicable in three ways. The first is simply that as head of department at Loughborough I inherited a very skilled and experienced departmental secretary ... The second was my personal realisation that an increasingly turbulent environment was placing demands on higher education which made the management challenge an intellectually stimulating one ... The third explanation is that I had a measure of that luck which Napoleon so valued in his generals: some key things went right – and thereby reinforced the gradual shift from academic to managerial roles.

(A. Webb 1994: 42)

If you are any good at it, and are interested, you would probably be well advised to pursue a managerial career. There are plenty of opportunities, and the academic world, as elsewhere, desperately needs good managers. Broadly speaking, there are three main managerial career routes within academic life, two of which are academic, and the other academic-related.

The first academic route, is the one which much of this chapter has been concerned with. You start as a lecturer and/or researcher, perhaps move on to running your department or centre, become more involved in the management of the university as a whole, and maybe end up in a senior university management role.

The second academic route focuses on the discipline rather than the institution. It would typically involve making increasing contributions to professional societies, editing journals, running conferences, contributing to the work of research councils, and so forth (see also Chapter 4, particularly the sections on **Conferences, seminars and societies** and **Journals and newsletters**).

The other, academic-related, route involves opting for an academic administrative career. Here, you are likely to work within the central administration of the university, though you might be located within a faculty or departmental office. Those entering this career path are likely to be as well educated as those becoming academics: nowadays, many have doctorates.

The academic-related career route leads on to assuming responsibility for particular branches of the administration, such as undergraduate or postgraduate admissions and progress, examinations, continuing education or validation arrangements. Other central administrative functions, such as personnel, finance and buildings, are headed by specialist professionals. For the general academic administrator, the career goal is likely to be to become an academic registrar or registrar.

For those with an inclination for this kind of work, academic administration can be at least as demanding as being an academic. The list of administrative roles identified and described in Box 8.14 makes clear the need for creative, insightful and hard-working administrative staff. At heart, academic management may be seen as a support role, though undoubtedly a key one. From this perspective, it is concerned with nourishing the life of the institution so that the academic staff are enabled to do their jobs effectively:

To achieve the goals of recognized high-quality teaching and research ... all that institutional managers can do is:
- establish, sustain and enhance an ethos in which these goals are pursued by all, which includes an accepted reward system;
- appoint and retain staff who are committed to these goals and able to pursue them;

Box 8.14: Administrative roles

- *The Foot Soldier* ... there are always things to be done, usually at short notice, that at best are less then fascinating ...
- *The Messenger.* Institutions exposed to the outside world must listen to what the world is telling them ... Listening for the messages and interpreting them is no task for an amateur. Conveying messages back is of equal importance.
- *The Prophet* ... One of the most valuable gifts that an administrator can bring to a university is that of foresight ...
- *The Junction Box.* An essential part of being a prophet (or indeed a messenger) is to make connections between unlikely subjects in the interests of producing desirable and acceptable change.
- *Houdini.* If you can find what the future is likely to bring (and a prophet is meant to do just that), you must find solutions to the problems that you identify ... Elegance of solution is not quite all, but very nearly.
- *The Priest* ... an administrator [must] be prepared to interpret the University's own version of the Bible and concordance ...
- *The Politician.* Politics is the art of the possible, the achievement of as much as one can without failing too obviously ... remember that more can always be achieved than cynics think.
- *The Auditor* ... do not be misled by a university's own statements about itself ... detached analysis is required ...
- *The Champion.* See the university as others see it, or you lose sight of the needs of the clients ...
- *Stakhanov.* Stakhanov is out of fashion these days, ironically because not only the administrator but all members of universities are expected to work whatever hours are needed to discharge the functions of their posts. Those who prefer to keep gentlemen's hours are likely to be given the leisure in which they can relax further.

(Kiloh 1994: 9–10)

- ensure an adequate infrastructure;
- provide the resources which allow the individual academic staff members to pursue the goals effectively and efficiently.

(Johnston 1996: 103–4)

Sources of further information

In this section we list a range of materials which you may find of interest in following up in more detail some of the issues discussed in this chapter. The emphasis is on recently published books in English. In each case, brief details are given as to contents and approach.

There is, of course, a vast literature on management. The literature on the management of higher education is, by contrast, much smaller but growing. It includes a glossy practitioner journal, *Managing HE: For Decision-makers in Higher Education*, published by Hobsons.

Ashcroft, K. and Foreman-Peck, L. (1995) *The Lecturer's Guide to Quality and Standards in Colleges and Universities*. London, Falmer Press.
Based on the reflective practitioner model, the text is interspersed with 'enquiry tasks'. Includes chapters on teaching and learning, student support, staff development, assessment and evaluation, course design, resource management, marketing and recruitment, and research.

Ashworth, A. and Harvey, R. (1994) *Assessing Quality in Further and Higher Education*. London, Jessica Kingsley.
Identifies sets of performance indicators in the areas of management, staffing, staff development, accommodation, equipment and resources, liaison and marketing, students, teaching and learning, curriculum, assessment and recording of progress; together with descriptions of what constitutes very good, good, satisfactory, unsatisfactory or poor performance.

Balderston, F. (1995) *Managing Today's University: Strategies for Viability, Change and Excellence*, 2nd edn. San Francisco, Jossey-Bass.
Revised version of basic American text.

Bland, D. (1990) *Managing Higher Education*. London, Cassell.
Includes discussion of the roles of ceremonial bodies, the principal, academic departments, administration and central services, and management and meetings.

Bocock, J. and Watson, D. (eds) (1994) *Managing the University Curriculum: Making Common Cause*. Buckingham, Open University Press.
Examines the changing context for higher education, and the roles of institutional heads, middle managers and lecturers.

Brodie, D. and Partington, P. (1992) *HE Departmental Leadership/Management: An Exploration of Roles and Responsibilities*. Sheffield, Committee of Vice-Chancellors and Principals.
Concise discussion of responsibilities, leadership models and management styles, team building and individual development.

Cuthbert, R. (ed.) (1996) *Working in Higher Education*. Buckingham, Open University Press.
Contains useful chapters on 'Managing the Employment Relationship', 'Managing How Academics Manage' and 'Work's Committees'.

Eggins, H. (1997) *Women as Leaders and Managers in Higher Education*. Buckingham, Open University Press.
Considers the context of higher education management and gender issues, case studies based on interviews with women in senior management, and change strategies such as work shadowing and networking.

Farrington, D. (1994) *The Law of Higher Education*. London, Butterworth.
The only British text on this subject, containing chapters on external influences, governance, management, employment, students, information, commercial activity, sponsored research and consultancy, land, buildings and equipment. Numerous references to case law.

Ford, P., Goodyear, P., Heseltine, R., Lewis, R., Darby, J., Graves, J., Satorius, P., Harwood, D. and King, T. (1996) *Managing Change in Higher Education: A Learning Environment Architecture*. Buckingham, Open University Press.
Details a method for assisting learning institutions in creating, implementing and maintaining their learning environment. Higher education, in this context, is treated as just another business.

Higher Education Quality Council (1995) *Managing for Quality: Stories and Strategies*. London, HEQC.

Based around 56 case studies, organized into ten sections which examine managing quality assurance systems, student feedback, modularization and curriculum development, reviewing and improving teaching and learning, student guidance and support, departmental leadership and managing staff resources, staff development, appraisal and promotion, assessment, examining and standards, promoting postgraduate work and research, managing structural changes and relationships.

King, C. (ed.) (1993) *Through the Glass Ceiling: Effective Senior Management Development for Women*. Eastham, Tudor Business Publishing Ltd.
Discusses whether there is a woman's way, meetings, working together with men and women, managing the boundaries, whether it's worth it, and how to take the next step. Useful bibliography and contact addresses.

Middlehurst, R. (1993) *Leading Academics*. Buckingham, Open University Press.
Considers the nature of leadership, organizational images, traditions and change in academe, leaders' roles. Based on surveys of heads of department and senior managers in the old university sector in the late 1980s and early 1990s.

Moses, I. and Roe, E. (1990) *Heads and Chairs: Managing Academic Departments*. St Lucia, University of Queensland Press.
Based on surveys and interviews in nine Australian universities. Contains chapters on how heads see themselves, how their staff see them, the academic, political and management dimensions of running a department, tensions, conflicts and rewards, skills and responsibilities.

Slowey, M. (ed.) (1995) *Implementing Change from within Universities and Colleges*. London, Kogan Page.
The ten core chapters present case studies of change led by heads of department, those working in cross-institutional roles and others.

Warner, D. and Crosthwaite, E. (eds) (1995) *Human Resource Management in Higher and Further Education*. Buckingham, Open University Press.
Essentially a top-down perspective. Includes chapters on managing change, managing diversity, rewarding performance, executive recruitment, employment law, developing managers, industrial relations strategies and managing information.

Warner, D. and Kelly, G. (eds.) (1994) *Managing Educational Property: A Handbook for Schools, Colleges and Universities*. Buckingham, Open University Press.
Pitched primarily at senior management. Includes chapters on property valuation, space management, external finance, investment appraisal, property law and energy management.

Warner, D. and Palfreyman, D. (eds) (1996) *Higher Education Management: The Key Elements*. Buckingham, Open University Press.
Includes chapters on organizational cultures, strategic planning, resource allocation, decision-making, support services, external relations and the management of personnel, students, research and the estate.

Whitchurch, C. (ed.) (1994) *A Handbook for University Administrators and Managers*. Sheffield, UK Universities' Staff Development Unit.
A useful guide for those making higher education management their career. Appendices list relevant organizations and contacts.

9 | DEVELOPING AN ACADEMIC CAREER

Introduction

This chapter considers how academic careers develop, and the strategies which you might use to develop your own career. It takes as its premise three key points. First, remaining in the same position and doing much the same job for the whole of a career can be stultifying and unchallenging. Second, being active rather than reactive is preferable as systems of higher education change. Third, the ideas behind 'lifelong learning' and 'multi-skilling' will apply to people in higher education as much as in other employment sectors.

The chapter is organized into five main sections:

- **Taking a lifetime perspective**, which argues the need to think about academic careers, and their relation to other aspects of life;
- **Continuing your development**, which discusses the varied institutional and personal strategies available;
- **Appraisal and promotion**, which considers when and how to argue for promotion, and what to do if unsuccessful;
- **Moving on and out**, which looks at the experience of moving between institutions and countries, and into and out of academic employment;
- **Conclusion**, which reviews where academic life and work may be going, and provides a realistic perspective on the academic's place in these developments.

At the end of the chapter a selection of sources of further information is listed.

Taking a lifetime perspective

We have already noted, from a collective standpoint, the inertia (though some would prefer the term conservatism) built into the academic enterprise as a

result of the often substantial investment needed to attain a special expertise in a particular field. Anyone who has spent long, arduous years in the
achievement of a close understanding of one particular knowledge area or
in the acquisition of a particular type of expertise, is unlikely without
hesitation to abandon it and repeat the process in favour of a new one.

(Becher 1989: 114–15)

We argued in Chapter 2 (see especially the section on **Academic roles and
careers**) that the nature of higher education, and of careers in general, is changing significantly, with a consequent impact upon academic careers in particular.
Yet academic life is not so beset by change that we cannot also recognize
important continuities. The academic roles of today remain broadly similar to
those of ten, twenty, thirty or even forty years ago.

The scale of the enterprise has undoubtedly mushroomed, and the productivity,
flexibility and multiple skills expected of academics have increased. The lecturer
of twenty years ago might well baulk at what is demanded of the lecturer today
– and many of them, of course, are the same people – but they would still recognize
the job. And, as the quotation above indicates, academics have invested so much
time in the development of their specialist skills and expertise, that they are
probably less than willing to seek to change either their field or their career,
except under extreme pressure.

Most of those who enter academic employment probably still do so early on
in their work careers: in their twenties or thirties, either immediately or soon
after a period of postgraduate education. Others undoubtedly enter academe later
on, after developing a work career elsewhere, or after a career break devoted to
caring for young children and/or older relatives. Some move into and out of
academic and related areas of work, or combine academic involvement with a
professional position outside the university.

Nevertheless, the majority are likely to view academic work as something
they intend to engage in for a significant period of time, perhaps (if not necessarily full-time) for their entire working career. They also tend to see academe as
an arena, much like their own initial education, in which they can expect to
develop and progress. That progression may initially be from a short-term and/or
part-time post to something more secure, or from lecturer to senior lecturer,
reader and professor. It is encouraged by the common practice of awarding
increments annually to permanent, full-time staff until they reach the top of
the scale.

In Chapter 3 we drew attention to the issues involved in balancing academic
careers. Most commonly, balancing is seen in terms of family and employment.
While academic work may appear to be relatively 'family-friendly', in that there
may be flexibility regarding when some of the work is done, this is not to say
that it is not demanding or that universities have 'family-friendly' employment
practices.

As a consequence, those who make substantial family commitments find that
this compromises or postpones outwardly successful careers. This, combined
with age and gender biases, contributes to the under-representation of women at

---

Box 9.1: Women talking about their academic careers

Despite all her achievements, Cynthia Cockburn remains the most open and unpretentious of scholars. 'Not having a degree I always felt hesitant about being a researcher, and put in that extra bit of effort,' she says. 'I greatly respect people who've achieved a formal education and in many ways I regret I haven't. But it's reassuring to find there are people and institutions that are open-minded and willing to judge a researcher on output rather than certification. Perhaps my career could be some encouragement to other women who find their direction late, or want to change track.'

A willingness to cross boundaries is something she [Mary Douglas] has noticed 'in the careers of other women. Sometimes the professional structures do not exert a strong enough grip, and in consequence they enjoy a freedom which others may envy, but pay a price of isolation which they may themselves regret . . . a move from being original to being bizarre which Margaret Mead's writings exemplified.'

'There are two ways of handling the ladder of mobility. One is to detach yourself, leave it all behind. For me [Susan Richards], strong family roots keep me going back there. My life is now very different, as part of the affluent middle class in the South East. I was lucky in having a warm supportive family who cared a lot for me, did not always understand where I was going, but none the less believed that anything I did was right as far as they were concerned.'

(Griffiths 1996b: 49, 89–90, 219–20)

---

higher levels within universities and colleges. There are plenty of examples of women (and doubtless some of men) who have enjoyed notable academic careers without neglecting their families (see Box 9.1), but these are closer to the exception rather than the rule, and few of them would say it had been easy.

Balancing in academic careers may also be viewed in terms of employment-related roles and tasks. Linking networking, teaching, research, writing and managing roles facilitates the development of a coherent, while flexible, academic identity. Yet, as Box 9.2 indicates, as individual careers develop so too do the nature of these roles and their linkages.

In this context, taking a lifetime perspective means recognizing the importance of thinking and planning broadly. This might involve thinking about where you would like to go in your academic career, what you might need to do in order to achieve your goals, and how all of this relates to the rest of your life. This kind of planning can be encompassed within a personal mission statement which: 'focuses on what you want to be (character) and to do (contributions and achievements) and on the values or principles upon which being and doing are based' (Covey 1992: 106). While a personal mission statement may change from time to time, as with organizational mission statements, it should be designed to provide the spirit within which daily decisions can be made.

Box 9.2: Career and role development

Networking
early career   – fellow graduate students
middle career – fellow researchers and teachers
late career   – invited to chair new network

Teaching
early career   – fellow graduate students and supervisor invite you to give
                 seminars
middle career – more research students, external examining
late career   – research student examiner, teaching quality assessor

Researching
early career   – research assistant
middle career – employ research assistants
late career   – research assistants now colleagues at other institutions,
                 reviewing research proposals

Writing
early career   – publish extracts from thesis
middle career – contributions to edited volumes, book and journal referee,
                 references for students
late career   – referee for professorial candidates

Managing
early career   – course team
middle career – journal board member, institutional committees, appraiser
late career   – national inquiry committee

In addition to developing a mission statement, goal setting means giving attention to specific employment-related aspects of career development. This might involve consideration of:

- *contexts*, e.g. what kinds of institution or department you would most like to work in and what kind of people you would like to work with;
- *role preferences*, e.g. what academic roles you would prefer to specialize in;
- *skills*, e.g. what particular skills or expertise you currently have or would like to develop and practise;
- *achievements*, e.g. what level of academic career you would like and what you would like to be remembered for.

Career development is not simply about reaching the top of a profession. Writing a mission statement and setting goals can be useful approaches in helping to find and retain a sense of direction and purpose, while recognizing the connectedness and balance that exists within careers. In an era of downsizing, multi- and flexi-skilling, these processes can help to maximize occupational chances across a lifetime, and be part of the armour of professionalism.

Continuing your development

> The taking of money for teaching and research also imposes a duty to engage
> in those activities ... It is, of course, notoriously difficult to prove how
> far academics discharge their contractual duty to engage in research ...
> Publication is a proper yardstick, but it is not the only one. The amount of
> research which goes into one article is capable of extreme variation ...
> Failure to discharge teaching duties is very much easier to prove ...
>
> (Russell 1993: 44–5)

The exercise of increasing control over the ways in which academics carry out
their professional duties is commonly discussed in relation to the growing managerialism in higher education and the impact of external quality assessments.
Institutions have responded by paying more attention to staff development activities as a way of controlling and even 'McDonaldizing' (Ritzer 1993) the academic
profession. The recent National Committee of Inquiry into Higher Education (1997)
has recommended a further strengthening of training programmes for academics.
From the organizational perspective, all of this might be necessary to compete
successfully in the higher education marketplace. At the individual level, continuing professional development remains a mechanism for enhancing personal
employability, as well as a professional responsibility to students, colleagues,
institution and discipline.

In addition to the opportunities offered by universities and colleges, and by
national organizations such as the Staff and Educational Development Association
(SEDA), professional associations, societies and trade unions also offer regular,
continuing programmes of staff development. Most courses are short, usually lasting
for an hour or two, rarely more than a day, and may focus on any of the academic
roles identified in this book, or on current developments and policy changes.

Increasing importance is being placed on the development of technical skills
in relation to, for example, new teaching technologies and telecommunications.
The consolidation of international links and the encouragement of collaborative
research may require additional language skills. Acquiring skills of these kinds,
even though essential, usually has to be squeezed into a rich schedule of priorities.
It is, therefore, worth checking what learning support may be available through the
institution. Many university language schools and computer services centres, for
example, offer courses designed for academic members of staff as well as students.

Some participation in staff development activities may be required by an institution or professional body, as part of initial or continuing professional development.
Beyond that, there may also be a more general expectation of some voluntary
participation where relevant: such activities are now commonly reviewed as part
of the appraisal process (see the next section on **Appraisal and promotion**).
Participation will also form part of a broader networking strategy (see Chapter 4,
particularly the section on **Conferences, seminars and societies**).

The most significant developmental opportunities available to academics –
beyond changing jobs, attending staff development events and conferencing – are
sabbaticals, fellowships, exchanges and secondments. These overlap to some
extent, and may be called by different names (see Box 9.3). They are typically

Box 9.3: Sabbaticals, fellowships, exchanges and secondments

Sabbaticals, or study leave, allow staff to have periods of time free from other responsibilities to focus on research, writing or development activities. At the University of Warwick, for example, academic staff are eligible to apply for one term's study leave after they have worked six terms. Not all institutions run such schemes, and some are more generous than others: all monitor what the recipients do with their sabbaticals carefully, and expect them to contribute significantly to research, and possibly teaching, quality assessments. Where an individual is not eligible for a sabbatical, or their institution does not run such a scheme, it may nevertheless be possible to negotiate some kind of leave of absence, perhaps unpaid.

Fellowships are offered by some higher education institutions, most notably by various Oxford and Cambridge colleges, and by some of the major national research funders (see Box 6.3), typically for a period of a year, though sometimes more or less. Their purpose is much the same as that of the sabbatical, to give the recipients time free from other responsibilities to concentrate on their research or writing, with perhaps some commitment to deliver a limited number of specialist lectures. Some are geared particularly at academics in the early part of their career, others at those who have already attained professorial level. Many are widely publicized and highly competitive. There may be restrictions on who is eligible to apply, relating to age, subject area and other factors.

Exchanges are schemes which allow two academics, usually working in similar positions in different institutions (and often different countries), to swop jobs for a period, usually at least a term. The development of European Community interests in higher education, notably through the Erasmus and Socrates schemes, has resulted in a mushrooming of such opportunities. Others are organized on a binational or bi-institutional basis. Typically, the academics involved take over each other's teaching and administrative responsibilities, though there may also be a research component.

Secondments are similar to exchanges, except that they are usually only one-way. Individual academics may be seconded to work for a period of time in another department, or perhaps in the central administration. They might also agree a secondment to an outside company or organization. While there, they will take on the range of responsibilities required by the role they are seconded to. The purpose of such arrangements may be to cover for a temporary shortage of staff, to gain experience in related areas of work and/or to build up networks for future development. In some cases – e.g. academics working in education departments spending time teaching in schools – such secondments are required by the national agencies responsible for overseeing their work. Work shadowing is a related kind of activity, where the individual spends time in another department or organization following, and perhaps assisting in, the work of someone else.

Box 9.4: Professional modes of learning

Courses and conferences
Professional interactions
Networking
Consulting experts
Personal research
Learning by doing
Learning by teaching

Source: Becher (1996: 46–52).

---

only available to full-time academic staff in permanent posts, though some similar opportunities are available to academic-related staff.

Sabbaticals, fellowships, exchanges and secondments are all powerful means of professional development, which can be taken advantage of at different points in your career. It is important to be aware of relevant opportunities in good time, to plan carefully how they will be used, and to make sure that colleagues and institution are supportive.

Most of the developmental opportunities and activities discussed so far in this section are organized by others, and are there for the individual academic to take advantage of, or not, depending on eligibility or interest. For those members of the academic profession who are in a post (short-term or part-time) which excludes such participation, it will, however, be necessary to take a more proactive approach.

Box 9.4 summarizes the developmental strategies identified in a study of professionals working in six different areas, each of them allied in some way to academic life. The first four of the seven 'professional modes of learning' listed – courses and conferences, professional interactions, networking and consulting experts – are discussed in Chapter 4. Personal research is considered in Chapter 6. The ideas of learning by doing and learning by teaching (see Chapter 5) illustrate the potential benefits of connecting different aspects of work, and developing them through practical activities and exposure to the reactions of others.

Developing the wider range of skills associated with academic work, such as counselling or public speaking, can be undertaken in a range of ways outside the employing institution. Box 9.5 gives an indicative list of providers. In addition, there is an enormous range of literature designed to provide guidance on personal career development for a more general audience. Box 9.6 provides some excerpts from these.

Keeping an eye on this literature – which can be found at the airport or railway bookstall, as well as in town-centre bookshops – is one, often quick and easy, way of staying informed about, and learning the language of, contemporary career-enhancing strategies. Such books are also likely to be read with interest by your manager! To provide context, these approaches can be combined with a

---

Box 9.5: Wider learning opportunities

University-provided short courses and classes: library, computer services and language departments

Adult education classes: in foreign languages, information technologies, interpersonal skills such as assertiveness, counselling, influencing skills, public speaking, voice

Skills exchange: with students, colleagues, friends

Distance learning: audio tapes for language learning, Open University courses on management

Self-development books: for the development of personal power and people management

All of these opportunities will have to be developed in your own time. Some, but not all, university-based courses may be free to staff members.

---

deepening knowledge of the debates and issues relevant to higher education. Following up the further reading in this book is a good starting point.

These, and related techniques, might form the basis of a personal developmental strategy which, over a period of time, should enable involvement in a wide range of institutional and disciplinary activities and roles. Box 9.7 provides a listing of some of the extra-institutional roles – from referee to reviewer, editor to board member, examiner to assessor – engaged in by one person, now a vice-chancellor. While you may not wish to take on such a range of academic roles, or may not have so many opportunities to do so, this does show that the scope for development is extensive. Don't miss your opportunities!

Appraisal and promotion

> Performance appraisal and career development are processes too often left to the bureaucracy, involving ritual meetings that cover rote questions and result in filled-out forms that join other forms in file drawers or on disks. Programs adopted by companies to help people cope with their lives and careers are sometimes undermined by managers who lack the skills for dealing with people – from discomfort at giving direct feedback to the inability to identify tricks of the trade that can improve performance.
>
> (Kanter 1997: 15)

The processes of appraisal and promotion have become more closely linked over the last decade, as appraisal schemes have been introduced and formalized in institutions of higher education. In some cases, there is a close and formal linkage, in that promotion is impossible if satisfactory appraisals have not been completed. In other cases, there is no direct linkage but, most probably, a clear but indirect association. Either way, while many people can identify with the views quoted above, do not fool yourself into thinking that the process is a formality.

Box 9.6: Self-development advice

To be meaningful, values must enter into the daily life of the organization, with violators punished and exemplars rewarded. That way, the organization will equate abstract statements of principle with concrete models and lessons. But the values must reflect enduring commitments, not ephemeral notions. Thus leaders who are tempted to manage through values had better be prepared to examine their own – and to put their actions where their hearts [or mouths?] are.

(Kanter 1997: 275)

Sun Tzu's Principles
 1 Learn to fight
 2 Show the way
 3 Do it right
 4 Know the facts
 5 Expect the worst
 6 Seize the day
 7 Burn the bridges
 8 Do it better
 9 Pull together
10 Keep them guessing
These ten principles form the foundation for competitive success. Learn them well!

(Krause 1995: 7)

Typical beliefs of great coaches:
You can't be a leader without a following
The autocratic boss is facing extinction
Investing ten minutes in coaching will save an hour
How to win friends and influence people – become a great coach

(Landsberg 1996: x)

Never walk down the hall without a document in your hands. People with documents in their hands look like hardworking employees heading for important meetings. People with nothing in their hands look like they're heading for the cafeteria. People with the newspaper in their hands look like they're heading for the bathroom.

(Adams 1996: 76)

Bids for promotion are unlikely to be successful if appraisals have not gone well, if only because many of the same people will be involved in both activities.

Regular staff appraisal was imposed on the British higher education system by the former Conservative government as a condition for agreeing a pay award. Before then, few universities or colleges had formal appraisal systems in place; appraisal now forms an essential part of all institutions' quality assurance procedures.

Appraisal schemes vary in detail from institution to institution. They typically involve a regular review of individual staff performance, progress and needs,

---

Box 9.7: A range of academic roles

Role	On whose behalf
Referee (articles)	Academic journal
Book reviewer	Academic journal/commercial publisher
Editor	Academic journal
Referee (book proposals)	Commercial publisher
Referee (grant proposals)	Grant-awarding body
Board member/chair	Grant-awarding body
External examiner (students' work)	Various universities
Referee (staff appointments and promotions)	Various universities
External reviewer (departmental reviews)	Various universities
Panel member (course validation)	Various universities
Academic auditor	Higher Education Quality Council
Assessor (teaching quality)	Funding council
Panel member (research assessment)	Funding council

Source: Finch (1997: 148).

---

perhaps every two years. While the focus is usually on full-time, permanent academic and related staff, other groups may also be involved. The process normally involves completing a review statement, covering recent experience of the range of academic roles, how these will develop in the near future, and identifying support or development needs. There then follows a meeting with one or more appraisers to discuss this statement, and the completion of a summary form, perhaps jointly, which will probably have to be agreed and signed by the head of department. An appraisal record will be maintained by the institution in some form.

The identity of appraiser(s) is usually determined by, or agreed with, the head of department. Increasingly, universities and colleges are offering training to appraisers, and staff are required to be appraised by someone who has specified competencies or, at least, has attended some form of training. Where you have some influence over the selection, choosing a person who you respect and who is well placed within your department or institution can be very important. This may or may not be a line manager, and may indeed be someone in another department. They are likely to be senior to you, or at least of equal status.

The aims of engaging with the appraisal process may be both instrumental and developmental. At the instrumental level, completing the process in a straightforward and successful fashion, and ensuring that a fair and positive account of your work goes on record, is crucial. In developmental terms, it may be possible to use the process for networking, for valuable advice on career

---

Box 9.8: Active and positive words

Action words: actively, accelerate, adapt, administer, analyze, approve, coordinate, conceive, conduct, complete, control, create, delegate, develop, demonstrate, direct, effect, eliminate, establish, evaluate, expand, expedite, . . . solve, strategy, structure, streamline, successfully, supervise, support, teach.

Self-descriptive words: . . . fair, forceful, imaginative, independent, logical, loyal, mature, methodical, objective, optimistic, perceptive, personable, pleasant, positive, practical, productive, realistic, reliable, resourceful, respective, self-reliant, sense of humour, sincere . . .

(Shepela 1986: 155)

Skills as verbs: achieving, acting, adapting, addressing, administering, advising, analyzing, anticipating, arbitrating, arranging, ascertaining, . . . integrating, interviewing, intuiting, investing, inventorying, investigating, judging, keeping, leading, learning, lecturing, . . . realizing, reasoning, receiving, recommending, reconciling, recording, recruiting, reducing, referring, . . . sensing, separating, serving, setting, setting-up, . . . undertaking, unifying, uniting, upgrading, using, utilizing . . .

(Bolles 1996: 218)

---

development and for better placing yourself for further development or future promotion.

It is most likely that the department and institution will see appraisal in much the same way, as a time-consuming but potentially useful activity, and one to be done as efficiently as possible. However, appraisals in universities, as in other organizations, have served multiple purposes. You may be informed that the appraisal process is developmental rather than in any way disciplinary. During the preparation of your review statement you may be encouraged to draw attention to any difficulties or challenges you are confronting, as well as to your achievements.

On the other hand, anecdotal evidence suggests that senior academics who themselves conduct appraisals, and sit on university-level committees, appear to be reluctant to have anything other than evidence of positive achievements recorded at the end of the process. This may suggest that in university management, a written record of a desire to learn something is taken as evidence of some deficiency. For these reasons, you may wish to consult Box 9.8, which offers some active and positive words (useful also for constructing a curriculum vitae: see the section in Chapter 3 on **Applying for a job**) with which to present a positive portrayal of your experience and activities.

You may consider, however, that the appraisal process is being used to criticize performance unfairly and/or deny further developmental opportunities. In such cases, it is important to be aware of provisions for third-party involvement or appeals when you and your appraiser and/or head of department cannot agree (see also the section on **Legal matters** in Chapter 8). Whatever happens, it is unwise to change or be pressured into changing a personal appraisal statement without good reason, and it is sensible to keep copies of all the relevant documents.

Seeking promotion is something that most academics do more than once during their careers. For staff on a part-time and/or short-term contract, the promotion sought may be to a full-time and/or more secure post. Once a more permanent position has been secured, interest focuses on moving up the promotional ladder from lecturer grade A to lecturer grade B, senior lecturer, reader and professor; or on the parallel research and academic-related routes.

Broadly speaking, and perhaps surprisingly, it is more difficult to gain promotion at the lower levels. This is simply because, like most complex organizations, higher education staffing is organized like a pyramid, with most people at any one time at or near the bottom. The limited number of more senior posts means that the competition for promotion is fierce. This is particularly so for those seeking their first secure post in academe, and for those seeking to negotiate the lecturer/senior lecturer divide (or its equivalent). However, while the competition may get less intense at higher levels, few, of course, ever get that far.

Box 9.9 suggests a series of promotional strategies to help you get on in academic life. While these are written with women in mind, and pay particular attention to the management route, most of them are of general applicability. They reflect the dual meaning of promotion, having to do both with strategies for getting known and with what is needed to move up a grade or post.

The detailed procedures for seeking promotion vary from institution to institution, but the following general guidance applies to most cases and levels:

- Promotions are usually only considered once a year: check the timetable.
- If you are unsuccessful, you may be disqualified from reapplying for a specified period. Make sure you apply at the most opportune time, therefore, though you may have to allow for initial refusal as part of a longer-term strategy.
- You will almost certainly need the support of your head of department in order to proceed with any hope of success. If you don't have this, and see no hope of persuading them to change their mind, you may have to accept your lot until they move on, or move on yourself (see the next section, **Moving on and out**).
- You will have to produce an up-to-date curriculum vitae, focusing on your recent experience and responsibilities, and detailing your publications.
- You and/or your head of department will need to make a case for your promotion, relating what you have achieved to the criteria for promotion established by your institution.
- You and/or your head of department or institution will need to identify a number of referees to comment upon your case. Some may come from within your department or institution, but the most important will probably come from other institutions, possibly from overseas. Cultivate a range of referees, both for different purposes and so that you need not always use the same ones. As we indicated in Chapter 4 (see the section on **Mentoring and partnerships**), mentoring relationships can be crucial to promotions.
- Your case will then be judged alongside others, and in the light of institutional policies and available finances.

Box 9.9: Promotional strategies

- Hard work, persistence, patience and staying power.
- Get qualified.
- Have confidence in your own ability.
- Maintain a sense of humour.
- Be aware that sexism and racism can affect your career.
- Don't lose your balance over sexist comments.
- Get support from: peers, tutors, networks, family, other professionals.
- Networking, nurturing and self-consciousness . . .
- Be instrumental; learn from others.
- Blame the system for negative experiences, not always yourself.
- As a manager, learn to pare things down to what is really important.
- Use all strategies, learn the rules of the system and play them.
- Learn discretion.
- Work out and utilise strengths of others and how to learn to compensate for weakness.
- Get better at decoding written messages . . .
- If developments cannot be achieved cooperatively, they should either be dropped, delayed or other methods of achieving change explored.
- Develop the courage to promote yourself; do not be squeamish.
- Take risks and seize opportunities; sometimes these might entail a change of direction or having a higher profile in an institution.
- Part of a feminist commitment must be to take up the challenges and compromises of management . . .
- Apply for good positions.

(Powney 1997: 53)

It is sensible to see gaining promotion as a long-term strategy. It is common to be rebuffed at least once. Obtaining feedback can help you put in a better case next time. Remember that, while many institutions may refer to the importance of managerial and teaching experience in making appointments and promotions, research and publications may count for more:

> In higher education, many – or most – new lecturers are appointed largely on the basis of their expertise in their subject disciplines. A major contributing factor may be their records of research publications in their fields. At more senior levels, subject-related expertise is seen as even more important. When it comes to applying for promotion, or for senior appointment at another institution, a track record of successful research publications is a vital component of the sort of *curriculum vitae* that gets one onto interview shortlists.
>
> (Race 1995b: 77)

Promotion is, however, usually easier to obtain if you are prepared to move between institutions, and cope with the upheaval or seek the challenges which that brings.

Box 9.10: A checklist for your next job

- know the organisation
- understand what the job is about
- know what you want and where you want to go
- be clear that this job will help you on your career path
- have a vision of yourself in the job
- plan how you will convince an employer that it is you they need
- work out what you will wear to the interview!

(King 1993: 112)

Moving on and out

Four strategies may be identified for academics to move on or out of their employing colleges or universities. These may help to develop careers more quickly and/or in different directions than is often the case when staying in the same institution. The four strategies are:

- moving between institutions;
- moving between countries;
- moving out of, and perhaps back into, academic employment; and
- retirement.

We will consider each of these in turn.

Moving between institutions is akin to seeking promotion, except that the presentation of your case is more in your own hands. The process involved is also much the same as that needed to secure your first academic job (see Chapter 3, particularly the sections on **Where to look for work**, **Applying for a job** and **The job interview**). The basics are a solid curriculum vitae, good referees and one or more suitable jobs to apply for! Most such opportunities are likely to be advertised in the press in the normal way, but networks are important sources for obtaining this kind of information before it is public knowledge, and can also give guidance on strategies and prospects for success.

Box 9.10 offers a checklist of points to bear in mind, which apply to both academic and non-academic posts. We would add to these the following pieces of advice:

- Don't undersell yourself: you are not likely to be appointed if you lack confidence, so use positive language.
- Don't, on the other hand, be over-ambitious: you are wasting your time in applying for posts you have no chance of getting.
- Be aware of your likely competition, and of what you have which makes you special.
- Remember that, as with promotion, you are more likely to be unsuccessful than successful, so regard applying for jobs elsewhere as a long-term strategy.
- Learn from your rejections, by requesting and acting upon all the feedback you can.

Box 9.11: Rough equivalents of career ranks for different countries and institutions

UK universities	UK universities (former polytechnics)	Australasian universities	North American universities
Professor	Professor	Professor	Professor
Reader/Senior lecturer	Reader/Principal lecturer	Associate professor/ Professor	Professor
Lecturer B	Senior lecturer	Senior lecturer	Associate professor
Lecturer A	Lecturer II	Lecturer	Assistant professor
	Lecturer I	Assistant/Associate lecturer	Instructor

Source: G. Webb (1994: 30).

Once people know you are on the lookout for a suitable post elsewhere, you may even find yourself head-hunted!

Moving between countries is similar in some ways to moving between institutions, but, of course, much more complicated and demanding. It used to be commoner in the times when Britain still had an Empire. You may be interested in working within another higher education system, or for an international organization based in another country. Start by developing and using appropriate networks to help build up knowledge of job opportunities in various countries. An awareness of different legal systems and cultural expectations, and of the varied ways in which higher education is organized in other systems (see Box 9.11, which lists career equivalents for academic posts in Australasia, the United Kingdom and the United States) is also important. Many countries use English as the language of instruction in higher education, but settling socially requires some openness to language learning. Most overseas university posts make generous allowances for partners and to support children's education.

It makes obvious sense to check out what you, and your family may expect. This can almost always be done by seeking out people who are still working, or have worked recently, in the place you are considering. Those who recruit you, or their British agents, will be able to put you in touch with such contacts.

While working abroad, it is wise to maintain contacts back home for when you wish or need to return. This point exemplifies the importance of planning ahead, and of having a longer-term career strategy. Getting back into academic employment at home can be problematic. It is rather too easy to be seen as having got out of touch or, even after only two years, to be seen as 'having been away too long'. Be prepared for this by:

- publishing internationally;
- preplanning joint international research projects;
- maintaining or making British personal and institutional links;
- exploring the possibility of taking research students with you;
- being active in networks;
- refreshing your knowledge of the current language for issues and developments in your professional areas;
- making contacts with the representatives of British higher education institutions in the country you are based;
- working on ways to emphasize the positive assets of your overseas experience;
- seeking a formal connection with a British university or college, such as visiting fellowship, or through offering a guest lecture or seminar.

Expect to be treated with some suspicion on your return, with your experience likely to be valued less than that of someone whose development has taken place entirely within the British system. If you and your partner have dual academic careers, re-entry is likely to be particularly difficult. One or other of you may have to restart at a lower level. Bear in mind, however, that people with international experiences have always enriched university cultures. If you remain alert to the reservations that people who have never worked abroad have, then working abroad can be an enriching personal and professional experience.

Moving out of academic employment is a particularly viable option in professional areas such as business and management, education, engineering and medicine, where it is normal to keep in close contact with professional practice outside academe. As we have indicated elsewhere, it is common both for academics to keep their hand in professionally, and for professionals to make some contributions to academic life. In such cases, the transitions into and out of academic life may be relatively straightforward, particularly when good contacts have been maintained.

Moving out of academic employment can be an important career strategy which accommodates periods of academic and non-academic work. It is unwise to give up academic employment, however, unless you have a strategy for maintaining your career. Nevertheless, there are some situations in which it may seem necessary to give up the demands of the job for a period, and where unpaid leave is not an option. In these circumstances, we cannot underestimate the importance of maintaining a reputation if you have any thoughts at all of resuming academic employment.

Try not to give up an institutional connection with the academy, even if for a while it means coming off the payroll. Access of this kind can be kept open by, for example, seeking an honorary position, or by undertaking some nominal duties, or by jointly supervising a research student. For those who can manage it, a period of low earnings and limited hours of employment can provide the space for original intellectual development. The danger is if you need to take, for financial reasons, short-term or part-time employment which does not readily fit into your 'career'. Be creative, therefore, in thinking about how hourly paid teaching in the local further education college, or tutoring for the Open

University, can contribute to your continuing academic identity. Finally, keep up membership of professional bodies and networks, and budget to attend, perhaps every two years, significant conferences.

In this entrepreneurial age, opportunities for self-employment or consultancy work may also be an option. Whether running a small business is a dream or an insurance policy, however, these are the circumstances under which it is essential to find out more about being self-employed. A short training course will alert you to legal and financial issues. If you earn an income from royalties or from consultancy you may already be deemed as 'self-employed' for taxation purposes.

Retirement gets us all at some point, unless we die in post. For many in recent years, given the straitened financial circumstances faced by most universities, early retirement has been an option. As with all things, retirement is likely to be easier to cope with when planned, though few universities appear to offer much in the way of assistance. The same considerations apply as for those who are, possibly temporarily, moving out of academic work. Keeping connections and maintaining engagement in some kind of academic activity requires a proactive strategy; though the glory of retirement, if the pension is adequate, is being able to choose what to do without any concern for your curriculum vitae.

It may be the case that you plan to have little or nothing further to do with academic life, but intend to spend the rest of your life gardening, painting or sailing. Good luck, but plan ahead. And don't forget all of the practical details: what, for example, are you going to do with all those books and papers you have accumulated over the years? And how are you going to manage without secretarial assistance (assuming that you had any while you were employed)?

Conclusion

> The university of 2004 will be evolving towards one with a small core of high quality full-time staff, more formally specialised than at present in terms of teaching and research skills, undertaking core teaching themselves, but also acting as creators and facilitators of high technology learning materials and forming the nodes of networks of part-time staff.
>
> (Williams and Fry 1994: 5)

There are many visions of where the university may be going, of which the above is just one. Most, like the above, are in essence simply a projection of current trends. None of these visions may seem particularly attractive to those working in academic life who have become accustomed to particular patterns of working, or who hark back to previous arrangements. Change always has an unsettling element, though it may also be liberating.

As we pointed out in Chapter 2, alongside such change there will also be a considerable continuity. The university is likely to remain a key institution for the foreseeable future, embedded within and closely connected to all aspects of society. Academic roles are also likely to remain much the same as they are now, though how they are distributed and carried out may change. The academic

---

Box 9.12: Assume that you're OK

1 Remember that poor self-esteem plagues most academic women.
2 Create a savings bank of support for your self-esteem, and dip into that bank whenever you need to.
3 Do not assume that those who have the power to evaluate your work at any point are objective or correct.
4 Realize that you will rarely or never feel or be completely prepared for whatever task you are about to do.
5 Do not assume that you are supposed to be able to meet the needs and answer the questions of everyone who expects you to do so.
6 Know that you – being human – will make some wrong choices and erroneous judgements, and don't panic about that.
7 When you feel you are doing badly, pretend that you are someone else – and ask yourself, 'How would I judge her/him?'
8 Don't spend a lot of time asking permission to do things.
9 Learn to recognize how much clout you really do have, understanding that this may be much different from official, 'legitimate', power.
10 Learn about physical and verbal ways to keep out of, or help extricate yourself from, a one-down position.
11 Remember that discrimination is illegal.
12 Ask yourself whether you really *want* to be like 'them'.
13 Determine for yourself that your goals include retaining your humanity, helping others to retain theirs, and acquiring and maintaining self-esteem and self-confidence.
14 Remember that if you do decide to play the traditional academic game in the traditional ways, there are steps you can take to be prepared.
15 Have an exit path, an idea of what you can do if you leave your present institution or academia altogether, to help alleviate any feeling of being trapped and totally dependent upon your current setting.

Source: Caplan (1994: 76–82).

---

life will, we fervently hope, retain its essential qualities of intellectual openness and enquiry.

For those starting or developing an academic career at this time, coping with these twin forces of change and continuity is essential. Hopefully, much that we have included in this book will be of assistance. We will end with two extracts designed to reassure and contextualize the nature of academic work.

The first extract (Box 9.12) starts from the recognition that academic work, like any kind of work, will be tough for most people at some time, and offers a series of practical suggestions for how to deal with this. Bear these in mind, and use them as required.

The second extract (Box 9.13) presents a summary image of the kind of academic some of us might like to be, more of our colleagues and managers might like to work with, and a few of us might even think we are.

Box 9.13: Is anyone out there really?

a truly inspiring teacher,
personable colleague,
and helpful mentor to junior faculty,
who actively serves the profession
and builds the home institution
while still finding time to write beautifully creative theoretical pieces
and to conduct flawless research
that is destined to be relevant,
now and forever,
to scientists seeking understanding
and to practitioners seeking solutions,
backed by megabuck funding
and the resources of the best university in the world,
which is pleased to see a research process that makes transparent the
    individual's independent contribution
while revealing the interpersonal skills of our team player,
whose inspiration comes from hard knocks and successes accumulated over
    years of high-prestige consulting or line-manager experience
in an international setting,
which makes it possible to live in laptop luxury
surrounded by a loving and productive family
and lifelong friends
who take pride in the community's appreciation of our superhero's selfless
    volunteer work,
not to mention those special talents that help the home team beat the local
    competition,
even on those occasional days when a wild party cuts into our superhero's
    usual eight hour sleep?

(Jackson 1996: 354–5)

The final word, however, must go to Elaine Showalter:

Not having any career ambitions meant that I did things without thinking them through, whereas now people have to plan. If I had been paradoxically more ambitious, I might have said 'well, it's not my idea to have children and to wait till later'. I just sort of had them because I thought that I would never amount to anything so what did it matter?

(*Times Higher Education Supplement*, 29/8/97, p. 15)

As her interviewer comments:

So that is what one needs to be successful: no ambition and no plan.

(Ibid.)

Sources of further information

In this section we list a range of materials which you may find of interest in following up in more detail some of the issues discussed in this chapter. The emphasis is on recently published books in English. In each case, brief details are given as to contents and approach.

Blumenthal, P., Goodwin, C., Smith, A. and Teichler, U. (eds) (1996) *Academic Mobility in a Changing World: Regional and Global Trends.* London, Jessica Kingsley.
Examines the internationalization of higher education, world regionalism, educational exchange programmes, academic mobility and cooperation.
Clyne, S. (ed.) (1995) *Continuing Professional Development: Perspectives on CPD in Practice.* London, Kogan Page.
Reviews the position of CPD in a range of professions in the 1990s, then looks at individual perspectives, including a series of 11 personal 'tales'.
Fisher, S. (1994) *Stress in Academic Life: The Mental Assembly Line.* Buckingham, Open University Press.
Considers the nature of stress, its role in everyday life and relation to health, stress in students and staff, and strategies for coping with stress.
Griffiths, S. (ed.) (1996) *Beyond the Glass Ceiling: Forty Women whose Ideas Shape the Modern World.* Manchester, Manchester University Press.
Contains biographies of women who have enjoyed considerable success within, or on the fringes of, the academic world.
Lie, A. and O'Leary, V. (eds) (1990) *Storming the Tower: Women in the Academic World.* London, Kogan Page.
Documents the issues which women face in building an academic career. The introduction presents statistical summaries of women's position in academe in the countries considered in the book: the United States of America, Netherlands, Jordan, Germany, Turkey, Norway, India and Britain. The remaining sections define the problems and explore the barriers to productivity facing academic women, present case studies and discuss approaches to change.
Morley, L. and Walsh, V. (eds) (1995) *Feminist Academics: Creative Agents for Change.* London, Taylor and Francis.
Contributions discuss 'feminist interventions in dominant organizations of knowledge production'. Gender, organization, culture, teaching, writing, research, class, 'race' and conferences are among the associated issues considered.
Webb, G. (1994) *Making the Most of Appraisal: Career and Professional Development Planning for Lecturers.* London, Kogan Page.
A personal guide with exercises, examples of career development materials, and case studies of academics facing different career dilemmas and decisions.
Willis, L. and Daisley, J. (1990) *Springboard: Women's Development Workbook.* Stroud, Hawthorn Press.
This text contains a series of exercises and case histories relating to assertiveness, networking, goal setting, stress, image management and curriculum vitae writing. The book is designed specifically for women.
Zuber-Skerritt, O. (1992) *Professional Development in Higher Education: A Theoretical Framework for Action Research.* London, Kogan Page.
Develops a theoretical model for improving the practice of learning and teaching in higher education. Emphasizes having a critical attitude, research into teaching, accountability and self-evaluation, and professionalism.

ORGANIZATIONS AND JOURNALS

In the following pages you will find descriptions and contact details for a range of organizations and journals which work within, and contribute to, British higher education. The list is organized alphabetically in two sections, covering general organizations and higher education journals. Neither of these lists is, of course, fully comprehensive, and their details change all of the time.

Telephone and fax numbers are given with UK dialling or area codes. Overseas readers should ignore the initial '0' and dial +44 followed by the number, where '+' represents the international access code, e.g. 011 in the United States.

General organizations

Association of University Teachers (AUT)
United House, 9 Pembridge Road, London W11 3JY
Tel: 0171 221 4370   Fax: 0171 727 6547
E-mail: hq@aut.org.uk
Web: http://www.aut.org.uk

One of the main trade unions for academic and related staff. Publishes newsletters and guidelines for good practice.

The British Academy
20–21 Cornwall Terrace, London NW1 4QP
Tel: 0171 487 5966   Fax: 0171 224 3807
E-mail: basec@britac.ac.uk
Web: http://www.britcoun.org

Grant-awarding body for scholars in the arts and humanities.

The Commission on University Career Opportunity (CUCO)
CVCP, 29 Tavistock Square, London WC1H 9EZ
Tel: 0171 387 9231   Fax: 0171 388 6256
E-mail: fiona.waye@cvcp.ac.uk

CUCO was set up by the Committee of Vice-Chancellors and Principals to remove all forms of discrimination across the university sector. It meets once a term, with a membership drawn from vice-chancellors, trade unions and industry.

The Economic and Social Research Council
Polaris House, North Star Avenue, Swindon SN2 1UJ
Tel: 01793 413000   Fax: 01793 413001
E-mail: xrel@esrc.ac.uk
Web: http://www.esrc.ac.uk

Exists to promote and support high-quality research and postgraduate training in the social sciences, and to increase understanding and meet the needs of research users, thereby enhancing economic competitiveness, effectiveness of public policy and the quality of life.

European Association for Institutional Research (EAIR)
c/o CHEPS, University of Twente, PO Box 217, 7500 AE Enschede, The Netherlands
Tel: + 31 53 489 35 79   Fax: + 31 53 489 40 47
E-mail: eair@cheps.utwente.nl

A European higher education society with members in 38 countries, comprising managers, policy-makers and researchers. EAIR organizes an annual forum, produces a newsletter and publishes *Tertiary Education and Management*.

The Leverhulme Trust
1 Pemberton Row, London EC4A 3EX
Tel: 0171 822 6938
E-mail: josbourne@leverhulme.org.uk
Web: http://www.leverhulme.org.uk

Grant-awarding body for researchers in the social sciences.

The Nuffield Foundation
28 Bedford Square, London WC1B 3EG
Tel: 0171 631 0566   Fax: 0171 323 4877

Grant-awarding body for researchers in the social sciences and sciences.

The Joseph Rowntree Foundation
Research Department, The Homestead, 40 Water End, York YO3 6LP
Tel: 01904 615911/2/3   Fax: 01904 620072
E-mail: resdept@jrfound.org.uk

Funds community-oriented research and development work.

The Society of Authors
84 Drayton Gardens, London SW10 9SB
Tel: 0171 373 6642   Fax: 0171 373 5768
E-mail: authorsoc@writers.org.uk
Web: http://www.writers.org.uk

The Society of Authors is an independent trade union and advises on negotiations with publishers, broadcasting organizations, theatre managers and film companies. It offers a number of services, including legal action and an emergency fund. The Society of Authors publishes *The Author* and produces *Quick Guides* on various aspects of writing.

Society for Research into Higher Education (SRHE)
3 Devonshire Street, London W1N 2BA
Tel: 0171 637 2766   Fax: 0171 637 2781
E-mail: srhe@mailbox.ulcc.ac.uk
Web: http://www.srhe.ac.uk/srhe

The SRHE brings together those with an interest in research and policy in higher education in the United Kingdom. It publishes two journals, *Higher Education Quarterly* and *Studies in Higher Education*, and (in association with the Open University Press) a substantial book series.

Staff and Educational Development Association (SEDA)
Gala House, Raglan Road, Edgbaston, Birmingham B5 7RA
Tel: 0121 440 5021
E-mail: office@seda.demon.co.uk
Web: http://www.seda.demon.co.uk

A professional association for staff and educational developers, in the United Kingdom. Its main activities are accreditation, conferences and events, networks and services to members, and publications.

The University and College Lecturers Union (NATFHE)
27 Britannia Street, London WC1X 9JP
Tel: 0171 837 3636   Fax: 0171 833 3636
E-mail: a.hart@natfhe.org.uk

The other main trade union, with members concentrated in the former polytechnics and colleges.

Women's Higher Education Network
c/o Jacquie Melia, Department of Rehabilitation, Faculty of Health Care and Social Work Studies, University of Salford, Brian Blatchford Building, Frederick Road, Salford M6 6PU

The Writers' Guild of Great Britain
430 Edgware Road, London W2 1EH
Tel: 0171 723 8074   Fax: 0171 706 2413
E-mail: posti@wggb.demon.uk
Web: http://www.writers.org.uk

The Writers' Guild is affiliated to the Trades Union Congress and represents professional writers in publishing, theatre, film, radio and television. It offers a range of services, help and advice for members, and has negotiated agreements on which writers' contracts are based with a range of organizations, including the BBC and independent television companies.

Higher education journals

European Journal of Education
European Institute of Education and Social Policy, Université de Paris IX-Dauphine, 1 place du Maréchal de Lattre de Tassigny, F-75116 Paris, France
Current editors: Tony Becher and Jean-Pierre Jallade

Published four times a year. Many special issues. Focus on educational policy and development throughout Europe, particularly at higher level.

Higher Education Digest
Quality Support Centre, 344–54 Gray's Inn Road, London WC1X 8BP
Tel: 0171 278 4411

Published three times a year. Contains detailed abstracts of recent policy statements and publications relating to British higher education, more detailed analyses of trends and developments, and journal and conference listings.

Higher Education Management
Brunel University, Uxbridge UB8 3PH
Current editor: Maurice Kogan

Focuses on institutional management of higher education.

Higher Education Quarterly
Institute of Education, University of London, 55–9 Gordon Square, London WC1N 0NT
Current editor: Gareth Williams

Published four times a year under the auspices of the Society for Research into Higher Education. Focus on policy analysis and discussion relating to higher education in Britain and overseas. Some special issues.

Higher Education Research and Development
Royal Melbourne Institute of Technology, PO Box 71, Bundoora, Vic. 3083, Australia
Tel: +61 3 9660 2979/9468 2339   Fax: +61 3 9639 0439/9467 8622
E-mail: pling@rmit.edu.au
Web: http://www.carfax.co.uk/her-ad.htm
Current editors: Elaine Martin and Peter Ling

Published three times a year. Focus on aspects of higher education which seek to improve practice through research, evaluation or scholarly reflection.

Higher Education Review
46 Mercers Road, London N19 4PR
Current editor: John Pratt

Published three times a year. A critical, problem-based journal, which aims to examine post-school developments world-wide.

Journal of Further and Higher Education
Edge Hill University College, St Helens Road, Ormskirk, Lancashire L39 4QP
Current editor: Jennifer Rowley

Published three times a year. Articles typically of 2500–3500 words, focusing mainly on management and administration, curriculum and staff development, and teaching and learning approaches in all areas of post-16 education and training.

Journal of Graduate Education
Brandon House, Bentinck Drive, Troon, Ayrshire KA10 6HX
E-mail: j.m.irvine@strath.ac.uk
Current editor: James Irvine.

A quarterly publication providing a forum for discussion on issues relating to the development of graduate education in the United Kingdom.

Journal of Higher Education Policy and Management
15–21 Pulteney Street, Adelaide 5000, South Australia, Australia
Tel: +61 8 223 3116/61 018 392 195 Fax: +61 8 232 1444
E-mail: gavin.moodie@unisa.edu.au
Current editors: Gavin Moodie and Vin Massaro

Published twice a year. Supports higher education managers by disseminating ideas, analyses and reports.

The New Academic
Staff and Educational Development Association, Gala House, 3 Raglan Road, Edgbaston, Birmingham B5 7RA
Tel: 0121 440 5021 Fax: 0121 440 5022
E-mail: office@seda.demon.co.uk
Web: http://www.seda.demon.co.uk
Current editor: Elisabeth Mapstone

Published three times a year. Short articles on current policies, practices and developments in teaching and learning in higher education.

Open Learning
Regional Academic Services, Open University, Walton Hall, Milton Keynes MK7 6AA
Tel: 01908 274066 Fax: 01908 655143
Current editor: Alan Tait

Published three times a year. Articles on open learning and distance education in Britain and overseas. The first section contains longer articles of up to 6000 words; the second section contains issues for debate, grassroots observations, research notes, conference reports and reviews, usually less than 2000 words.

Quality in Higher Education
University of Central England in Birmingham, 90 Aldridge Road, Perry Barr, Birmingham B42 2TP
Current editor: Lee Harvey

Published three times a year. Focuses on theory, practice and policy relating to the control, management and improvement of quality in higher education.

Research in Post-compulsory Education
School of Education, University of Wolverhampton, Gorway Road, Walsall WS1 3BD
Tel: 01902 323257   Fax: 01902 323177
E-mail: fa1809@wlv.ac.uk
Current editors: Neil Moreland and Geoffrey Elliott

Sponsored by the Further Education Research Association and published three times a year. Aims to cover the whole sphere of post-compulsory education, including adult, further and community as well as higher education.

Research into Higher Education Abstracts
Centre for Higher Education Management, Anglia Polytechnic University, Danbury Park, Main Road, Danbury, Essex CM3 4AT
Current editor: Ian McNay

Published three times a year under the auspices of the Society for Research into Higher Education. Provides brief summaries of the contents of current journal articles and books relating to higher education.

Studies in Higher Education
Centre for Higher Education Development, Liverpool John Moores University, 10 Rodney Street, Liverpool L1 2TE
Current editor: Mantz Yorke

Published three times a year. Focus on analyses of teaching and learning arrangements and strategies within higher education. Articles of between 5000 and 7000 words.

Teaching in Higher Education
Division of Education, University of Sheffield, Education Building, 388 Glossop Road, Sheffield S10 2JA
Current editor: Len Barton

Published three times a year. Concerned with the relationship between teaching and research, the constraints within which teaching operates, staff and course development, the student voice, innovation and change.

Tertiary Education and Management
University Office, University of Aberdeen, Regent Walk, Aberdeen AB24 3FX
Tel: 01224 272094   Fax: 01224 273717
E-mail: unisec@admin.aberdeen.ac.uk
Current editor: Roddy Begg

The journal of the European Association of Institutional Research. Published twice a year.

Times Higher Education Supplement
Admiral House, 66–8 East Smithfield, London E1 9XY.
Fax: 0171 782 3300
E-mail: theslet@thes.co.uk
Web: http://thesis.newsint.co.uk

A weekly newspaper containing news, analysis, features, reviews and advertisements for all interested in British higher education.

REFERENCES

Acker, S. (1994) *Gendered Education*. Buckingham, Open University Press.

Ackerman, R. (1986) 'Middle-aged Women and Career Transitions' in S. Rose (ed.), *Career Guide for Women Scholars*. New York, Springer-Verlag, pp. 102–8.

Adams, S. (1996) *The Dilbert Principle: A Cubicle's-eye View of Bosses, Meetings, Management Fads and Other Workplace Afflictions*. London, Boxtree.

Allan, D. (1996) 'Talking the Tightrope' in D. Allan (ed.), *In at the Deep End: First Experiences of University Teaching*. Lancaster, Unit for Innovation in Higher Education, pp. 38–46.

Altman, B. and Post, J. (1996) 'Beyond the "Social Contract": An Analysis of the Executive View at Twenty-five Large Companies' in D. Hall (ed.), *The Career is Dead: Long Live the Career*. San Francisco, Jossey-Bass, pp. 46–71.

Alvesson, M. and Willmott, H. (1996) *Making Sense of Management: A Critical Introduction*. London, Sage.

Arnold, J. (1997) *Managing Careers into the 21st Century*. London, Paul Chapman.

Ashcroft, K. and Foreman-Peck, L. (1995) *The Lecturer's Guide to Quality and Standards in Colleges and Universities*. London, Falmer Press.

Ashford, S. (1996) 'The Publishing Process: The Struggle for Meaning' in P. Frost and M. Taylor (eds), *Rhythms of Academic Life: Personal Accounts of Careers in Academia*. Thousand Oaks, Calif., Sage, pp. 119–28.

Atkins, M. (1995) 'What Should We Be Assessing?' in P. Knight (ed.), *Assessment for Learning in Higher Education*. London, Kogan Page, pp. 25–33.

Barling, J. (1994) 'Work and Family: In Search of More Effective Workplace Interventions' in C. Cooper and D. Rousseau (eds), *Trends in Organizational Behaviour*, Vol. 1. Chichester, John Wiley, pp. 63–73.

Becher, T. (1989) *Academic Tribes and Territories: Intellectual Enquiry and the Cultures of Disciplines*. Milton Keynes, Open University Press.

Becher, T. (1996) 'The Learning Professions', *Studies in Higher Education*, 21(1), 43–55.

Becher, T. and Kogan, M. (1992) *Process and Structure in Higher Education*, 2nd edn. London, Routledge.

Bird, E. (1996) 'Interdisciplinary Ideals and Institutional Impediments: A Case Study of Postgraduate Provision' in L. Morley and V. Walsh (eds), *Breaking Boundaries: Women in Higher Education*. London, Taylor and Francis, pp. 149–59.

Blackmore, P. and Wilson, S. (1995) 'Learning to Work in Higher Education: Some Staff Perceptions', *British Journal of In-service Education*, 21(2), 223–34.

Bland, D. (1990) *Managing Higher Education*. London, Cassell.

Blaxter, L., Hughes, C. and Tight, M. (1996) *How to Research*. Buckingham, Open University Press.

Boice, R. (1995a) 'Writerly Rules for Teachers', *Journal of Higher Education*, 66(1), 32–60.

Boice, R. (1995b) 'Developing Writing, Then Teaching, amongst New Faculty', *Research in Higher Education*, 36(4), 415–56.

Bolles, R. (1996) *What Color is Your Parachute? A Practical Manual for Job-hunters and Career-changers*. Berkeley, Calif., Ten Speed Press.

Bradbury, M. (1975) *The History Man: A Novel*. London, Secker & Warburg.

Brennan, J. and Ramsden, B. (1996) 'Diversity in UK Higher Education: A Statistical View' in J. Brennan (ed.), *Special Digest Report*. Milton Keynes, Open University Quality Support Centre, pp. 2–15.

Bronstein, P. (1986) 'Applying for Academic Jobs: Strategies for Success' in S. Rose (ed.), *Career Guide for Women Scholars*. New York, Springer-Verlag, pp. 3–26.

Brooks, A. (1997) *Academic Women*. Buckingham, Open University Press.

Brooks, D. and Brooks, L. (1997) *Seven Secrets of Successful Women: Success Strategies of the Women who Have Made It – and How You Can Follow Their Lead*. New York, McGraw-Hill.

Brown, G. and Atkins, M. (1988) *Effective Teaching in Higher Education*. London, Methuen.

Brown, G., Bull, J. and Pendlebury, M. (1997) *Assessing Student Learning in Higher Education*. London, Routledge.

Burns, E., Dydo, E. and Rice, W. (eds) (1996) *The Letters of Gertrude Stein and Thornton Wilder*. New Haven, Conn., Yale University Press.

Caplan, P. (1994) *Lifting a Ton of Feathers: A Woman's Guide for Surviving in the Academic World*. Toronto, University of Toronto Press.

Carter, I. (1990) *Ancient Cultures of Conceit: British University Fiction in the Post-war Years*. London, Routledge.

Central Statistical Office (1997) *Social Trends 27*. London, HMSO.

Clark, B. (1983) *The Higher Education System: Academic Organization in Cross-national Perspective*. Berkeley, University of California Press.

Clegg, S. (1996) 'Creating a Career: Observations from Outside the Mainstream' in P. Frost and M. Taylor (eds), *Rhythms of Academic Life: Personal Accounts of Careers in Academia*. Thousand Oaks, Calif., Sage, pp. 37–53.

Colgan, F. and Ledwith, S. (1996) 'Women as Organisational Change Agents' in S. Ledwith and F. Colgan (eds), *Women in Organisations: Challenging Gender Politics*. Basingstoke, Macmillan, pp. 1–43.

Collinson, D., Knights, D. and Collinson, M. (1990) *Managing to Discriminate*. London, Routledge.

Commission on University Career Opportunity (1997) *A Report on Policies and Practices on Equal Opportunities in Universities and Colleges in Higher Education*. London, CUCO.

Committee of Vice-Chancellors and Principals, Standing Conference of Principals, Committee of Scottish Higher Education Principals *et al.* (1996) *A Concordat on Contract Research Staff Career Management*. London, CVCP.

Committee on Higher Education (1963) *Report*, Cmnd 2154. London, HMSO.

Cooper, C. (1990) 'Coping Strategies to Minimise the Stress of Transitions' in S. Fisher and C. Cooper (eds), *On The Move: The Psychology of Change and Transition*. New York, John Wiley, pp. 315–27.

Court, S. (1994) *Long Hours, Little Thanks: A Survey of the Use of Time by Full-time Academic and Related Staff in the Traditional UK Universities*. London, Association of University Teachers.

Covey, S. (1992) *The Seven Habits of Highly Effective People: Powerful Lessons in Personal Change*. London, Simon and Schuster.

Cox, B. (1994) *Practical Pointers for University Teachers*. London, Kogan Page.

Cryer, P. (1997) 'How to get ahead with a PhD', *Times Higher Education Supplement*, Research Opportunities Supplement, 16 May, p. i.

Daly, M. (1979) *Gyn/Ecology: The Metaethics of Radical Feminism*. London, Women's Press.

Davies, C. and Holloway, P. (1995) 'Troubling Transformations: Gender Regimes and Organisational Culture in the Academy' in L. Morley and V. Walsh (eds), *Feminist Academics: Creative Agents for Change*. London, Taylor and Francis, pp. 7–21.

Davis, D. and Astin, H. (1990) 'Life Cycle, Career Patterns and Gender Stratification in Academe: Breaking Myths and Exposing Truths' in S. Lie and V. O'Leary (eds), *Storming the Tower: Women in the Academic World*. London, Kogan Page, pp. 89–107.

Davis, K. (1997) 'What's a Nice Girl Like You Doing in a Place Like This? The Ambivalences of Professional Feminism' in L. Stanley (ed.), *Knowing Feminisms*. London, Sage, pp. 184–96.

Diski, J. (1988) *Rainforest*. Harmondsworth, Penguin (first published 1987).

Eaglestone, R. (1996) 'Three-part Harmony', *The Guardian Higher*, 3 December.

Economic and Social Research Council (1997) *Social Sciences: News from the ESRC*, 35. Swindon, ESRC.

Ellington, H. and Race, P. (1993) *Producing Teaching Materials: A Handbook for Teachers and Trainers*, 2nd edn. London, Kogan Page.

Elsey, B. and Kinnell, M. (1990) 'Introduction' in M. Kinnell (ed.), *The Learning Experiences of Overseas Students*. Buckingham, Open University Press, pp. 1–11.

Entwistle, J. (1997) 'Is She a News Reader or a New Darwinist?' *Times Higher Education Supplement*, Research Opportunities Supplement, 16 May, p. iv.

Entwistle, N. (ed.) (1994) *Teaching and the Quality of Learning*. London, Committee of Vice-Chancellors and Principals.

Farrington, D. (1994) *The Law of Higher Education*. London, Butterworth.

Finch, J. (1997) 'Power, Legitimacy and Academic Standards' in J. Brennan, P. de Vries and R. Williams (eds), *Standards and Quality in Higher Education*. London, Jessica Kingsley, pp. 146–56.

Finch, J. and Morgan, D. (1991) 'Marriage in the 1980s: A New Sense of Realism?' in D. Clark (ed.), *Marriage, Domestic Life and Social Change: writings for Jacqueline Burgoyne*. London, Routledge, pp. 55–82.

French, K. (1995) 'Men and Locations of Power: Why Move Over?', in C. Itzin and J. Newman (eds), *Gender, Culture and Organizational Change: Putting Theory into Practice*. London, Routledge, pp. 54–67.

Fukami, C. (1996) 'Herding Cats Part Deux: The Hygiene Factor' in P. Frost and M. Taylor (eds), *Rhythms of Academic Life: Personal Accounts of Careers in Academia*. Thousand Oaks, Calif., Sage, pp. 321–4.

Fulton, O. (1996) 'The Academic Profession in England on the Eve of Structural Reform' in P. Altbach (ed.), *The International Academic Profession: Portraits of Fourteen*

Countries. Princeton, NJ, Carnegie Foundation for the Advancement of Teaching, pp. 391–437.

Gallos, J. (1996) 'On Becoming a Scholar: One Woman's Journey' in P. Frost and M. Taylor (eds), *Rhythms of Academic Life: Personal Accounts of Careers in Academia*. Thousand Oaks, Calif., Sage, pp. 11–18.

Gibbs, G. (1992) 'Control and Independence' in G. Gibbs and A. Jenkins (eds), *Teaching Large Classes in Higher Education: How to Maintain Quality with Reduced Resources*. London, Kogan Page, pp. 37–59.

Gibbs, G. and Habeshaw, T. (1989) *Preparing to Teach: An Introduction to Effective Teaching in Higher Education*. Bristol, Technical and Educational Services Ltd.

Gilbert, L., Hallett, M. and Eldridge, N. (1994) 'Gender and Dual-career Families: Implications and Applications for the Career Counseling of Women' in W. Walsh and S. Osipow (eds), *Career Counseling for Women*. Hillsdale, NJ, Lawrence Erlbaum, pp. 135–64.

Goldschmidt, W. (1990) *The Human Career: The Self in the Symbolic World*. Oxford, Blackwell.

Green, M. and McDade, S. (1991) *Investing in Higher Education: A Handbook of Leadership Development*. New York, American Council on Education.

Griffiths, S. (1996a) 'Ann Oakley' in S. Griffiths (ed.), *Beyond the Glass Ceiling: Forty Women whose Ideas Shape the Modern World*. Manchester, Manchester University Press, pp. 176–83.

Griffiths, S. (ed.) (1996b) *Beyond the Glass Ceiling: Forty Women whose Ideas Shape the Modern World*. Manchester, Manchester University Press.

Griffiths, S. (1997) 'The Struggle for Equality'. *Times Higher Education Supplement*, 6 July, p. 19.

Halsey, A. (1995) *Decline of Donnish Dominion: The British Academic Professions in the Twentieth Century*, revised edition. Oxford, Clarendon Press.

Hardy, T. (1974) *Jude the Obscure*. London, Macmillan (first published 1896).

Harrison, R. (1992) *Employee Development*. London, Institute of Personnel Management.

Hart, E. and Bond, M. (1995) *Action Research for Health and Social Care: A Guide to Practice*. Buckingham, Open University Press.

Heward, C., Taylor, P. and Vickers, R. (1997) 'Gender, Race and Career Success in the Academic Profession', *Journal of Further and Higher Education*, 21(2), 205–18.

Higher Education Statistics Agency (1996) *Higher Education Statistics for the United Kingdom 1994/95*. Cheltenham, HESA.

Hill, K. (1996) 'My First Seminars' in D. Allan (ed.), *In at the Deep End: first Experiences of University Teaching*. Lancaster, Unit for Innovation in Higher Education, pp. 47–51.

Holmes, O. (1976) 'Thesis to Book: What to Get Rid of' in E. Harman and I. Montagnes (eds), *The Thesis and the Book*. Toronto, University of Toronto Press, pp. 63–73.

Hughes, C. and Tight, M. (1995) 'Linking University Teaching and Research', *Higher Education Review*, 28(1), 51–65.

Jackson, S. (1996) 'Dealing with the Overenriched Work Life' in P. Frost and M. Taylor (eds), *Rhythms of Academic Life: Personal Accounts of Careers in Academia*. Thousand Oaks, Calif., Sage, pp. 351–5.

Jacobson, H. (1984) *Coming from Behind*. London, Black Swan (first published 1983).

Janes, D. (1996) 'The Junior Lecturer' in D. Allan (ed.), *In at the Deep End: First Experiences of University Teaching*. Lancaster, Unit for Innovation in Higher Education, pp. 78–81.

Jarillo, J. (1993) *Strategic Networks: Creating the Borderless Organization*. Oxford, Butterworth-Heinemann.

Johnson, L. (1996) *Being an Effective Academic*. Oxford, Oxford Centre for Staff Development.

Johnston, R. (1996) 'Managing How Academics Manage' in R. Cuthbert (ed.), *Working in Higher Education*. Buckingham, Open University Press, pp. 101–18.

Kanter, R. (1997) *Frontiers of Management*. Harvard, Harvard Business Review.

Kiloh, G. (1994) 'The Higher Education Administrator and Manager in the 1990s and Beyond' in G. Whitchurch (ed.), *A Handbook for University Administrators and Managers*. Sheffield, UK Universities' Staff Development Unit, pp. 5–10.

King, C. (ed.) (1993) *Through the Glass Ceiling: Effective Senior Management Development for Women*. Eastham, Tudor Business Publishing Ltd.

King, C. (1995) 'Making It Happen: Reflections on a Varied Career' in M. Slowey (ed.), *Implementing Change from within Universities and Colleges*. London, Kogan Page, pp. 41–9.

King, C. (1997) 'Through the Glass Ceiling: Networking by Women Managers in Higher Education' in H. Eggins (ed.), *Women as Leaders and Managers in Higher Education*. Buckingham, Open University Press, pp. 91–100.

Kirkwood, G. (1991) 'Education in the Community' in B. O'Hagan (ed.), *The Charnwood Papers: Fallacies in Community Education*. Ticknall, Derbyshire, Education Now Books.

Kolb, D. and Fry, R. (1975) 'Towards an Applied Theory of Experiential Learning' in C. Cooper (ed.), *Theories of Group Processes*. London, John Wiley, pp. 33–57.

Kram, K. (1996) 'A Relational Approach to Career Development' in D. Hall (ed.), *The Career Is Dead – Long Live the Career: A Relational Approach to Careers*. San Francisco, Jossey-Bass, pp. 132–57.

Krause, D. (1995) *The Art of War for Executives*. London, Nicholas Brealey.

Kronenfeld, J. and Whicker, M. (1997) *Getting an Academic Job: Strategies for Success*. Thousand Oaks, Calif., Sage.

Lambert, S. (1990) 'Processes Linking Work and Family: A Critical Review and Research Agenda', *Human Relations*, 43(3), 239–57.

Landsberg, M. (1996) *The Tao of Coaching: Boosting Your Effectiveness at Work by Inspiring and Developing Those around You*. London, HarperCollins.

Lankshear, C., Gee, J., Knobel, M. and Searle, C. (1997) *Changing Literacies*. Buckingham, Open University Press.

Laurillard, D. (1993) *Rethinking University Teaching: A Framework for the Effective Use of Educational Technology*. London, Routledge.

Lewis, S. (1994) 'Role Tensions and Dual-career Couples' in M. Davidson and R. Burke (eds), *Women in Management: Current Research Issues*. Liverpool, Paul Chapman, pp. 230–41.

Limerick, B. (1995) 'Accommodated Careers: Gendered Career Paths in Education' in B. Limerick and B. Lingard (eds), *Gender and Changing Educational Management*. Rydalmere, NSW, Hodder Education, pp. 67–78.

Locke, L., Spirduso, W. and Silverman, S. (1993) *Proposals that Work: A Guide for Planning Dissertations and Grant Proposals*, 3rd edn. Newbury Park, Calif., Sage.

Maddux, R. (1994) *Team Building: An Exercise in Leadership*, 2nd edn. London, Kogan Page.

Magolda, M. (1992) *Knowing and Reasoning in College: Gender-related Patterns in Students' Intellectual Development*. San Francisco, Jossey-Bass.

Mahony, P. (1988) 'Oppressive Pedagogy: The Importance of Process in Women's Studies', *Women's Studies International Forum*, 11(2), 103–8.

Marshall, J. (1995) *Women Managers Moving On: Exploring Career and Life Choices*. London, Routledge.

McNay, I. (1996) 'Work's Committees' in R. Cuthbert (ed.), *Working in Higher Education*. Buckingham, Open University Press, pp. 119–29.

Millard, R. (1991) *Today's Myths and Tomorrow's Realities: Overcoming Obstacles to Academic Leadership in the 21st Century*. San Francisco, Jossey-Bass.

Moghissi, H. (1994) 'Racism and Sexism in Academic Practice: A Case Study' in H. Afshar and M. Maynard (eds), *The Dynamics of 'Race' and Gender: Some Feminist Interventions*. London, Taylor and Francis, pp. 222–34.

Morgan, G. (1993) *Imaginization: The Art of Creative Management*. Newbury Park, Calif., Sage.

Morgan, G. (1997) *Images of Organization*, 2nd edn. Thousand Oaks, Calif., Sage.

Morley, L. and Walsh, V. (1996) (eds) *Breaking Boundaries: Women in Higher Education*. London, Taylor and Francis.

Moses, I. and Roe, E. (1990) *Heads and Chairs: Managing Academic Departments*. St Lucia, University of Queensland Press.

Murphy, K. (1996) 'Getting Published' in P. Frost and M. Taylor (eds), *Rhythms of Academic Life: Personal Accounts of Careers in Academia*. Thousand Oaks, Calif., Sage, pp. 129–34.

National Committee of Inquiry into Higher Education (1997) *Report*. London, NCIHE Publications.

Nicholson, M. and West, M. (1988) *Managerial Job Change: Men and Women in Transition*. Cambridge, Cambridge University Press.

Nicholson, N. (1990) 'The Transition Cycle: Causes, Outcomes, Processes and Forms' in S. Fisher and C. Cooper (eds), *On the Move: The Psychology of Change and Transition*. Chichester, John Wiley, pp. 83–108.

Oakley, A. (1989) *The Men's Room*. London, Flamingo (first published 1988).

O'Leary, V. and Mitchell, J. (1990) 'Women Connecting with Women: Networks and Mentors' in S. Lie and V. O'Leary (eds), *Storming the Tower: Women in the Academic World*. London, Kogan Page, pp. 58–74.

Oshagbemi, T. (1996) 'Job Satisfaction of UK Academics', *Educational Management and Administration*, 24(4), 389–400.

Ozga, J. and Walker, L. (1995) 'Women in Education Management: Theory and Practice' in B. Limerick and B. Lingard (eds), *Gender and Changing Educational Management*. Rydalmere, NSW, Hodder Education, pp. 34–43.

Pascall, G. (1997) *Social Policy: A New Feminist Analysis*. London, Routledge.

Perkin, H. (1987) 'The Academic Profession in the United Kingdom' in B. Clark (ed.), *The Academic Profession: National, Disciplinary and Institutional Settings*. Berkeley, University of California Press, pp. 13–59.

Phillips, E. and Pugh, D. (1994) *How to Get a PhD: A Handbook for Students and Their Supervisors*, 2nd edn. Buckingham, Open University Press.

Powney, J. (1997) 'On Becoming and Being a Manager in Education' in H. Eggins (ed.), *Women as Leaders and Managers in Higher Education*. Buckingham, Open University Press, pp. 49–62.

Race, P. (1994) *The Open Learning Handbook*, 2nd edn. London, Kogan Page.

Race, P. (1995a) 'What Has Assessment Done For Us – and To Us?' in P. Knight (ed.), *Assessment for Learning in Higher Education*. London, Kogan Page, pp. 61–74.

Race, P. (1995b) 'Competent Research: Running Brook or Stagnant Pool?' in B. Smith and S. Brown (eds), *Research, Teaching and Learning in Higher Education*. London, Kogan Page, pp. 75–87.

Ramsden, B. (1996) 'Academic Staff: Information and Data' in R. Cuthbert (ed.), *Working in Higher Education*. Buckingham, Open University Press, pp. 23–33.

Ramsden, P. (1992) *Learning to Teach in Higher Education*. London, Routledge.

Ritzer, G. (1993) *The McDonaldization of Society*. Thousand Oaks, Calif., Pine Forge.

Rose, S. (1986) 'Building a Professional Network' in S. Rose (ed.), *Career Guide for Women Scholars*, New York, Springer-Verlag, pp. 46–56.

Russell, C. (1993) *Academic Freedom*. London, Routledge.

Russell, J. (1994) 'Career Counseling for Women in Management' in W. Walsh and S. Osipow (eds), *Career Counseling for Women*. Hillsdale, NJ, Lawrence Erlbaum, pp. 263–326.

Rust, C. (1991) *Surviving the First Year: The Experiences of New Teaching Staff in Higher Education*. Birmingham, Standing Conference on Educational Development.

Sadler, D. (1990) *Up the Publication Road: A Guide to Publishing in Scholarly Journals for Academics, Researchers and Graduate Students*, 2nd edn. Campbelltown, NSW, Higher Education Research and Development Society of Australasia.

Scott, P. (1995) *The Meanings of Mass Higher Education*. Buckingham, Open University Press.

Scott, P. and Watson, D. (1994) 'Managing the Curriculum: Roles and Responsibilities' in J. Bocock and D. Watson (eds), *Managing the University Curriculum: Making Common Cause*. Buckingham, Open University Press, pp. 33–47.

Seagren, A., Cresswell, J. and Wheeler, D. (1993) *The Department Chair: New Roles, Responsibilities and Challenges*. Washington, DC, ERIC Clearinghouse on Higher Education.

Segerman-Peck, L. (1991) *Networking and Mentoring: A Woman's Guide*. London, Piatkus.

Seyd, P. and Moran, M. (1997) 'Politics and the ESRC Research Grants Board: Opportunities and Problems'. *PSA News* (the newsletter of the Political Studies Association of the United Kingdom), 9(2), 5.

Shaw, J. and Perrons, D. (1995) 'Introduction – Gender Work' in J. Shaw and D. Perrons (eds), *Making Gender Work: Managing Equal Opportunities*. Buckingham, Open University Press, pp. 1–11.

Shepela, S. (1986) 'Changing Career Directions: Life outside the Academic Mainstream' in S. Rose (ed.), *Career Guide for Women Scholars*. New York, Springer-Verlag, pp. 139–57.

Shmerling, L. (1993) *Job Applications: The Winning Edge*. Melbourne, Macmillan Educational.

Skilbeck, M. and Connell, H. (1996) 'International Education from the Perspective of Emergent World Regionalism: The Academic, Scientific and Technological Dimension' in P. Blumenthal, C. Goodwin, A. Smith and U. Teichler (eds), *Academic Mobility in a Changing World: Regional and Global Trends*. London, Jessica Kingsley, pp. 66–102.

Smith, B. and Brown, S. (1995) 'Research, Teaching and Learning: issues and challenges' in B. Smith and S. Brown (eds), *Research, Teaching and Learning in Higher Education*. London, Kogan Page, pp. 11–18.

Snow, C. (1951) *The Masters*. London, Macmillan.

Spurling, A. (1997) 'Women and Change in Higher Education' in H. Eggins (ed.), *Women as Leaders and Managers in Higher Education*. Buckingham, Open University Press, pp. 37–48.

Stanley, J. (1995) 'Pain(t) for Healing: The Academic Conference and the Classed/Embodied Self' in L. Morley and V. Walsh (eds), *Feminist Academics: Creative Agents for Change*. London, Taylor and Francis, pp. 169–82.

Stanley, L. (1990) 'Feminist Praxis and the Academic Mode of Production: An Editorial Introduction' in L. Stanley (ed.), *Feminist Praxis: Research, Theory and Epistemology in Feminist Sociology*. London, Routledge, pp. 3–19.

Stenhouse, L. (1984) 'Library Access, Library Use and User Education in Academic Sixth Forms: An Autobiographical Account' in R. Burgess (ed.), *The Research Process in Educational Settings: Ten Case Studies*. Lewes, Falmer Press, pp. 211–33.

Stokes, C. (1996) 'Entering the Fray' in D. Allan (ed.) *In at the Deep End: First Experiences of University Teaching*. Lancaster, Unit for Innovation in Higher Education, pp. 1–8.

Thomson, R. and Mabey, C. (1994) *Developing Human Resources*. Oxford, Butterworth-Heinemann.

Tsui, A. (1997) 'From the Editor', *Academy of Management Journal*, 40(1), 5–8.

Tuckman, H. and Pickerill, K. (1988) 'Part-time Faculty and Part-time Academic Careers' in D. Breneman and T. Youn (eds), *Academic Labour Markets and Careers*. Lewes, Falmer Press.

UK Universities' Staff Development Unit (1994) *Staff Development for Teaching and Learning: Towards a Coherent and Comprehensive Approach*. Sheffield, UKUSDU.

Vaitilingam, R. (1997) 'Economists in the Media', *Social Sciences: News from the ESRC*, 34, 8.

Vines, G. (1996) 'Cynthia Cockburn' in S. Griffiths (ed.), *Beyond the Glass Ceiling: Forty Women whose Ideas Shape the Modern World*. Manchester, Manchester University Press, pp. 44–50.

Wagner, L. (1995) 'A Thirty-year Perspective: From the Sixties to the Nineties' in T. Schuller (ed.), *The Changing University?* Buckingham, Open University Press, pp. 15–24.

Watson, D. (1994) 'Living with Ambiguity: Some Dilemmas of Academic Leadership' in J. Bocock and D. Watson (eds), *Managing the University Curriculum: Making Common Cause*. Buckingham, Open University Press, pp. 77–85.

Webb, A. (1994) 'Two Tales from a Reluctant Manager' in S. Weil (ed.), *Introducing Change from the Top in Universities and Colleges*. London, Kogan Page, pp. 41–55.

Webb, G. (1994) *Making the Most of Appraisal: Career and Professional Development Planning for Lecturers*. London, Kogan Page.

West, L. (1996) *Beyond Fragments: Adults, Motivation and Higher Education, A Biographical Analysis*. London, Taylor and Francis.

Wheeler, S. and Birtle, J. (1993) *A Handbook for Personal Tutors*. Buckingham, Open University Press.

Wilbur, H. (1995) 'On Getting a Job' in A. Deneef and C. Goodwin (eds), *The Academic's Handbook*. Durham, NC, Duke University Press, pp. 115–27.

Williams, G. and Fry, H. (1994) *Longer Term Prospects for British Higher Education: A Report to the Committee of Vice-Chancellors and Principals*. London, Institute of Education.

Willis, L. and Daisley, J. (1990) *Springboard: Women's Development Network*. Stroud, Hawthorn Press.

Woods, P. (1985) 'New Songs Played Skilfully: Creativity and Technique in Writing up Qualitative Research' in R. Burgess (ed.), *Issues in Educational Research: qualitative methods*. Lewes, Falmer, pp. 86–108.

Woolf, V. (1995) *Killing the Angel in the House*. Harmondsworth, Penguin.

Zelmer, A. and Zelmer, L. (1991) *Organising Academic Conferences*. Campbelltown, NSW, Higher Education Research and Development Society of Australasia.

Zimmer, W. (1990) *On Writing Well: An Informal Guide to Writing Nonfiction*. New York, HarperCollins.

INDEX